YOU DON'T HAVE TO BE RICH TO GO CAMPING!

Bushcraft eliminates the need for expensive equipment. With one sharp tool you can survive comfortably and safely in the wilderness.

Bushcraft equips you to face nature on its own terms, making use of natural materials. Much of Bushcraft will be new to even the most experienced camper, but its techniques are useful for all campers.

Bushcraft teaches you how to recognize edible, safe foods. It diagrams every rope and knot you will need, illustrates every method of making a fire and every kind of shelter. Follow this comprehensive guide.

"Superior . . . comprehensive . . . doesn't stop with little tips on water, refrigeration and selection of sites as most of the others do."—*Journal Outdoors*

"Through this book, an individual's ability to adapt and improve can be developed to a remarkable degree."
—*Pittsburgh PA Press*

D0819336

BUSHCRAFT

A SERIOUS GUIDE TO SURVIVAL AND CAMPING

Richard Graves

WARNER BOOKS

A Warner Communications Company

WARNER BOOKS EDITION

Copyright © by Dymock's Book Arcade Ltd.
Published by arrangement with Schocken Books. All rights reserved,
which includes the right to reproduce this book or portions thereof in any
form whatsoever.

ISBN 0-446-85491-3

Library of Congress Catalog Card Number: 74-185329

Cover photo by Bill Cadge

Warner Books, Inc., 75 Rockefeller Plaza, New York, N.Y. 10019

Ⓦ A Warner Communications Company

Printed in the United States of America

Not associated with Warner Press, Inc., of Anderson, Indiana

First Printing: March, 1978

10 9 8 7 6 5 4 3 2 1

CONTENTS

BUSHCRAFT

THE PRACTICE OF BUSHCRAFT shows many unexpected results. The five senses are sharpened, and consequently the joy of being alive is greater.

The individual's ability to adapt and improvise is developed to a remarkable degree. This in turn leads to increased self-confidence.

Self-confidence, and the ability to adapt to a changing environment and to overcome difficulties, is followed by a rapid improvement in the individual's daily work. This in turn leads to advancement and promotion.

Bushcraft, by developing adaptability, provides a broadening influence, a necessary counter to offset the narrowing influence of modern specialisation.

For this work of bushcraft all that is needed is a sharp cutting implement: knife, axe or machete. The last is the most useful. For the work, dead materials are most suitable. The practice of bushcraft conserves, and does not destroy, wild life.

R.H.G.

1.

ROPES AND CORDS

One of the first needs in Bushcraft is the ability to join poles or sticks. The only method available is by the use of lashings.

To use lashings however, it is necessary to have, find or make, materials for this purpose.

The ability to spin, or plait fibres into ropes or cords is one of the oldest of man's primitive skills. The method is simple, and follows precisely the same stages that are made use of by today's complicated machines.

The material from which to spin or plait ropes or cords is in abundance everywhere. Any fibrous material which has reasonable length, moderate strength and is flexible or pliable can be used. These are the three things to look for, and they can be found in many vines, grasses, barks, palms, and even in the hair of animals.

The breaking strains of handmade ropes and cords varies greatly with different materials, consequently it is essential that the rope or cord be tested for the purpose for which it will be used, before being actually put to use.

The uses to which these hand-made ropes and cords

can be put, apart from lashing, is almost endless, and some few are included in this book.

THE MAKING OF ROPES AND CORDS

Almost any natural fibrous material can be spun into good serviceable rope or cord, and many materials which have a length of 12 to 24 inches, or more can be braided or plaited. Ropes of up to 3 and 4 inches diameter can be 'laid' by four people, and breaking strains for bush-made rope of one inch diameter range from 100 lbs. to as high as 2,000 or 3,000 lbs.

BREAKING STRAINS

Taking a three lay rope of 1 inch diameter as standard, the following table of breaking strains may serve to give a fair idea of general strengths of various materials. For safety sake always regard the lowest figure as the breaking strain unless you know otherwise.

Green Grass . . . .   100 lbs. to   250 lbs.
Bark Fibre . . . .   500 lbs. to 1,500 lbs.
Palm Fibre . . . .   650 lbs. to 2,000 lbs.
Sedges . . . . .2,000 lbs. to 2,500 lbs.
Monkey Rope (Lianas) . . . . .   560 lbs. to   700 lbs.
Lawyer Vine (Calamus) . . . .½ inch dia. 1,200 lbs.
Double the diameter quadruples the breaking strain.
Halve the diameter, and you reduce the breaking strain to one fourth.

PRINCIPLES OF ROPE MAKING MATERIALS

To discover whether a material is suitable for rope making it must have four qualities.

It must be reasonably long in the fibre.

It must have 'strength.'

It must be pliable.

And it must have 'grip' so that the fibres will 'bite' onto one another.

GRASS BARK
LENGTH

TWIST

PLIABLE

There are three simple tests to find if any material is suitable.

First pull on a length of the material to test it for strength. The second test, to be applied if it has strength, is to twist it between the fingers and 'roll' the fibres together; if it will stand this and not 'snap' apart, tie a thumb knot in it, and gently tighten the knot. If the material does not cut upon itself, but allows the knot to be pulled taut, then it is suitable for rope making, providing that the material will 'bite' together and is not smooth or slippery.

You will find these qualities in all sorts of plants, in ground vines, in most of the longer grasses, in some of the water reeds and rushes, in the inner barks of many trees and shrubs, and in the long hair or wool of many animals.

Some green freshly gathered materials may be 'stiff' or unyielding. When this is the case try passing it through hot flames for a few moments. The heat treatment should cause the sap to burst through some of the cell structure, and the material thus becomes pliable.

3

STIFF   PLIABLE

Fibres for rope making may be obtained from many sources:

> Surface roots of many shrubs and trees have strong fibrous bark;
>
> Dead inner bark of fallen branches of some species of trees and in the new growth of many trees such as willows;
>
> In the fibrous material of many water and swamp growing plants and rushes;
>
> In many species of grass and in many weeds;
>
> In some sea weeds;
>
> In fibrous material from leaves, stalks and trunks of many palms;
>
> In many fibrous-leaved plants such as the aloes.

GATHERING AND PREPARATION OF MATERIALS

In some plants there may be a high content of vegetable gum and this can often be removed by soaking in water, or by boiling, or again, by drying the material and 'teasing' it into thin strips.

Some of the materials have to be used green if any strength is required. The materials that should be green include the sedges, water rushes, grasses, and lianas.

Grasses, sedges and water rushes should be cut and never pulled. *Cutting above ground level is 'harvesting,' but pulling up the plant means its 'destruction.'*

It is advisable not to denude an area entirely but to work over a wide location and harvest the most suitable material, leaving some for seeding and further growth.

4

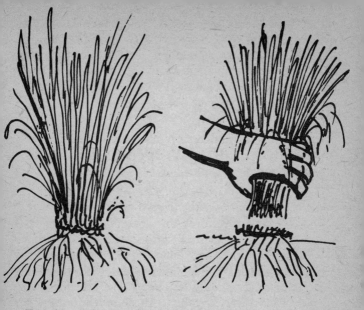

For the gathering of sedges and grasses, be particularly careful therefore to '*harvest*' the material, that is, cut what you require above ground level, and take only from the biggest clumps.

By doing this you are not destroying the plant, but rather aiding the natural growth, since your harvesting is truly pruning.

You will find that from a practical point of view this is far the easiest method.

Many of the strong-leafed plants are deeply rooted, and you simply cannot pull a leaf off them.

Palm fibre in tropical or sub-tropical regions is harvested. You will find it at the junction of the leaf and the palm trunk, or you will find it lying on the ground beneath many palms. Palm fibre is a 'natural' for making ropes and cords.

Fibrous matter from the inner bark of trees and shrubs is generally more easily used if the plant is dead or half dead. Much of the natural gum will have dried out and when the material is being teased, prior to spinning, the gum or resin will fall out in fine powder.

There may be occasions when you will have to use the bark of green shrubs, but avoid this unless it is absolutely essential, and only cut a branch here and there. *Never ever cut a complete tree just because you want the bark for a length of cord.*

TO MAKE CORD BY SPINNING WITH THE FINGERS

Use any material with long strong threads or fibres which you have previously tested for strength and pliability. Gather the fibres into loosely held strands of even thickness. Each of these strands is twisted clockwise. The twist will hold the fibre together. The strands should be from ⅛″ downwards—for a rough and ready rule there should be about 15 to 20 fibres to a strand. Two, three or four of these strands are later

This illustration shows the general direction of twist and the method whereby the fibres are bonded into strands. In similar manner the twisted strands are put together into lays, and the lays into ropes. Illustrated in this diagram is a two strand lay.

twisted together, and this twisting together or 'laying' is done with an anti-clockwise twist, while at the same time the separate strands which have not yet been laid up are twisted clockwise. *Each strand must be of equal twist and thickness.*

The person who twists the strands together is called the 'layer,' and he must see that the twisting is even, that the strands are uniform, and that the tension on each strand is equal. In laying, he must watch that each of the strands is evenly 'laid up,' that is, that one strand does not twist around the other two. (A thing you will find happening the first time you try to 'lay up.')

When spinning fine cords for fishing lines, snares, etc., considerable care must be taken to keep the strands uniform and the lay even. Fine thin cords of no more than one-thirty-second of an inch thickness can be spun with the fingers and they are capable of taking a breaking strain of twenty to thirty lbs. or more.

Normally two or more people are required to spin and lay up the strands for cord.

Many native people when spinning cord do so unaided, twisting the material by running the flat of the hand along the thigh, with the fibrous material between hand and thigh and with the free hand they feed in fibre for the next 'spin.' By this means one person can make long lengths of single strands.

This method of making cord or rope with the fingers is slow if any considerable length of cord is required.

A more simple and easy way to rapidly make lengths of rope of fifty to a hundred yards or more in length is to make a rope-walk and set up multiple spinners in the form of cranks. The series of photographic illustrations on the succeeding pages show the details of rope spinning.

In a rope walk, each feeder holds the material under one arm and with one free hand feeds it into the strand which is being spun by the crank. The other hand lightly holds the fibres together till they are spun. As the lightly spun strands are increased in length they must be supported on cross bars. Do not let them lie on the ground. You can spin strands of twenty to one hundred yards before laying up. Do not spin the material in too thickly. Thick strands do not help strength in any way, rather they tend to make a weaker rope.

Layout of a rope walk.

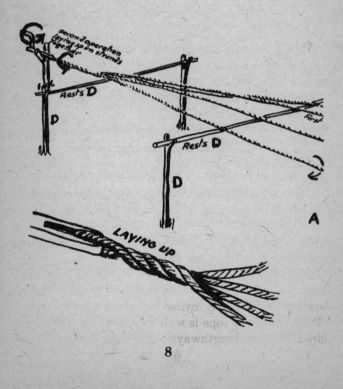

SETTING UP A ROPEWALK

When spinning ropes of ten yards or longer it is necessary to set cross bars every two or three yards to carry the strands as they are spun. If cross bars are not set up the strands or rope will sag to the ground, and some of the fibres will tangle up with grass, twigs or dirt on the ground. Also the twisting of the free end may either be stopped or interrupted and the strand will be unevenly twisted.

The easiest way to set up crossbars for the rope walk is to drive pairs of forked stakes into the ground about six feet apart and at intervals of about six to ten feet. The cross bars must be smooth, and free from twigs and loose portions of bark that might twist in with the spinning strands.

The cross bar A is supported by two uprights, and pierced to take the cranks B. These cranks can be made out of natural sticks, morticed slab, and pegs, or if available, bent wire. The connecting rod C enables one man to turn all cranks clockwise simultaneously. Crossbars supporting the strands as they are spun are shown D. A similar crank handle to C is supported on a fork stick at the end of the rope walk. This handle is turned *in reverse* (anti-clockwise) to the cranks C to twist the connected strands together. These are 'laid up' by one or more of the feeders.

Always make it a rule to turn the first strand clockwise, then the laying up of the strands will be done anti-clockwise and the next laying will again be clockwise.

Proof that your rope is well made will be if the individual fibres lie lengthways along the rope.

9

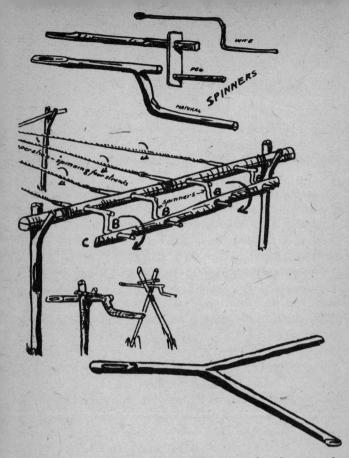

In the process of laying up the strands, the actual twisting together, or laying will take some of the original 'twist' out of the strand which has not yet been laid. Therefore it is necessary to keep twisting the strands whilst laying together.

When making a rope, too long to be spun and laid in one piece, a section is laid up, and coiled on the ground at the end of the rope walk farthest from the cranks. Strands for a second length are spun, and these strands are married or spliced into the strands of the first sec-

Bark fibre being spun into strands using a single crank handle.

Spinner-feeder on right with bundle of material under his right arm feeds in material.

Joining the strands prior to lay up.

Testing the rope of bark fibre, breaking strain 1" diameter, about 800 lbs.

tion and then the laying up of the second section continues the rope.

The actual 'marrying' of the strands is done only in the last lay, which when completed makes the rope. The ends where the strands are married should be staggered in different places. By this means rope can be made and extended in sections to a great length.

After your complete length of rope is laid up, pass it through fire, to burn off the loose ends and fibres. This will make your rope smooth and most professional looking.

Close up of the finished rope.

LAYING THE STRANDS

The strands lie on these crossbars as they are spun. When the strands have been spun to the required length, which should be no more than about a hundred feet, they are joined together by being held at the far end. They are then ready for laying together.

The turner, who is facing the cranks, twists the ends together *anti-clockwise*, at the same time keeping his full weight on the rope and which is being layed up. The layer advances placing the strands side by side as they turn.

Laying up is very fast when the layer is experienced. He quickly gets the feeling of the work.

It is important to learn to feed the material evenly, and lay up slowly, thereby getting a smooth even rope. Do not try to rush the ropemaking. If you do you will have uneven, badly spun strands, and ugly lays, and poor rope. Speed in ropemaking only comes with practice. At first it will take a team of three or four up to two hours or more to make a 50-yard length of rope of three lays, each of three strands, that is nine strands for a rope with a finished diameter of about 1 inch. With practice the same three or four people will make the same rope in 15 to 20 minutes. These times do not include time for gathering material.

In feeding, the free ends of the strands twist in the loose material fed in by the feeder. The feeder must move backwards at a speed governed by the rate at which he feeds. As the feeder moves backwards he must keep a slight tension on the strands.

BAD LAYING | GOOD LAYING

MAKING ROPE WITH SINGLE SPINNER

Two people can make rope, using a single crank.

A portion of the material is fastened to the eye of the crank, as with the multiple crank, and the feeder holding the free ends of this strand against the bundle of loose material under his arm feeds in, walking backwards. Supporting crossbars, as used in a ropewalk, are required when a length of more than 20 or 30 feet is being spun.

FEEDING

If the feeder is holding material under his left arm, his right hand is engaged in continuously pulling material forward to his left hand which feeds it into the turning strand. These actions done together as the feeder walks backwards govern the thickness of the strands. *His left hand, lightly closed over the loose turning material, must 'feel' the fibres 'biting' or twisting together.*

When the free end of the turning strand, which is against the loose material under his arm takes in too thick a tuft of the material he closes his left hand, and so arrests the twist of the material between his left hand and his bundle. This allows him to tease out the overfull 'bite,' with his right hand, and so he maintains a uniform thickness of the spinning strand. There is a knack in 'feeding' and once you have mastered this knack you can move backwards, and feed with considerable speed.

THICKNESS OF STRANDS

Equal thickness for each of the strands throughout their length, and equal twist are important. The thickness should not be greater than is necessary with the material being used. For grass rope, the strand should not be more than ¼-inch diameter, for coarse bark or palm not more than ⅛ or 3/16, for fine bark, hair or sisal fibre not more than ⅛-inch.

For cords the strand should be no more than one-sixteenth inch in diameter.

Fine cords cannot be made from grass, unless the fibres are separated by beating out and 'combing.'

The correct amount of twist is when the material is 'hard,' that is, the twist is tight.

FAULTS COMMON WITH BEGINNERS

There is a tendency with the beginner to feed unevenly. Thin wispy sections of strand are followed by thick hunky portions. Such feeding is useless. Rope made from such strands will break with less than one-quarter of the possible strain from the material.

The beginner is wise to twist and feed slowly, and to make regular, even strands rather than rush the job and try and make the strands quickly. Speed, with uniformity of twist and thickness, comes only with practice. In a short time when you have the 'feel' of feeding, you will find you can feed at the rate of from thirty to sixty feet a minute.

Thick strands do not help. It is useless to try and spin up a rope from strands an inch or more in thickness. Such a rope will break with less than half the potential strain of the material.

Spinning 'thick' strands does not save time in ropemaking.

LIANAS, VINES AND CANES

Lianas and ground vines are natural ropes, and grow in sub-tropical and tropical scrub and jungle. Many are of great strength, and useful for bridging, tree climbing and other purposes. The smaller ground vines when plaited give great strength and flexibility. Canes, and stalks of palms provide excellent material if used properly. Only the outer skin is tough and strong, and this skin will split off easily if you bend the main stalk away from the skin. This principle also applies to the splitting

16

of lawyer cane (calamus), all the palm leaf stalks and all green material. If the split starts to run off, you must bend the material away from the thin side, and then it will gradually gain in size, and come back to an even thickness with the other split side.

BARK FIBRES

The fibres in many barks which are suitable for rope making are close to the innermost layer. This is the bark next to the sap wood.

When seeking suitable barks of green timber, cut a small section about three inches long, and an inch wide. Cut this portion right from the wood to the outer skin of the bark.

Peel this specimen, and test the different layers. Green bark fibres are generally difficult to spin because of 'gum' and it is better to search around for windfallen dead branches and try the inner bark of these. The gum will probably have leached out, and the fibres separate very easily.

Many shrubs have excellent bark fibre, and here it is advisable to cut the end of a branch and peel off a strip of bark for testing. Thin barks from green shrubs are sometimes difficult to spin into fine cord and it is then easier to use the lariat plait for small cords.

Where it is necessary to use green bark fibre for rope spinning (if time permits), you will find that the gum will generally wash out when the bark is teased and soaked in water for a day or so.

After removing from the water allow the bark strips to partly dry out before shredding and teasing into fibre.

PLAITING

One man may require a considerable length of rope, and if he has no assistance to help him spin up his material he can often find reasonably long material (say, from 1 ft. to 3 ft. or more) and using this material he can plait (or braid) and so make suitable rope. The usual three plait makes a flat rope, and while quite good, has not the finish or shape, nor is it as 'tight' as the four or lariat plait. On other occasions it may be necessary to plait broad bands for belts or for shoulder straps. There are many fancy braids and plaits which you can develop from these, but these three are basic, and essential for practical woodcraft work.

A general rule for all plaits is to work from the outside in to the centre.

THREE PLAIT

Take the right-hand strand and pass it over the strand to the left.

Take the left-hand strand and pass it over the strand to the right and repeat alternately from left to right.

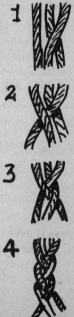

18

FLAT FOUR PLAIT

Lay the four strands side by side. Take the right-hand strand as in Fig. 1 and lay it over the strand to the left.

Now take the outside *left*-hand strand as in Fig. 2 and lay it under the next strand to itself and over what was the first strand.

Take what is now the outside *right*-hand strand, and lay it over the first strand to its left.

Take the outside left strand and put it under and over, the next two strands respectively moving towards the right.

Thereafter your right-hand strand goes over one strand to the left, and your left-hand strand under and over to the right, as shown in Fig. 4.

BROAD PLAIT

To commence. Take six, seven or more strands, and hold them flat and together.

Take a strand in the centre and pass it over the next strand to the left, as in Fig. 1.

19

Take the second strand in the centre to the left and pass it towards the right over the strand you first took so that it points towards the right as in Fig. 2.

Now take the next strand to the first one and weave it under and over as in Fig. 3.

Weave the next strands from left and right alternately towards the centre as in Fig. 4, 5, 6.

The finished plait should be tight and close as in Fig. 7.

TO FINISH OFF

Take one of the centre strands, and lay it back upon itself as in Fig. 1.

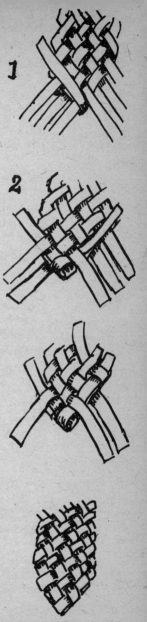

Now take the first strand which it enclosed in being folded back, and weave this back upon itself as in Fig. 2.

Take a strand from the opposite side, and lay it back and weave it between the strands already plaited.

All the strands should be so woven back that no strands show an uneven pattern, and there should be a regular under-over-under of the alternating weaves.

If you have plaited tightly there may be a difficulty in working the loose ends between the plaited strands.

This can be done easily if you sharpen a thin piece of wood to a chisel edge, and use this to open the strands sufficiently to allow the ends being finished to pass between the woven strands.

Roll under a bottle to work smooth after finishing off.

21

ROUND OR LARIAT PLAIT ... FOUR STRANDS

1. Lay the four strands together side by side, as in Fig. 1, and cross the right-hand centre strand over, and then around the left-hand strand.

2. Take the left-hand outside strand, and pass it over the two crossed strands, and then under the right-hand one of the two, so that it is pointing towards the left, as in Fig. 2.

3. Take the free right-hand strand, and pass it over the two twisted strands to the left and completely round the left-hand one of the two, as in Fig. 3.

4. Repeat this with the outside left-hand strand as in Fig. 4.

5. Repeat with the right-hand strand as in Fig. 5.

6. The finished plait should look like this.

CLIMBING WITH FOOTLOCK

Ascent of a cliff face, using a footlock on a grass rope. The grass rope was 3 strand 3 lay of 2 inches diameter.

23

CAUTION

Prior to trusting your life to a bush-made rope, always test it. Tie one end to a tree and put three or four fellows onto the other end. Have them take the strain gently until finally all their weight is on the rope. If they cannot break it, then it is safe for one man at a time to use it to climb or descend a cliff face.

When climbing up a bush-made rope always use the foot-lock, and when descending never slide down the rope. *Climb* down again using the same footlock.

The footlock offers a measure of safety, and the climber is so secure that he can actually stand on the rope and rest without his body weight being carried entirely on his arms. To prove this, use the footlock, and clasp the rope to your body with your arms. You will find that you are 'standing' on the rope and quite secure.

By means of the footlock you can climb to any height on the rope, stopping to rest when your arms tire.

The footlock is made by holding onto the rope with both hands, lifting the knees, and kicking the rope to the outside of one foot. The foot on the oppo-

24

site side to the rope is 'pointed' so that the toe picks up the rope, which is pulled over the foot which was against the rope, and under the instep of the foot which 'picked' it up.

The two feet are brought together, and the rope is now over the instep of one foot, and under the ball of the other. Then, to secure the grip, and lock the rope; the feet are placed one on top of the other so that the rope is clamped down by the foot on top.

By straightening the knees, and raising the hands, the body is lifted, and a fresh grip taken for the next rise.

In descending, the body is bent, the hands lowered, and the footlock released, and a fresh grip taken with the feet at a lower level on the rope.

It is advisable to wear boots or shoes when climbing bush-made ropes.

This method of descending is much safer than sliding. In sliding there is grave risk of bad rope burns to hands and legs.

'ABSYLE' FOR ROCK DESCENT

The 'Absyle' is used for rock work, generally for descending, though it can be used on some faces for ascent.

In the 'Absyle' the body is upright, but the legs are stretched out, and the feet pressed against the rock face.

The rope passes down between the thighs, around one thigh and diagonally up and across the upper half of the body and over the shoulder opposite

Photo with acknowledgment to "S.M. Herald"

Absyle used for descending rock face. This bush-made grass rope is 3 strand 3 lay of about 2 inches diameter. Breaking strain approx. 400 lbs.

to the leg under which it passes. The rope may be gripped with one hand.

In descending, the free hand pulls the rope over the shoulder. This leaves a loop below the thigh, and the feet are 'walking' down the rock face until the thigh is again snug in the loop. The 'Absyle' used for descending makes it practically impossible to fall.

In ascending a rock face which has an extreme slope but is not vertical, the feet are 'walked' up the rock face, the body is pulled up the rope, and the slack, hanging below the legs, is pulled up with one hand and fed over the shoulder. By this means the climber can 'sit' on the rope and rest. When using the 'Absyle' it will be found that bare feet, sandshoes or spiked shoes give a better grip on the rock face than plain leather soles.

TYING SPLIT CANES AND VINES TOGETHER

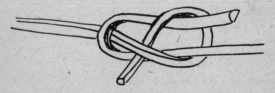

These materials will only tie with special knots and it is a safe rule to tie with the *outside of the skin on the outside bend of the knot*, as in A. If you try to tie with the inside of the material on the outer surface of the bend (as in B), it is probable that the material will either crack or snap off, and you may reject it as useless. The knots which are most suitable for tying these canes and vines are:

Joining knots: Sheet bend, Reef knot, and fisherman knot.
Securing knots: Timber hitch.

When pulling the knot taut, do so gently. If you snap the joining knot the material may either cut itself or break. If the canes or vines are brittle through greenness try heat treatment.

USES FOR BUSH-MADE ROPES

There are many occasions when bush-made ropes can be extremely useful ... for climbing or descending a short cliff face; for climbing a tree; for a rope bridge; for a safety-line across a fast or flooded river.

SINGLE ROPE LADDER WITH STICKS

A single rope ladder is made by opening the lays of the rope and inserting cross sticks each about 8 inches long as shown with an equal amount protruding on either side of the rope. These cross sticks must be secured to the rope, and it is necessary to lash the rope above and below the sticks. The distance between the sticks should be from 15" to 18".

To climb a rope ladder, hold the rope with both hands, bend the knees, and draw both feet up together and lay them with even pressure on the next cross sticks. When the footing is secure, raise the hands and continue the action, which is somewhat like that of a toy monkey on a string.

Bush single-rope ladders have the advantage that they can be used easily by people who may not be able to climb by ordinary means. They provide an easy means of ascending and descending a cliff or a lookout.

SINGLE ROPE LADDER WITH CHOCKS

This type of ladder has the advantage of being portable and quickly made. The chocks of hardwood are about 6" diameter and 2" deep, and are suitably bored to take the diameter of the rope. Splice an eye at the top end and seize in a thimble to lash the rope head securely. To secure the chocks, put two strands of seizing between the strands of the rope and then work a wall knot.

ROPE BRIDGE

Two ropes are spun. They must be very strong and thoroughly tested. They are anchored to either side of the river, either to convenient trees or to anchors as shown.

When these ropes have been stretched taut, light 'A' frames are made. The number required depends upon the length of the decking.

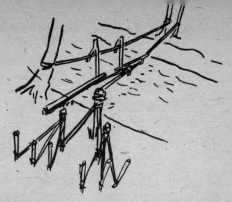

The first 'A' frame is hooked onto the ropes and pushed forward with a stick. The footing, a straight sapling, is dropped down onto the crotch of the frame, and the bridge builder walks out along this, and hooks on the next 'A' frame, pushing it out the required distance, and repeats the process till the far bank is reached. Rope bridges must not be overloaded—one at a time is a safe rule. If Monkey vines, Lianas, or Lawyer vines (Calamus) are available instead of bush-made rope, use any of these. They are much stronger and will make a bridge strong enough for 4 to 6 men at a time.

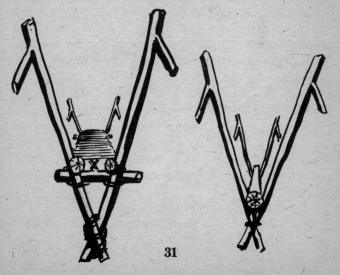

TO MEASURE THE DISTANCE ACROSS A RIVER OR GORGE

Select a mark on the opposite bank 'A,' and then drive a stake on the near bank 'B.' Walk at right angles for a known number of paces and put in another marker stake 'C,' and continue an equal number of paces and put in a third marker 'D.'

Turn at right angles away from the river, and keep moving back until the centre marker stake and the mark on the other side of the river are in line 'E.'

Measure the distance from the third or last marker peg 'D' to this point 'E,' and this distance will equal the distance across the river.

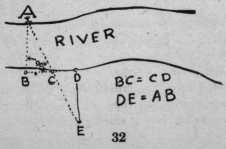

TO GET A ROPE ACROSS A NARROW DEEP RIVER

Fasten a stout stick to the end of the rope. The rope must be in the middle of the stick. Select a forked tree on the opposite bank. Throw the free end of the coiled line with the stick across the river to the tree. After many casts when it has caught, test with two or three people to make sure the line is secure. Fasten the near end of the rope to a convenient anchor, and then the person crossing the line (usually the lightest member of the party) hangs onto the line, lifts his legs and hooks them over the rope, with his feet towards the opposite bank. By this means he can work himself across the river, fasten the rope, and do all the work which has to be done on that side of the river.

SAFETY LINE FOR RIVER CROSSING

A bush rope can be spun to serve as a safety line for crossing flooded or fast rivers. The rope is taken across by one member of the party, and fastened to an anchor on the opposite bank. As a safety line it should be above water level. The person crossing should stand on the downstream side of the rope, and face upstream. He crosses by moving his feet sideways, one step at a time, and holding all the time to the rope which helps him keep his balance. If by chance the current is so strong that it sweeps him off his feet, his grip on the line will save him from being washed downstream, and he can work his way shoreward hand over hand, until he is in a less strong portion of the current where he can regain his footing.

1-2-3 ANCHOR

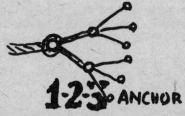

A very stout stake is driven into the ground, at an angle of about 45°, and to the foot of this the main rope to be anchored is fastened. To the head of this stake two ropes are secured and these are fastened to the foot of two stakes to the rear. The heads of these stakes are in turn tied back to the foot of three other stakes. This anchor will hold secure under almost all conditions.

ANCHORING A PEG IN SAND

The only way to anchor a rope into soft sand is to attach it to a peg, and bury the peg in the sand.

Scrape a trench in the sand to a depth of between a foot and eighteen inches, deeper if high winds or very stormy weather are expected. Pass the rope round the centre of the peg; scratch a channel for it at right angles to the peg trench.

Fill in the trench and rope channel, and fasten the free end of the rope to the standing end with a stopper hitch (see page 5), and pull taut. The buried peg should hold a tent rope in sand under all normal weather conditions.

BUSH WINDLASS

A bush windlass, capable of taking a very heavy strain on a rope can be made by selecting a site where a tree forks low to the ground, with the fork facing the direction in which the pull is required. Alternatively, a stout fork can be driven in and anchored with the "1-2-3" method.

The windlass portion is a forked log. The forks are notched to take the lever (up to seven feet long). The rope is passed round the roller a few times so that it locks upon itself. (If the fork of the roller is long, the rope may pass through the fork.)

This type of bush windlass has many uses.

2.

HUTS
AND THATCHING

Little skill is needed to make a comfortable, thatched, weatherproof hut using only material locally available.

Such huts can be expected to have a useful service life of 4 to 6 years without maintenance. With maintenance, such as renewing lashings, and repairs to ridge thatch, the life is anything up to 20 years.

Where rammed earth is used for walls, the life of the structure is indeterminate. Many earth wall buildings have stood undamaged for hundreds of years.

The building of a thatched hut from local materials is a creative exercise. Design must provide for the anticipated weather conditions. Finding suitable materials almost anywhere presents no problem, but considerable organisation may be required to collect the material. For the actual structure and thatching, good teamwork is required.

The final hut, with its promise of long periods of protection and shelter, is the result of combination of head work and hands. With this comes the inward reward of having created a weather-proof hut out of nothing except the natural materials garnered from the surrounding area.

Circular hut 20 feet diameter at ground; no nails or man-made materials used in its construction. Time of erection, 12 to 18 man hours. Left half is thatched with palm leaves—right half thatched with eucalypt branches. Shortly after erection there was 4½ inches of rain in 75 minutes. The inside of the hut was completely dry after this terrific drenching.

Thatched Huts

The making of huts and shelters for occasional or continuous use from exclusively local materials and without the aid of any man-made equipment is not difficult. In place of nails, lashings, either of vine, bark strips or other fibrous material are used (see pages 71, 72 and 73). Framework is of round poles. Weatherproof roofing is provided by thatching with long grass, ferns, reeds, palm leaves, sea weeds, bark sheets, split shingles or even sods of clayey turf.

The material you will use depends on what there is in your vicinity. The shape, size and details of your hut are governed by the length of your occupation; the number of people that have to be sheltered; the local climatic conditions against which you want shelter; and, of course, the time available for construction.

If there are one or two to be sheltered for a few nights only in a temperate climate, a simple lean-to thatched shelter will suffice and this can be built in one to three hours, but if there are eight or ten in your party and they require shelter for a few months against cold and bad weather, then a semi-permanent hut complete with doors, windows, and a fireplace for heating, and built-in bunks will be required, and to do this properly might take two or three days.

It is assumed that a good knife, hatchet or axe is available and that the workers are willing. The structures shown here are merely examples of what can be done. When it comes to planning your hut, you are your own architect and your own builder. If there are several people in the party, organise the labour so that no hands are idle — have one or two fellows cutting poles, another carrying them to the site, a fourth stripping bark for lashings (see Chapter 1 "Ropemaking"), and set the others gathering material for thatching.

Collect all the material for your structure before you start to build, stack it in orderly piles where it will be most convenient. Your main structure poles in one pile; your battens for thatching in another pile; your bark strips or vines shredded down for immediate use; and your thatching material neatly stacked in several piles close to the work.

When you are ready to start building, have every man on the site. Organise the labour of erection of the main framework, and then break your team up into small gangs for lashing on battens and completing details of framework. By this means you will save hours of labour and you will succeed in building a better hut.

There is nothing to it really, except intelligence. Plan

and organise to keep everybody's fingers busily engaged.

DESIGN

There are three main designs of huts: a simple lean-to hut, suitable for fine warm weather; an enclosed pyramidal hut, suitable for cold, inclement conditions; and a long hut, which if open is suitable for mild climates, or if completely walled is suitable for cold conditions.

Refinements such as doors (yes, doors that swing on hinges) and windows may be added to suit your pleasure. And when your hut is completed, then there is the all important matter of furnishing it—but first let us look at what the backwoods man can build for his new season camp.

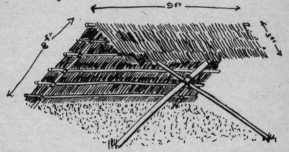

This would be suitable for a short summer shelter for two fellows. It can be put up in one to three hours.

This long hut, about twelve feet by ten feet wide, will house five to twelve men, depending on the bunking arrangements, and can be built in about 40 man hours.

39

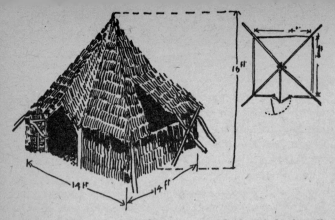

This pyramidal hut, 14 feet square inside the 5 ft. high walls, is comfortable, and an excellent cold weather camp for from eight to sixteen men, according to the bunking arrangements. It can be put up in about 20 man hours.

SECTIONAL LEAN-TO HUTS

Small one and two man lean-to huts can be easily constructed in an hour or two by making and thatching two or three frames which are from seven to nine feet in length and three feet six to four feet deep.

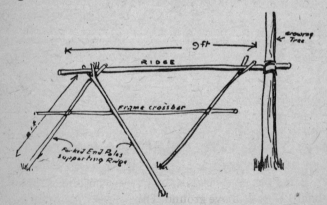

Framework for Sectional Lean-to Shelter.

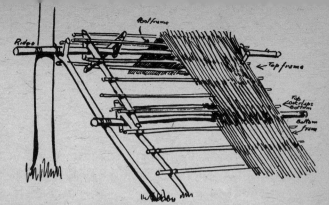

Labels on image: Ridge, Front frame, Top frame, Top overlaps bottom, Bottom frame

Three Thatched Sections attach to Crossbar and Ridge.

These frames, built of battens, are lashed on to two fork sticks. The forks are in the form of hooks at the upper end. The framework for these one or two man shelters is simple to construct.

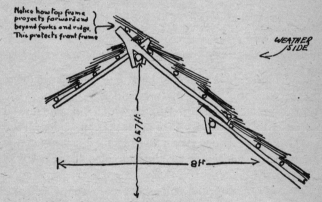

Labels on image: Notice how top frame projects forward and beyond forks and ridge. This protects front frame, WEATHER SIDE, 6 to 7 ft, 8 ft

Assembly on framework of sections.

Note how top of top frame projects forward beyond fork and ridge. This protects front frame, and saves the work of ridge thatching. If raised bunks (see Chapter 3) are being put in, it is advisable to have bottom of thatch about 1'6" to 2' above ground. This raises ridge height to 1' to 1'6" and side poles become 10 to 11 ft. instead of 8 to 9 ft.

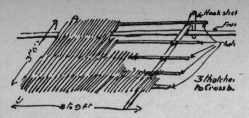

Section of assembly.

Permanent Lean-To Huts

The permanent lean-to hut using a tree for bracing is simple and quick to erect.

Cutaway section of frame for hut sited between two saplings.

The ridge pole is raised against the tree by means of the two end forked poles to the required height, between eight to ten feet, depending on the width. The end forked poles should be at an angle of not less than 45 deg. If the length of ridge is more than 10 to 12 feet, it is advisable to put in another one or two forked poles about halfway along.

On to the end forked poles lash a crossbar ("A") and lash it again to the upright tree. This crossbar has lashed to its front end a pole ("B") connecting and lashed to the ridge, and also the front eaves pole ("C"), and also the front thatching battens.

Thatching battens are lashed on to the two rear forks. The distance apart for the thatching battens varies: it may be anything from 6 to 12 in., depending on the length of thatching material being used. A general guide is that battens should be distant about one-fourth of the average length of the thatching material. (See pages 55-63.)

An upright in the form of a light fork may be placed under the front corners to the front eave pole. Wall thatch battens are lashed horizontally from the rear forked poles to this upright to wall in the ends of the hut. Wall pegs are driven in along the rear at whatever height is required and to these wall pegs thatching battens are also lashed.

Forked poles should be not less than 3 to 4 in. in diameter—thatching battens from 1 to 2 in. Ridge pole about 3 to 4 in.

Use dry timber or dead timber wherever possible. It is lighter to handle and its use avoids destruction of the bush. When making wall pegs bevel off the head—they will then drive into the ground without splitting. (See page 73.)

Pyramidal Huts

The pyramidal hut, having a square base, is particularly useful where it is desired to make the fullest possible use of wall and floor space.

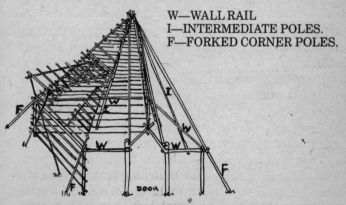

W—WALL RAIL
I—INTERMEDIATE POLES.
F—FORKED CORNER POLES.

Pyramidal hut, showing window frame, thatch battens and main structure.

The construction is very much the same for a circular hut except for the intermediate poles. Erection time is considerably less for the pyramidal hut. In this type of hut it is more efficient, when lashing on thatching battens, to make one lashing at each corner secure the two thatching battens, and when the span between fork poles becomes six feet or less to lash only to the corner poles, omitting the lashing to the intermediate poles. If the span between corner poles is greater than six feet it is necessary to lash battens to the intermediate poles.

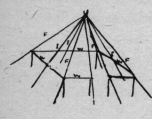 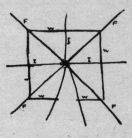

F—FORK POLES
I—INTERMEDIATE POLES
W—WALL POLES

LONG HUT

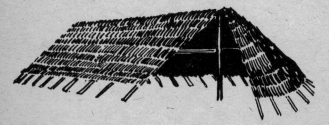

Hut, sixty feet long, twenty feet wide, by sixteen feet high, built by five men in four days.

The end portion of this structure is basically the same as one-half section of the pyramid hut.

44

The length can be extended to any required distance by prolonging the ridge pole and using additional supporting fork poles. If the ridge is extended and in two or more lengths, these should be lashed together, and it is advisable to notch the ridge so it will sit snugly in the interlocking forks.

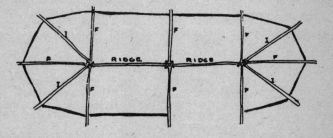

Plan of Long Hut. Intermediate poles required if fork poles are more than 6 ft. apart.

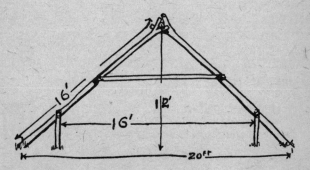

When the span is more than 12 ft. lash collar ties on to forks and intermediate poles.

Wall pegs are driven in at a convenient wall height and thatching battens are lashed down. Refinements such as "lift up" sections for light and ventilation can be added if required.

Step by Step Construction of a Circular Hut

(1)
First Construction: 30 minutes after start-off with four men on the job.
Note three fork poles to which have been lashed two rafters each, also entrance ridge and entrance poles with wall poles in position.

(2)
1 Hour After Start: The basic structure is completed, a start is made with the thatch battens and wall battens, the door fork is swung.

(3)
Lashing on the thatching–battens to the rafters. Note how the lower battens must be strong enough to bear a man's weight.

(4)
One and a half hours after start: Thatching battens are nearly all lashed on, door is complete, ready for thatching.

(5)
Two and a half hours after start: The door is completely thatched, and the thatching is well under way on the roof.

(6)
Two and a half hours after start: Three rows of roof thatch laid. The hut, which was 15 ft. diameter from wall to wall, was completed one hour later, or three and a half hours after the start. No nails or purchased materials were used. This hut would be serviceable and weatherproof for six to ten years.

POLES AND STRUCTURES

All slopes to be completely waterproof should be not less than 45 deg. (although a 40 deg. slope will shed water). A slope that is 45 deg. is useful and will give good headroom. To work out the most efficient size of poles for main structure it is advisable to discover first the length of pole required and then the approximate diameter, excluding bark. It will be found that the proportion of spread to pole length at 45 deg. slope is as 4 to 3 between base of poles.

Example: If spread at base of poles is 20 ft., then pole length to ridge or crown of hut will be 15 ft. This proportion is constant and wall space or height is not allowed for in the calculations. In general, a wall height of 3 ft. to 4 ft. is sufficient.

Diameter of timber inside bark can be roughly calculated by allowing a minimum of 1 inch diameter at butt for each four to five feet of length. Thus, if a pole is 10 ft. in length, the diameter of wood clear of bark at butt should be not less than 2½ ins. or, if the pole is 20 ft. long, the diameter at butt should be not less than 5 ins.

If the span is relatively wide, or the timber used relatively light, it is advisable to strengthen the structure and prevent sagging or inward bending of the main poles by putting cross ties or collar ties so that the thrust or weight is thrown from one pole on to the pole opposite. (See page 44.)

BRACING

Similarly with bracings, if long huts or lean-to type of huts are being built and there is no strong support, such as a growing tree, it is advisable to lash in diagonal braces that extend if possible from ground at one end to ridge at the other end. These bracings will make even a light hut quite storm-proof.

DOORS AND WINDOWS

Refinements such as doors and windows are completely practical in thatch huts, and very little extra work is involved. Windows are simply two (or three) fork sticks cut off short below the fork and with one long end projecting.

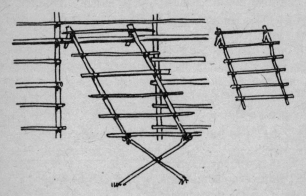

Window frames hook on to thatch batten above window opening.

Thatch battens are lashed to these fork sticks and the framework is lifted up and hung on to one of the thatch battens of the hut. In the general thatching of the hut this window space beneath the windows is left unthatched and the window frame is thatched as a complete unit. It is advisable to leave the window frame rather wider than the opening. It can be propped open at the bottom and still preserve a fair slope. If the window is very wide it is advisable to use three fork sticks. There should be at least six inches overlap of the window and roof thatch at the sides. The loose ends of the thatching above the window frames should be allowed to come directly on to the window thatch, and should completely cover sewing of the top thatching of the window frame.

Doors, if required, are similar to the gate frame shown, but with two uprights lashed across the fork. To these two uprights the horizontal thatching battens are secured.

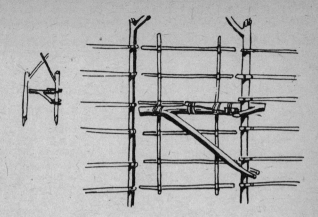

The hinging of the door frame is obtained by a combination of hook and fork.

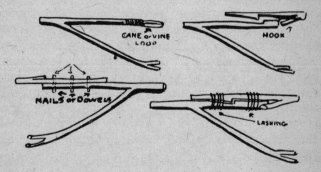

CANE or VINE LOOP

HOOK

NAILS or DOWELS

LASHING

There are several means whereby the door hinge can be assembled.

TREE SWINGING SHELTER

In swampy country, or in areas which are badly snake infested, a very simple swinging bunk can be made by one man in a day.

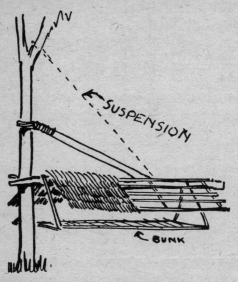

The forked frame stick must be very strong, both at the fork on the tree and at the main juncture. Either a cane or vine loop or a hook may be used at the top section. It is also advisable to have a vine or cane rope from the extreme end of the main frame to as high up in the tree as it is practical to reach for additional suspension.

The frame poles for thatch battens are lashed separately with a square lashing to the bottom of the forked frame stick, and, in order to give rigidity, a short cross stick is lashed horizontally to each of the opposite sides of the frame poles.

When thatching, thatch one row on one side, and then the row on the opposite side. This will help to strengthen the framework and keep it correctly balanced.

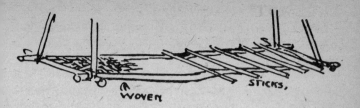

WOVEN   STICKS,

The bunk is made separately.

The main frame of the bunk is simply four poles lashed together to form a rectangle about three feet by seven. The space between the poles to form the bunk proper can be either woven or made with crossed sticks as for the camp bed (see Chapter 3).

THATCHING MATERIALS

Materials suitable for thatching range from long grass, reeds, rushes; most of the long stalked ferns, such as bracken, etc.; palm leaves of all types, and, as a last resource, many pliant leafy branches.

Long grass and reeds are most satisfactory when used dry or partly dry. It is advisable if you are going to use these materials to cut and stook them first so that they may get a chance to season before being used on the roof.

There are two good reasons for this: first is that in drying out most of these materials, if green and exposed to hot sun, tend to shrink on one side and turn and curl in shrinking, so reducing the coverage value for thatching. The other is the general tendency of all green materials to shrink, and therefore the thatching stitches become loose, and the thatch may slip from the stitches and be blown away in the first breeze.

When the materials are well seasoned the stitches will not slacken because there is very little shrinkage, and the thatch will stay down securely.

With most of the bracken ferns it is advisable to thatch with the material green, and sew it down very tightly. This also applies if you are forced by circumstances to use green branches. These do not make a very efficient thatch and their use is not recommended except in emergency.

In a general way, the use of bracken and reeds for thatching is doing a very good service to the land generally. Bracken is injurious to cattle, and reeds choke watercourses, so that removing these two pests and putting them to practical use is quite a good thing to do.

If branches of trees or shrubs are to be used, seek out a dead branch with some of the leaves still on it. Shake the branch. If the leaves immediately fall from it, the material is almost useless and will only serve you for a day or so. If the leaves withstand this shaking, the plant will probably serve your purpose fairly effectively. Some trees and shrubs drop their leaves within a few hours of being cut. Such are useless.

The palm leaves are best used for thatching when they are dead. You will find great quantities lying under the palms and these are excellent material. They may be brittle and inclined to break if you start collecting them in the middle of a hot summer day.

The best time to collect dead palm for your thatching is either early in the morning when the leaves are softened by the overnight dew, or after rain. It is always advisable to wet the leaves down before you start sewing them on the thatching battens. This damping down softens the brittle leaves, makes them lie flat, and ensures that you get a better coverage.

THATCHING METHODS

There are almost as many different methods of thatching as there are different materials. Each different method has its own peculiar advantage and applications for certain types of material.

The methods you are most likely to find of use are either to sew the thatch on to the thatch battens, which is called "Sewn Thatching," or to tuft the material on in bundles, which, appropriately, is called "Tuft Thatching."

Instead of sewing on to the battens you may find it more convenient to tie a pliant stick on to the thatching batten at convenient intervals, using the pressure of this stick tightly tied to the thatch batten to hold the thatch material secure. This is called "Stick Thatching."

There are also several methods by which the thatching materials may be secured to the thatching battens on the ground, and these thatching battens are then laid on to the framework, overlapping like long tiles.

Or with some of the palms the palm stalk itself may be used either as the thatch batten, or to hold the palm leaf itself in the desired position. All these methods are self explanatory, and briefly dealt with on the following pages.

PRINCIPLES OF WATERSHED IN THATCHING

Thatching may be either for shade or to give protection against rain. Thatching for shade presents no problems. If the thatch is thick enough to break up the sun's rays, that is all that is required.

Thatching for protection against rain or, under certain conditions, wind, will be effective only if certain principles are observed. It is interesting to watch the behaviour of drops of water on thatch. The drops run down the topmost strands, until they come to the very end of the blade of grass or other material. There the drop gathers size and, when it is big enough, and heavy enough, it falls off and on to the blade immediately beneath.

If the stitching interrupts the smooth continued course of the water droplets, then the water will follow the stitching because it is at a steeper angle. It will creep along the stitch and when it reaches the lowest point, on the underside of the thatching batten, the drop will gradually build up until it becomes too heavy to remain on the sewing material. Then you will complain that the "thatching leaks". Thatch will never leak if the stitching is properly covered.

It is this quality of "coverage" rather than thickness which makes a thatch waterproof. Windproofing lies largely in the "tightness" and thickness of the thatching.

SEWN THATCHING

Stitch at bottom of first thatch on lowest thatching batten. The second layer must overlay the stitching of the first row and include the top section of the underneath layer in the actual stitch. It is better to have each layer held by three rows of stitching. The stitching of every row MUST be completely covered by the free ends of the next layer above it.

To sew thatching make a thatching needle by cutting a dead, straight grained stick one inch thick and about 18 inches long. Sharpen one end and rub it fairly smooth

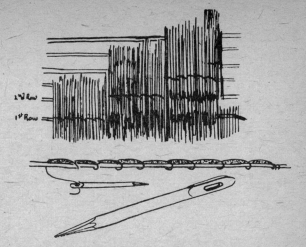

on a stone. Narrow the other end till it is about one quarter of an inch thick, but the full width of the stick. This end should be flattened for about three inches.

About two inches from the end cut an eye carefully through the flat side. This eye should be about one quarter inch wide and at least half an inch long.

Lay the thatching material with the butts towards the roof and the lower end on the lowest batten. Secure one end of the sewing material with a timber hitch (see page 68) to the thatching batten, thread the other end through the eye of the thatching needle and sew in the ordinary manner to the thatching batten. To avoid holes where the sewing may tend to bunch the thatching together, pass the needle through the thatch at the angle indicated in the sketch and push thatch over the crossing of the stitches.

STICK THATCH

With this stick thatch, ties about two feet apart are fastened on to the thatching batten. The thatching stick is tied at one end, the thatching material placed under it, and when the tie, fixed on the thatching batten is reached, the stick is tied down, thus binding the thatching to the batten. This method of securing thatching is useful when long lengths of material for sewing are not readily available.

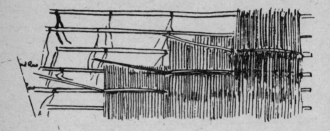

The overlapping and general principles of sewn thatching are followed.

TUFT THATCHING

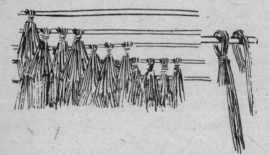

This method is excellent if the material is fairly long, say, two or three feet, and pliable. It is very suitable for reeds and sedges. The thatching material is gathered into small sheaves about an inch or so thick. The butt end is bent over the thatching batten, and a few strands are then twisted round the sheaf a few times and pushed through the bunched up material to hold the end secure. The tuft is then slipped along the thatching batten to lie alongside the preceding tuft. This thatch makes a very neat job from inside. It is secure in all weather, and requires no tying material. If sedge or sword grasses are being used it is advisable to put a pair of socks or gloves on your hands to avoid cuts.

It is important that the long free ends overlap the two or three preceding rows. Do not push the tufts up too tight. There can be about half an inch or more between the bent-over ends on the thatching battens. This open space will be covered by the free ends on the next row.

STALK THATCH

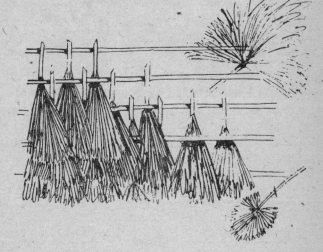

This method is very quick to apply and quite efficient. It is suitable for either the plicate type of palm leaf (as shown above) or the pinnate type (shown overleaf). The stalks are simply woven between the thatch battens. The natural bend forced on the stalks will exert sufficient pressure to hold the leaves securely in position. This is the quickest and easiest of all thatching methods, and quite efficient if the palm leaves are well bunched and have a good overlap to give watershed.

SPLIT STALK THATCH

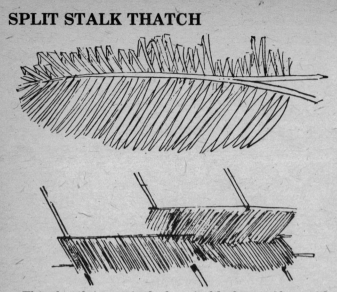

This thatch is particularly suitable for very long pinnate leaves. The centre rib of the palm frond is split. These split ribs are tied together and secured to the thatching battens with a good overlap. This method eliminates the need for thatching battens and is very efficient if suitable material is easily available.

WOVEN THATCH

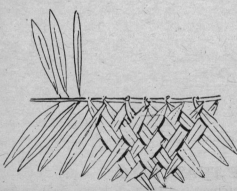

If time permits and the materials are readily available, an alternative method to the split stalk thatch is the woven thatch. The pinnate fronds are laid flat on the ground and the leaves from one side are laid over and woven between the leaves on the other side. The entire stalk is then tied on to the framework, observing the same principle of overlap which applies to the other methods.

SEWN BATTEN THATCH

With other long, broad-leaved materials the leaves may be bent over sticks on the ground and a thin sliver of split cane or other suitable material used to sew the two sections of the leaves together. The sticks are then tied to the framework as for split stalk thatching. This method is very neat and efficient for certain materials. If green material is to be used make certain that it will not curl as it dries out. Many grass materials will curl into thin strips, and the thatch will be almost ineffective. Dead material is generally best.

RIDGE THATCHING

In thatching the ridge it is essential to cover the

stitching of the topmost row of thatching. If this stitching is covered there will be complete protection. If it is inadequately covered there will be a leak along the ridge.

The ridge thatch therefore must curl completely over the ridge pole or, better still, over a false ridge pole or, alternatively, it may stand up from the ridge and, if bound tightly, will make an efficient watershed. For pyramidal and circular huts this last is the most efficient method.

SEWN RIDGE THATCHING

With very long material two heavy poles may be slung on slings, so that they lie on either side and hold the outside edges of the ridge thatch material down.

Another method of thatching a ridge is to tie on two battens to the top of the topmost layer of thatching. The ends of the ridge thatching material sewn to these two battens must overhang the sewing of the topmost layer.

An alternative method is to sew the ridge material on to three poles, one of which acts as a false ridge, and the other two, which are sewn tightly, hang over the ridge some twelve or eighteen inches on either side of the centre pole. This ridge thatch material can be sewn on the ground in lengths of from six to twelve feet, and when the roof is ready for ridging these are laid over the actual ridge proper and the two side poles allowed to hang on either side, covering the top layer of stitching.

CROWN RIDGE THATCH

A third method of ridge thatch is to make a "crown" and overlap this over the ends of the top layer of thatching.

GUTTERING

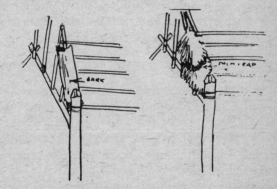

Under some conditions it may be necessary to put a "valley" in the roof, and this will require guttering. Efficient guttering can be made from wide sheets of bark inverted so that they lie with the hollow side in the valley. An alternative is the use of hollowed-out palm trunks or the extra-wide leaves of the plicate palms can be laid to overlap each other. Considerable care must be taken with this guttering if you are to have a watertight roof.

FLASHING

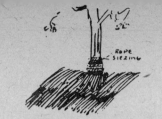

There are occasions when flashing may be required. For instance, there may be a tree growing through the roof where the ridge pole is held up, or for some reason some of the structural poles or tree trunks may project through the roof thatch. When flashing is required, simply spin up a length of thin rope from grass or other soft fibrous material (see Chapter 1 "Ropemaking") and bind thatching round the tree or pole. Continue the binding an inch or two above top of the thatching material. Make sure that it is tight and secure. The rain will run down the tree trunk, come to the flashing binding and, seeping over it, come on to the thatch, from where it is led by natural flow to the thatch of the roofing.

Rammed Earth

This method of building makes a permanent structure which is well insulated and low in cost. The only materials required for the walls are earth containing certain wide proportions of clay and sand or other gritty particles. The earth must also be free from organic materials such as grass, roots and the like.

Rammed earth buildings can either be built by erecting forms or by ramming earth in blocks (like large bricks) and laying these in courses.

Foundations and footings are made by setting large stones in clay in the foundation trench. Clay is in many ways better than concrete for rammed earth buildings, because it is impervious to moisture.

If concrete foundations are used, then it is necessary to put in a dampcourse, but with clay and stone no dampcourse is needed.

Foundations

The foundations (footings), as shown here, are large stones set in clay. The foundations extend from six to nine inches above ground level. Foundation trench is 2 ft. wide by 1 ft. deep, and lined with at least one inch of clay. After laying the stones in the clay, they are rammed to make a firm bed.

The advantage of this method of laying foundations is that there is no cost, and the method is speedy.

One man can dig and lay fifteen to twenty feet of foundation in a day.

The foundation must extend above ground level so that in the event of very heavy rain the surface run-off will not reach to the rammed earth wall.

SOIL QUALITIES FOR RAMMED EARTH

Any "heavy" loamy soil is suitable for rammed earth building. The soil must be just right for its moisture content. To find out the right "consistency", roll up a ball of the earth (about the size of a golfball) between the palms and drop it from a height of about one foot. If the ball breaks up, the soil is too dry, and moisture must be added before ramming.

If the ball does not break from a foot high drop, then hold the ball above the head and drop it again. If the ball does not shatter into small fragments with a six or seven foot drop, then the soil is too moist and must be allowed to dry out before ramming.

The qualities in the soil are easily determined. There should be not more than 70 per cent sand, and not less than 30 per cent. There should be not more than 70 per cent clay and silt, and not less than 30 per cent.

To discover if the soil is all right for rammed earth

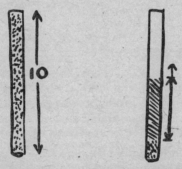

If Sand or Grit is between three-tenths and seven-tenths soil will be O.K.

work, take a glass tube ten inches long, or, alternatively, divide a glass tube into ten equal divisions. Dry some of the earth, crumble it to fine powder, and fill the tube. Take the exact quantity which was in the tube and put it into a billy or dish, and wash thoroughly in running water until all the clay and silt particles have been washed out. Dry the remainder and then put back into

—Photo by John Culliton.

This photo shows a rammed earth Hostel in course of erection. This hostel is to provide snow accommodation for 20 people. It is 35 ft. by 22 ft., 8 ft. walls, 1 ft. thick. The total cost of the building is estimated to be under $300. The only materials bought are iron for the roof, timber for roof, and floor, doors, windows, and 5 bags of cement for facing of the rammed earth wall and also for a 3-inch top sill for same.

the tube. The level will tell you the approximate percentage of clayey content that was in the soil.

If the soil has too much clay it will crack; if too little clay or too much sand or organic matter it will crumble.

FORMS

Forms can be made and bolted together, and in these the earth can be rammed or, alternatively, moulds can be made and the earth rammed into these to form blocks, and these blocks are then laid in courses like large bricks.

If forms are used they need not be more than two or three feet high and six to eight feet long. The forms are held by bolts which, when tightened up, clamp the form to the wall.

When ramming, shovel in three or four inches of earth and ram until the earth "rings". This is quite a definite sound, unmistakable from the soft "thud thud" of the first ramming strokes.

Ramming is hard work, and tiring.

When the layer is "ringing", throughout its length, shovel in another three or four inches of soil, and repeat.

Rammers should be from 6 to 8 lb. A hardwood base, about 4 in. x 4 in. x 10 in. long, handle maybe a 5 ft. length of gaspipe.

If moulds are used they must be of a design which can be quickly "knocked down" to remove the rammed earth block, and as quickly re-assembled.

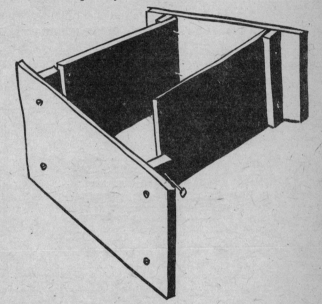

One man can fill and ram about nine to twelve cubic feet in a day.

Rammed earth walls should be at least nine to ten inches in thickness for an eight-foot wall, or twelve to fifteen inches if a top structure or greater height are required.

Rammed earth walls may be protected from driving rain either by providing a wide overhang to the eave, by plastering with a cement or lime mortar, or by giving a cement "skin" by brushing on a thick cement-sand mixture (one-to-two proportion). However, even without the cement skin, rammed earth will stand up to a hundred years or more of weather.

Log Cabins

Where timber is plentiful and white ants (termites) not prevalent and a structure of permanence is required, the Log Cabin is suitable. It is permanent, solid, and easy to build. The construction is simple. Cut your logs (which should be of roughly uniform diameter) to within a few inches of the required lengths. Lay the bed logs, which should be the heaviest logs. See that these are laid square. Where the end logs lie across the back and front logs, halve or scarf the sites for the logs.

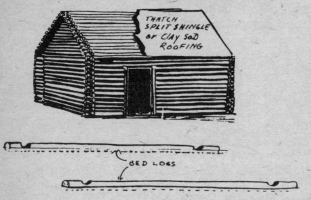

THATCH SPLIT SHINGLE or CLAY SOD ROOFING

BED LOGS

The remainder of the construction follows exactly the same method. The logs are carved into each other.

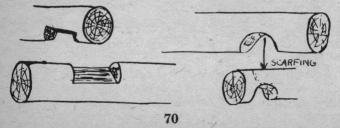

SCARFING

70

These are two methods of scarfing logs for building. The flat surface of the bottom log always "falls" outwards, so that when any rainwater blows in it will not find a place for easy lodgement, but will drain away because of the natural slope of the bottom of the scarf. Chinks between the logs should be filled with clay.

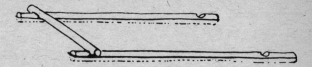

MATERIALS FOR LASHINGS

In bushcraft work it is assumed that no manufactured materials are available, and therefore in hut making lashing must be used when no nails are available. Rope, too, may be unprocurable, and it is then necessary to know what natural materials can be used and how.

For lashing, sewing, and tying, any ground or tree vine which has length, strength and pliability will serve. Length, of course, is visible and easily found, but tests for strength and pliability should be applied. The test for strength is simply to exert a steady straight pull on the material. You will be able to judge its breaking strain if under sixty or eighty pounds. The test for pliability is to tie a thumb knot in the vine and gently pull the knot tight. If the vine snaps or cuts upon itself, it lacks pliability and must be discarded.

In addition to ground and tree vines, the outer skin of the long leaves of most palms may be used for ties. To harvest these, nick the hard outer shell with a cut about one-quarter inch wide and an eighth of an inch deep. Start the outer cane splitting, and to prevent it "running off" *bend the thick portion away from the thin*.

This is most important. If you pull the thin strip and bend it away from the main stalk, it will split for a few feet and then "run off." This principle of bending AWAY from the tendency to run off applies to all canes, palms, vines, bamboos and barks.

BARKS

The inner bark of many shrubs and trees, alive or dead, also makes excellent lashing material. Strip down to the required thickness, but watch out for weak places.

SPECIAL KNOTS

Many of the sedges have length and strength and may be used for lashing and sewing work.

Nearly all the bulrushes can serve as lashings, and many of the "sword grasses" or sedges, but be careful handling these, as the razor-sharp edge can make nasty little cuts in your skin which poison easily. If handling any of the sword grasses, put a pair of socks on your hands and so save your skin.

SEDGES AND BULRUSHES

These green materials require special knots if they are to be used to best advantage. For example, the customary start of a square lashing is with a clove hitch (see also Chapter 6 "Knots and Lashings"), but a clove hitch on "green" bush material is useless. The natural springiness in the material will cause the start of the knot to open. ALWAYS start a lashing with a timber hitch, as shown above.

RIGHT   WRONG

And ALWAYS see that the free end passes straight through the "eye" and does not come back against the eye. If it does, it will probably cut itself.

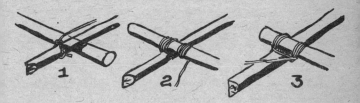

1   2   3

Start your lashing with a timber hitch, as Fig. 1; make three to six complete turns around the two poles, and "work" them together as you tighten the lashing at each turn (Fig. 2).

The frapping turns (Fig. 3) follow. These frapping turns close the lashing in, and tighten the whole job. Finish off by passing the free end of the material through an opening of the lashing and finish with a couple of half hitches pulled tight.

JOINING GREEN MATERIALS

An overhand knot (Fig. 1) will often serve, but if the material "cuts," try a sheet bend (Fig. 2) or a reef knot (Fig. 3). There are many ways of joining green materials either by plaiting or by spinning into rope. These are fully explained in Chapters 1 and 6.

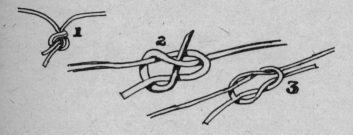

WALL PEGS

Wall pegs, and all stakes which are to be driven into the ground, must be straight, have the head bevelled and the foot pointed. This is shown on the illustration on the left. Avoid pointing with a single cut, as illustrated on right.

3.

CAMPCRAFT

With the only tool, a machete or a sharp knife, it is
practical and easy to set up a camp in comfort. Every-
thing one needs for bed, table, seats and chairs, cooking,
and even lighting is usually available in the area immediately around the camp.

A small amount of knowledge is needed and some of
this is given in this book.

Campcraft, like all the other skills in bushcraft develops the powers of observation to a remarkable degree,
and with this the ability to adapt or improvise.

It is applicable by all who camp, regardless of whether
the camping is a once-a-year venture with a car and
auto tent, or a weekend adventure with a pack on one's
back.

There need be no discomfort for anyone in camping if
they have knowledge of how to set up a camp in comfort.

A properly made camp bed can be as restful as an
inner spring mattress, and no food is more flavoursome
than when cooked in the out-of-doors.

If the camper does not know how to camp in comfort
there will be times during heavy rain when wood ap-

pears too wet to take fire, or when the wind is so high that the heat of the fire is blown under and away from the water in the billy the camper is trying to boil, or when ants or bush rats find the food supply.

This book shows many things you can do to make your camping more comfortable, and considerably safer.

PEGS AND STAKES

Campcraft without equipment is totally different from campcraft with equipment . . . and in some ways, "doing without" can be more fun. This Bushcraft book shows things that you can make and do in camp when you have no equipment except a cutting tool. Some items will be new to even the most experienced camper, and there will be much that is of value to the Boy Scout and his brother in woodcraft.

Camping without equipment calls for a really sharp tool, and a good deal of common sense. A good machete is probably the most useful of all tools for bush work. Mostly you will want sticks, either for pegs or stakes, or forks or hooks, and these generally can be cut from windblown branches close to the site of your camp. *It is always preferable to use dead timber rather than growing wood. By using dead (but not rotten) wood you are clearing the forest floor of debris, and by avoiding cutting green wood you are helping to conserve the forests.*

BUSH CAMPCRAFT

Even a simple item like a stake or a peg must be cut properly, and if it is to be driven into the ground it must have the head bevelled and the toe properly pointed.

THIS IS THE RIGHT WAY

This stake will drive cleanly into the ground. It will not split when being driven because the head is properly bevelled.

Both these stakes will be a failure. One will not drive because it has a bend, and this deflects the blow. The other will either split at the head, or drive crooked, because the toe is cut at an angle.

THESE ARE WRONG

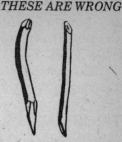

FORKS

Generally the correct sort of fork to select is one with a perfectly straight drive from the head to the toe, and with the forked stick coming off at an angle. A fork which is to be driven into the ground must have the head bevelled and the toe pointed.

There is a perfectly straight drive from the bevelled head right through to the toe. This fork will drive into the ground and stand securely.

THIS FORK IS CORRECT

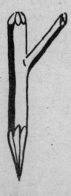

These forks cannot be driven. *Left:* If you try to hit one of the forks, the blow will be deflected by the angle. If you try to hit in the crotch, the fork will split. *Right:* Because the main stick is not straight, this fork will not go into the ground.

THESE FORKS ARE WRONG

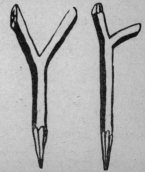

Most beginners think that the wrong way will work out all right ... everyone does ... the first time; then you learn that it pays to spend five minutes finding the right shaped stake or fork, rather than trying to make do with a poorly selected stick.

HOOKS

Unless hooks are to be driven into the ground, less care is required for their selection.

After you have selected the stake, fork or hook, and before you trim it, make sure that the wood, though dead, is not rotten. The inner wood must be sound.

THIS HOOK WILL DO THE JOB

AND SO WILL THIS

DRIVING STAKES

Stakes can be driven into the ground either by using the back of an axe for a maul, or if an axe is not available, a large stone, held in the two hands, and "pulled" down to the head of the stake, will drive quite effectively. When using a stone, if it is flat, use the edge rather than the flat. The edge will put more weight behind the drive, and there will be less chance of the stone breaking in two with the force of the blow. If stones of a convenient size are not available, a club with one flat face can be quickly fashioned with a tomahawk or heavy knife, and this will serve effectively.

CAMP KITCHENS

The camp kitchen should be sited so that the breeze will not blow the smoke into the cook's face. This is quite easy when you know which direction the winds blow, both in the morning and the evening. The morning breeze (*anabatic*, if you want to be technical) blows up the valley, because the warm air of the valley floor rises; and the evening breeze (*catabatic*) blows down the valley. Therefore set your kitchen so that the cook will face neither up valley nor down valley from the fire, but sideways. Thus the smoke will blow past him, and he can cook in comfort.

The kitchen should be sited on a slight rise so that during rain it will not be flooded. The fireplace, in badly drained ground, should be built up a few inches above ground level. Select the place for your fire, and build the kitchen round it.

FIREPLACES

If stones are available, build a wall to enclose the fire. This wall should be about nine or ten inches high, and the opening should be parallel to the valley. Do not take stones from a watercourse. They will explode in the fire.

You will want a means of suspending your billies, and the most simple is a stick across the end walls.

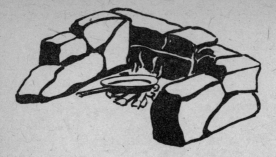

A trench fireplace is an efficient cooking place, but only suitable in clayey soil and if there is no likelihood of flooding.

A third method is a single stick, lying over one of the end stones, and with its farther end held down either under a hooked stake or by a heavy stone.

Two simply erected tripods of interlocking forked sticks at either end, with a cross stick, is another method of suspending your billies over the fire. This latter has the advantage that, by changing the base of the tripods, the height of the billy above the flames can be varied.

Another method to suspend your billies is by an overhead stick supported by two forked stakes driven into the ground at either end of the stone wall.

The best method of all, in a permanent camp, calls for a single straight stake driven into the ground at one side of the fireplace, and from this single stake a swinging gantry is hung. The height of the gantry on the upright

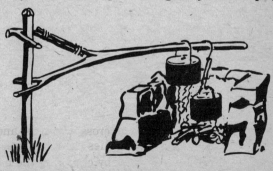

stake can be adjusted to any height above the fire. It will swing free of the flames, and the billies can be taken off without burning your fingers. Although it may take five minutes to make, it will save burnt fingers and spilt or spoilt meals.

In flooded country, or in a marsh or swamp land, it may be impossible to find a spot of dry land on which to light a fire. One way to overcome this is to build a raised platform with its floor a few inches above the water level. The sticks which make the base of the platform are covered with a thick layer of mud. On this you can light your fire and cook your meal.

In the absence of stones, and where green wood of no value (such as sucker growth) is plentiful, a reflector fireplace may commend itself to you, particularly if the location is windy. The reflector should be on the windward side of the fire, so that the wind, passing over it, draws the flames up to the top of the reflector and then across.

When you want to boil a billy quickly in an open space in a very high wind, the flames will be blown away if the billy is suspended. Woodsmen have a trick that is worth using under such conditions. Place the billy on the ground, and build the fire to windward and on both sides of the billy. The wind will blow the hot flames around the sides and your billy will soon boil.

BILLY HOOKS AND FIRE TONGS

All of these methods of suspending billies over a fire are improved with the use of billy hooks, and these can be easily made by cutting a few hooked sticks about half an inch in diameter, and varying in length from, say, six to ten inches. At the end farthest from the hook, a single deep nick is cut into the wood, so that the direction of the cut is away from the hook. The wire handle of the billy will sit safely in this nick and the billy stick from which the billy hooks hang will be sufficiently far from the flames so that there will be little chance of it being burnt through.

It is preferable to cut the nick on the side opposite to the hook.

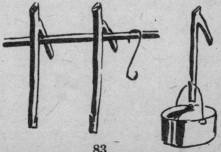

ADJUSTABLE WIRE
BILLY HOOK

It is worth while making a couple of adjustable wire billy hooks if you go camping frequently. The advantages of being able to have one billy high above the flames so that it can simmer gently, and another right down over the fire to boil quickly, is apparent.

The adjustable billy hook is held at whatever height you set it by the link which locks it securely.

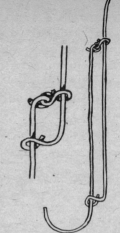

In addition to your billy stick and billy hooks, you would be well advised to make a pair of fire tongs. They will take only a few minutes, but may save a badly burnt hand.

Another improvised pair of fire tongs uses a narrow but long fork, and a single stick through its crotch.

WOODSHED

And finally, you will want to be prepared against a spell of wet weather, and so you'll need a small woodshed. Only then will there be a supply of dry kindling and wood after heavy rain.

The ground dimensions of your woodshed should be at least three feet by four, and about three feet high at the front. It should be to windward of your fireplace, so that windblown sparks will not fall on dry bark or other tinder.

FIREWOOD AND FIRE IN RAIN

Firewood gathered from the ground after rain will be damp and unsuitable for a good fire. This applies to winter conditions and in rain forest, except after a long drought. It is far wiser, if you want a good fire, to pull down dead branches standing on trees for your firewood store. This wood is always reasonably dry.

When cutting thick sticks into short lengths, an easy way is to make deep cuts, opposite each other, on either side of the stick, and then, taking the stick, bring it down sharply on to a convenient log or rock, with the cut area at the point of impact. One sharp blow will generally break the wood, and you will save yourself the work of cutting right through the wood.

Always cut and store an ample supply of firewood in your woodshed in a standing camp. You never know when you may get a spell of rainy weather. Lighting a fire with wood soaked after a heavy night's rain is not easy, even for the expert, and you'll appreciate your store of dry wood.

After rain or heavy dew, you can start a fire by picking a big handful of thin dead twigs from nearby bushes. Hold these in your hand and apply the match flame to the end of the twigs. Keep twisting and turning until the whole handful is well alight.

If the twigs are too wet you may have to make a few "fuzz" sticks. Select dead wood standing from a shrub and break into sticks about ¾-inch thick and ten inches long. Cut away the wet outer wood, and trim the dry wood down in feathers. Three or four of these "fuzz" sticks will start your fire.

If it is raining heavily at the time, start your fire in your tent, and carry the twigs or "fuzz" sticks when well alight to the fireplace in your billy. Shield the early fire from the rain with your body. A slush lamp (page 108) will always start a fire, even with wet twigs.

The bandage in your first-aid kit previously soaked in kerosene will give you a starter for a fire. The kerosene will not affect the usefulness of the bandage.

You can make one match light two fires by splitting the match. Hold the point of a sharp knife just below the head of the match and press down sharply. When using a split match to light a fire prime the twigs with dry grass or teased dry bark fibre.

BOILING AND BAKING WITHOUT UTENSILS

In emergency you may want to boil water, or cook food in boiling water, and you have no billy or utensil of any kind. This difficulty can be overcome by scooping a shallow hole in the ground and lining it with your groundsheet, some newspaper, a shirt, or any material which will hold the water. Build a quick fire of small sticks in which to heat twenty or thirty stones each two or three inches in diameter. Be very careful not to take these stones from a creek bed. Such stones may explode in the fire and injure you.

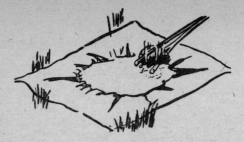

Fill the shallow hole with water, and when the stones are nearly red hot, which will take at least ten minutes, lift them one at a time from the fire with a pair of fire tongs and put gently into the water in the hole. The hot stones will not burn the paper or cloth, and five or six stones will bring a couple of quarts of water to boiling point in a matter of two or three minutes. Boiling temperature can be maintained for an indefinite period by putting in the other stones singly. Remove the cold stones when you put the hot ones in.

BARK DISH OR COOLAMIN

One method of improvising a cooking utensil is to make a bark dish, or Aboriginal "Coolamin".

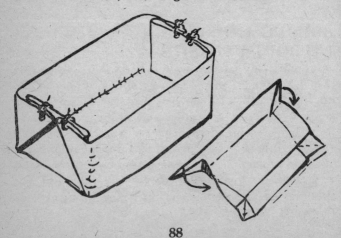

A flat piece of bark, of a species which will not split easily (the bark of many trees has this quality; one is the *ficus* family, or "fig trees"; test first by stripping a small piece of bark from one of the branches), is softened in the hands, and then the two ends are folded as in the illustration and pinned with a thin, sharpened peg or tied to hold them in position.

A coolamin can be used for all sorts of cooking with hot stones.

It is necessary to use the bark of green trees for a coolamin. If the sap is coloured, particularly if it is white or whitish and you can't be sure it is "latex" or "rubber", be extremely careful not to get it in your eyes. Many saps can "burn" your skin, or blind you temporarily.

Meat can be grilled by using a forked stick with the fork ends sharpened. Alternatively, you can place a flat stone in the fire and get it nearly red hot. This hot flat stone should be removed from the fire and dusted clean. Place the meat to be cooked on it, and the meat will grill perfectly.

Baking can be done by making a stone oven, in which you light the fire and, when the stones are "sizzling" hot, draw the fire out of the oven, and place your scone or meat in the heated cavity. It will cook perfectly, and cannot burn, because the temperature is falling all the time.

An oil drum or large tin, if available, can be made into a good oven. Coat it thickly with several inches of clay. Build your fire either in the drum or tin, which is used like the stone oven, or alternatively, set the tin over a trench fireplace, and build one fire in the trench and another on top of the tin.

Another ready-made oven is to fire a hollow log or old stump. When the hollow is alight, place your cooking (covered on top and underneath) inside. You will have to watch all the time your food is cooking, because the fire may be too fierce and burn the baking. If the fire gets too fierce, damp it off with splashes of water.

The best baking is done by wrapping the food in either a coating of clay or damp paper, and then burying it in the hot dust beneath your camp fire. Food can be left for six to eight hours without spoiling if the fire is not built up. The food will not overcook and you can rely on it being tender. This is one of the best ways to cook freshly-killed meat, which would otherwise be tough. When cooking fish and game by this method, it is not necessary to pluck, skin or "draw" the carcase. The intestines will shrivel up, and the outer skin, whether fur or feathers, will peel off when you unwrap the clay or paper.

A variation of this method of "primitive" cooking is to dig a hole which is lined with stones. This hole is "fired" with a quick fire so that the stones are thoroughly heated. When the fire has died down and there is only hot white ash left, the food, wrapped as before, is placed on the heated stones, and the whole covered over with the dirt removed in the digging of the hole. In this, as in the previous method of cooking, the food will not spoil or be burnt, and can be left for six to eight hours.

The cooking methods outlined are adaptable to the needs of the moment. For instance, it would be waste of time to build a stone fireplace on which to cook a single meal when on a walking tour. It would be far easier to select a suitably sheltered position in the lee of an earthy bank or rock. On the other hand, in a standing camp, time is well spent in making a good fireplace, secure against wind and bad weather. It is assumed that the reader has sufficient common sense to use the cooking method and fireplace best suited to his needs and to clear trash away from the neighbourhood of the fire, also never to leave a fire burning in a vacant camp.

An egg can be baked by placing it in the hot ashes of your fire. But first you must pierce the shell and inside skin to allow the steam to escape. The egg will blow up if this is not done.

Water which is very muddy, dirty or stagnant can be clarified and sterilised and made quite safe for drinking by filtering and boiling with hot stones. A good filter is made from a pair of drill trousers with one leg turned inside out and put inside the other leg. The cuff is tied, and the upper part held open by three stakes driven well into the ground. Fill with the dirty water, and then drop in the hot stones. The water will filter through, and must be caught either in a billy or bark dish and poured back until the dirt has been filtered out and the water is boiling.

CAMP FURNITURE

TABLES

A camp table and seats are worth making if there are five or six people in a standing camp, even if only for a few days. The best pattern of camp table is one which also carries the seats, and which will not become unbalanced or unsteady, even though several people sit on one side.

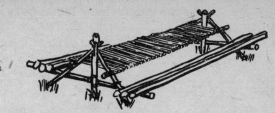

This is about the best style of camp table you construct. When you make it do not use green wood, but search through the bush and you will find dead timber, which is lighter in weight and quite strong, for forks and poles.

SHOWING THE FRAMEWORK WITH TABLE TOP POLES AND SEAT POLES.

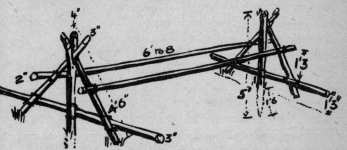

For the framework select two forked stakes at least three inches thick and four to five feet long. The length depends upon the soil, and how far you will have to drive the stakes into the ground to make them quite secure. The lower end of each stake is sharpened and the head bevelled. The first stake should be driven well into the earth, so that the lowest part of the crotch of the fork is three feet above the ground. The prong of the fork should be pointing out from the length of the table. When this stake is set, measure off the length you want your table, say, from four to seven feet, and drive in the other stake with its prong also pointing outwards—that is, away from the first stake. This stake must also be driven the same depth into the ground as the first stake. Cut four strong straight stakes, four feet six to five feet in length, and at least two and a half inches thick. Place

these with one end in the crotch of the forks, and at right angles to the line of the forked stakes. Note where the sticks cross each other in the forks, and scarf out cuts in each, so that the two will nest together in the crotch. These side poles carry the table poles and the seat poles, so they must "seat" securely in the forks.

On to these side poles, and about two feet above ground level, two strong poles, two inches thick, are securely lashed. These poles are for the table, and later straight sticks are laced side by side across these poles for the actual table top.

Fifteen inches above ground level, two very strong poles, three inches thick and seven or eight feet in length, are lashed. These lashings must be very tight to make these two poles secure to the two side poles and also to the forked stakes you first drove into the ground. These poles serve both as a bracing to carry the seat.

Your table is now ready for finishing. Cut short, straight sticks for the top. You will need eight sticks for every foot in length of table top. The method of lacing these to the table top poles is shown in the sketch below.

2"
to
3"

The seat-sticks—at least three to four inches thick —are cut a foot longer than the length of the table. You will need at least three of these seat-sticks for each side. They are not lashed to the cross poles, but allowed to lie on them, so that the distance of the seat from the table can be adjusted by either pushing the sticks back or pulling them in.

SHOWING HOW TO BRACE YOUR TABLE IF THE GROUND IS SOFT OR SANDY.

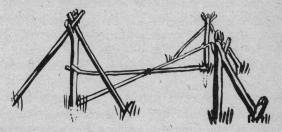

If the ground is soft, or loose sand, your table will require bracing, and this can be done simply by two diagonal braces from the table level of each of the forked stakes to the foot of the other. Where the bracings cross, they should be lashed. An alternative is to cut two five-foot forks and brace with these so that they "jam" below the forks of the stakes in the ground. Their own butts must be firmly seated on the ground and held from slipping by a stout peg driven well in the ground.

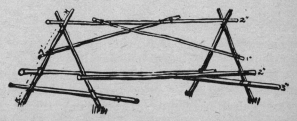

This type of structure is recommended for a portable table. When securely lashed the whole table is extremely strong. A fly thrown over the top bar can be used to give shade.

95

Another type of camp table, suitable for dry country, is to simply dig two trenches, two or three feet apart on their inside edges, and at least ten to twelve inches deep. This is only suitable when the earth is clayey or firm enough to be dug in clean sods. Sods are used to give height to the seat. When digging such a table, remember to replace the sods when you leave the camp site.

When using an earth table it is advisable to weave a couple of grass mats to lay over the seat. These will keep your clothes clean, and only take a few minutes to make on a camp loom. (See page 103.)

CAMP CHAIRS

A comfortable camp chair can be made in ten or fifteen minutes and will give you hours and hours of comfort. Select two stout forked sticks, four feet long and three inches thick. The forks must be at a wide angle, and cut with the straighter of the two prongs about nine to ten inches long, and the other wide angled prong about twelve to fifteen inches. Cut another stout forked stick about four feet in length, and leave the prongs of this sufficiently long to hold the two sticks you have previously cut.

SHOWING THE THREE MAIN STICKS REQUIRED FOR A CAMP CHAIR.

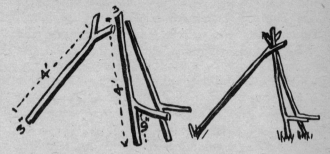

Across the seat portion of the chair, lash straight sticks about an inch thick, and continue these up the back of the chair. On the seat portion they must be close together, but on the back they can be spaced two or three inches apart.

SHOWING THE FRAMEWORK OF A CHAIR USING HOOKED STICKS.

There may be difficulty in finding two sticks with wide angled prongs, in which case you can make your chair by using two hooked stakes. The crotch of the hook should be about eight inches above the end of the stick, and the sticks themselves should be about three feet six inches long.

Two side poles, each about five feet long, are laid one

each through the hooked portion of the sticks, which have their upper ends lashed together. These two poles are lashed together behind the chair, and a forked pole, leading from the upper end where the hooked stakes are lashed, comes back to these two side poles and is lashed again. This gives you the framework for your chair.

Occasionally you will find a pair of twisty sticks which, lying on the ground, will look like this—

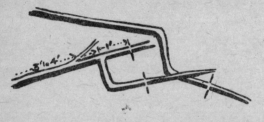

but, if you are quick to see the opportunity they present, you will convert them into a seat like this:

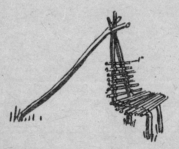

A good bushman makes himself comfortable wherever he may be. The simplest seat, of course, is either to roll up a log, or failing that, to select your site where a fallen tree will serve you. Such are not always to be found, and you can often make a comfortable seat by using a few stones to build up a platform, and between these you can lay two or three poles for your seat.

CAMP SEAT

A very comfortable fireside camp seat can be made by driving two short stakes into the ground, so that the forks are pointing outwards, that is, away from the opposite stake. The bottom of the forks should be from 8 to 10 inches above the ground level.

Two back forked stakes about three feet six inches long are driven into the ground, 15 to 18 inches behind these two short stakes. These back stakes should be driven in on a slight angle, leaning away from the two forward forks. The forks of the rear stakes should point outwards.

Both short and long stakes should be not less than two inches thick and the fork at least one and a half inches thick.

The short stakes should be at a convenient distance from the fireplace, anything from three feet to six feet, depending upon the size fire you usually build.

Cut two cross-bars, each about 3 inches thick, and cut nicks in these so they fit snugly in place in the forks, and connect front and rear forks.

Lengthways, lay straight smooth sticks, one to two inches thick. These must be close together. Along the back, that is to the tall stakes, lash similar sticks from 2 to 3 inches apart.

This makes an excellent fireside camp seat, and the comfort it gives you will well repay the half-hour it took to build.

CAMP BEDS

A sound night's rest is worth ten minutes' toil. Time spent in making a camp bed that will keep you both comfortable and warm is time well spent.

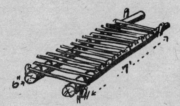

Cut two poles six or seven inches thick, and about seven feet long. Lay these parallel to each other, three feet apart; and to prevent them rolling, put pegs at head and foot, driven well into the ground with about a foot of the peg above the pole. Cut about twenty or thirty straight, strong sticks, three and a half feet long, and lay these every four inches across the two poles. Now on top of these cross sticks place two poles, three to four

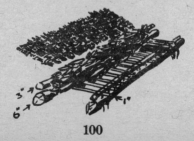

inches thick and seven feet long. They should lie against the pegs driven in to hold the two "bed" poles secure.

At the head end of the bed, lay about half a dozen cross sticks on top of these last two poles. Now cut green brushwood, fern, or waste green stuff, such as sucker growth, or weedy bush material, and put this so that the main stalks are lengthways along the bed. Pile it high between the two top poles, and lying across the cross sticks. The resulting bed will be as springy and comfortable as any you have ever slept on in your life.

If you are going to be in camp for a long period, you had better make yourself a camp mattress from grass on the camp loom (see page 103), and if bedding is short you can weave a covering from dried grass on the same loom, and sleep as warm and snug as if you were between the blankets in your own bed at home.

CAMP BED OFF THE GROUND

A framework, similar to the table, with the table top only, is made, and the two poles are overlaid with sticks exactly as for the bed on the ground. When making a bed

off the ground it is not necessary to have the forks as high as for the table. A camp bed should always be built off the ground in bad snake country, or in areas where ground pests such as leeches, ants, scrub-mites, chiggers or ticks are liable to be troublesome.

An alternative to the forked stakes and ground poles is the use of two piles of stones to support the sidepoles.

CAMP BED USING A COUPLE OF BAGS

A very comfortable camp bed can be made by setting up the two forked stakes as for the preceding camp bed, and two side poles are placed into the crotches of these so they are about 45 degrees slope. Two long, straight poles are cut, and passed through the two sides of two bags (holes are cut in the bottoms of each of the bags to allow the poles to pass through). The closed ends of the bags

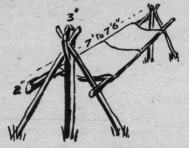

are towards the ends of the poles, and the bags overlap a few inches in the middle. The two bed poles with the bags are laid one on either side of the angle poles. The weight of the body, lying on the bags, keeps the side poles pulled well down on the angle poles. If the weather is cold, or greater comfort is required, a stuffing of dried grass or bracken fern inside the bags will serve to give greater softness, and also make this type of bed warmer.

STICK HAMMOCK

A camp loom is set up (see Camp Loom, page 103), and

the hammock is woven, using vines, twisted bark fibres, grass rope or any suitable material for the weaving, and sticks about one inch thick for the cross parts. The hammock should be at least three feet wide by six feet six inches long. The end two spreaders should be two inches thick, and from these short lengths of rope are brought to the central rope by means of which the hammock is suspended. Ropes from each of the four corners will also serve to suspend the hammock. A grass mattress, also woven on the camp loom, makes an excellent cover for the hammock.

CAMP LOOM

Two stout forked stakes, about two inches thick, are cut and driven into the ground with their lower prongs three feet above the ground, and facing away from the direction you wish to work. The distance between the stakes should be at least six inches wider than the widest article you want to weave. Across the forks a cross bar, about one inch thick, is laid. It is advisable to trim this cross bar of twigs and roughnesses. It should be fairly strong.

Eight or nine feet from the cross bar, and on the side farthest from the prongs, a row of straight, smooth stakes, each about four feet long, is driven into the ground so that there are about two inches between the centres of the stakes. These stakes should be trimmed of any side twigs or roughnesses. A weaving bar, a few inches longer than the width of the row of stakes, is cut and laid on the ground, parallel and about six inches in front of this row of stakes.

Your camp loom is now ready to be set up for weaving.

An alternative to the row of stakes, and a considerable improvement if a situation is available, is to select a site where two trees are at a convenient distance apart. At ground level, and about seven feet above the ground, two stout cross bars, two inches thick, are lashed to the tree trunks, and to these crossbars a series of smooth vertical sticks are lashed at top and bottom. These sticks are about two inches apart at centres.

TO WEAVE ON A CAMP LOOM

Lengths of the weaving material are tied to the stakes as shown, brought back over the cross bar, and then forward and between the stakes, and then tied to the weaving bar in front of the row of stakes. (This is the "weft" of your weaving.) A ball of material is tied to the outside strand, and then passed between the two rows of strands (this is the warp), with the weaving bar lying on the ground. The weaving bar is lifted above the weft, and the ball returned again between the weft threads. Repeat by alternately lifting and lowering the weaving bar.

CAMP MATTRESS OR STICK HAMMOCK

The weft or long strands are set up as for weaving, but instead of warp (cross strands), tufts of grass, fern or other material (or sticks if for a stick hammock) are passed between the weft. In weaving a camp mattress it is advisable to put in a warp tie every second or third lift. This binds the sides and prevents the outside weft strands spreading.

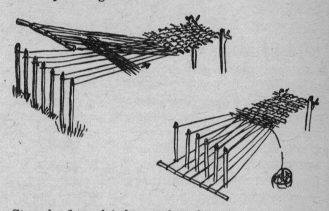

Strands of sun-dried grass, loosely spun, can be woven into a covering for a camp bed if you are without blankets. When weaving for this purpose, make sure that the warp strands are pushed closely up to each other. Do not try and make a camp blanket too heavy. It is better to make two light grass coverings than one heavy one . . . it is a number of layers, rather than extreme thickness of one layer, which keeps you warm.

WEAVING A CAMP HAMMOCK

Normally a hammock is made by using the netting tie, and netting needle (not shown in this book), but a serviceable hammock can be woven on the camp loom from bush materials. The ball of warp is passed around the weft threads to form an overhand knot on the lower lay of the weft, and these knots, pulled tight, make the weaving secure.

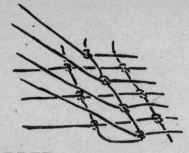

BUSH LADDER

A bush ladder is easily made. Select two long, straight poles cut to equal length. Lash the thin ends together. Spread the butts or thick ends so that they are about two and a half to three feet apart. To these lash the rungs, and make certain that the lashings are good and tight. Lashing the rungs is made easier if you lift the butts on to a log or a couple of big stones. This will allow you to pass the lashing material more easily under the poles.

SINGLE ROPE LADDER

Cut as many hardwood chocks, 1½ to 2 inches thick, as you require for your ladder. These are placed every fifteen to eighteen inches apart. The chocks should be about four in-

ches across and can be cut from
either square or round timber.
Bore a hole through the centre
of each chock. This hole should
not be more than one-eighth
inch larger than the diameter of
the rope.

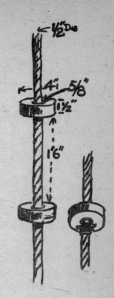

Thread the rope through the
holes in the chocks and then,
starting at one end, open the
strand of the rope and slip in a
half-inch thick hardwood peg
about three inches long. Bind
the rope below the peg. Slide the
chock down, and measure off
the distance to the next step. If
desired, bind above the chock to
prevent the feet pulling it up
when climbing.

SWINGING SHELTER

A forked pole, at least four to five inches thick, and
eight feet long, with a side branch coming off at right
angles to the fork and four to five feet below it, is required. To the side branch a rope or very strong vine loop
is secured, passed around a tree trunk, and then bound
very securely back on to the side branch. The long arm of
the pole should be horizontal and six to seven feet above
the ground.

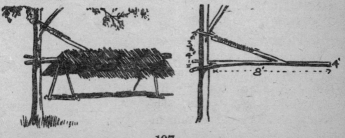

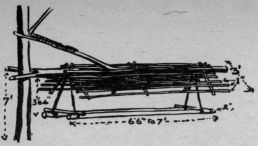

To make the shelter top, lash three 3-ft. stakes, each about 2 inches thick, to each side of the pole. They should slope down at an angle of about forty-five degrees, and can be held outwards by lashing braces across.

Lengthways to these poles lash thatching battens, each about 1 inch thick and eight feet long. These should be six inches apart. They are then thatched with grass, fern palms or reeds. (Branches and tree leaves are useless.)

The bed is suspended from the centre pole by ropes or vines to the two long sides, which are held apart by lashing two cross-bars at head and foot. The bed is then made up like the camp bed.

This shelter can be swung round the tree trunk to take advantage of sun or shade or get better protection from the weather.

SLUSH LAMP

A lamp for your camp is made by filling an old tin or small hollow piece of branch with clayey earth, packed tight at the bottom. The earth should come to about an inch from the top of the tin. Into this a twig is pushed and a piece of old cotton rag, or very finely teased bark fibre, is wound round the twig to serve as a wick. Fat from your cooking is poured on top of the earth, and when the wick is lit the lamp burns with a clear flame. The amount of light can be controlled by the size of wick.

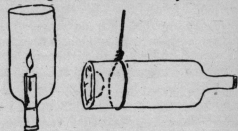

A CANDLE HOLDER FROM A BOTTLE

An open flame in a tent is dangerous, and a candle holder or glass cover for a slush lamp can be made by cutting off the base of a clear glass bottle. A very easy way to cut the glass cleanly is to heat a piece of thin wire to red heat. Bend this around the bottle where you want to cut it (alternatively, tie a piece of greese-soaked string round the bottle and burn it), and then, when the hot wire or burning string is around the bottle, immerse the bottle in cold water. The glass will break off evenly at the place where the wire or string encircled it.

NOGGIN

On many trees you will see lumpy growths or "burls", varying in size from a few inches to a foot or more. These are covered completely over with bark, and if you examine one closely you will find that under the bark the wood is all solid, and the growth is complete, without any holes where branches might have once grown.

Cut off the lump by making a scarf an inch or so above and another below the growth. A side-cut with your axe will then slice the wood with the burl completely free. Roughly trim the surplus wood, and with a gouge clean out the wood from the centre of the burl. This is very easy, because the grain follows the curves of the growth. Leave a handle in the form of a lip, and if you so wish, bore a hole through this handle and put a leather loop through the hole. A coconut shell makes an excellent noggin.

CLOTHES PEGS

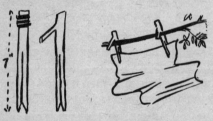

Clothes pegs are quickly made by taking a number of half-green sticks, about seven inches long, and splitting them, first binding the end so that they will not split right along their length. A better way is to use a forked stick, hooking the hook part on to a branch.

CAMP BROOM

A bundle of green straight sticks, each not much thicker than a matchstick, is collected and bound

tightly to a central handle. The business end of the broom is then trimmed off.

BUSH HOE

Select a dead or half-dead branch of hardwood, four to six inches thick, with a side branch from five to six feet long and an inch and a half thick coming off it at a fairly wide angle. Trim the side branch so that it is smooth. With your machete or tomahawk, trim the main branch so that it is a "hook" to the handle part. See that it is sharpened to a chisel edge. This bush hoe is quite an efficient digging tool, particularly if the digging end is fire hardened.

BUSH SLED

There are occasions when it is necessary to move a heavy load, and for this purpose a bush sled can be easily made from a forked branch of a tree. The branch is cut with the prongs of the fork a couple of feet behind the end of the main branch. A rope or other means of towing the sled is fastened on to this main part of the branch, and across the forks a few straight sticks are laid, and the load placed on top of these.

CAMP LARDER

A camp larder is simply a platform, roofed over with thatch and with the sides thatched so that it is dark and cool inside. Darkness will help to keep flies away, and coolness will help to prevent food going bad. An excellent improvement to a camp larder is a water tin suspended above the thatch, with a few pieces of cotton rag to siphon water on to a thatched roof. This is almost a camp refrigerator. The temperature inside such a larder, if built in a shady position and with a good breeze, will be easily twenty to forty degrees below the shade temperature outside.

Other methods of storing food in camp away from animals include placing it in a hollow log wedged in the crotch of a tree, or suspending it from a bough, or making a platform and suspending this from a branch in a

shady position. If ants are a pest, suspending the platform is probably one of the best ways to keep them away from your food. If they do find the cord, you can prevent them from travelling along to your food by tying a kerosene-soaked rag around the cord. Another method is to break a bottle off above the neck, pass the cord through the cork, and then, after packing clay around the rope where it passes the neck, fill with water. Water will soak down the rope and the bottle will need frequent filling.

Usually in camp, one's travelling clothes become crushed and soiled. This can easily be prevented by making a simple coat and trousers hanger. If you take off your good clothes immediately you arrive in camp and put them on this coathanger, they will remain fresh and uncreased.

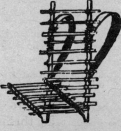

This "Adirondack" pack is a good method of carrying gear in camp. The cross sticks are tightly lashed to the two hooked sticks. Shoulder straps are plaited from reeds or made from wide strips of soft bark.

CAMP SUN CLOCK

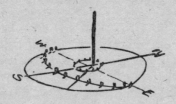

Select a patch of bare earth near your camp. It must be level, and open to the sun all day. Stick a peg in the centre of this patch, and with a length of cord as a loop around the peg, scratch a circle on the ground. This must be at least five feet across. From the peg, which is now the centre of the circle, carefully draw a line TRUE north. This must be accurately TRUE, and not Magnetic. Extend this line to cut the southern side of the circle, and then draw in accurate East-West lines crossing at the circle's centre.

Divide the circumference of the circle into twenty-four equal divisions. Each of these divisions will be fifteen degrees.

Now have a look at your map and find out what degree of latitude you are in. Measure this in degrees on the outside circle, working from where it is cutting the East-West line. Put a small peg on each side of the circle's edge to mark the latitude degrees.

Be careful to note whether your latitude is North or South of the Equator. Stretch the cord over the two pegs and mark where it crosses the North-South line. Now put a peg on the North-South line where the cord crosses it. Next, put two other pegs at either end of the East-West line so that the "degree" pegs on the circle are at

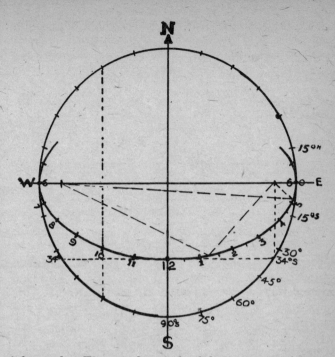

right angles. Tie a cord to each of these pegs, and have
the cord pass round the peg on the North-South line. Lift
the cord over the centre peg, and with the point of your
knife, scratch an ellipse on the ground, so that it touches
the circle where the East-West line crosses, and also
touches the point on the North-South line where the
peg is.

Connect up the fifteen degree marks on the circle by
means of the cord and parallel with the North-South
line. Where the cord crosses the ellipse, put a small peg
very firmly into the ground.

There will be thirteen of these pegs, and they will
follow the curve of the ellipse. These are the hour pegs,
starting from 6 a.m. on the left, where the West line cuts
the circle, 12 noon on the North-South line, and 6 p.m.
on the right where the East line cuts the circle.

115

You must now know how to find where to place the shadow stick. This depends on the sun's position North or South of the Equator.

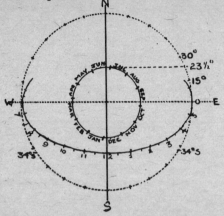

TO FIND THE SUN'S POSITION
NORTH OR SOUTH OF THE EQUATOR

Draw another circle inside the big circle using the same centre. The radius of this circle must be equal to 23½ degrees of the big circle. Divide this circle into twelve equal divisions and mark June at the North side; July, etc., follow clockwise. Divide June into four equal divisions, and do the same with December (at the South end). Offset ALL divisions one-fourth in a clockwise direction. The North-South line will now pass through the third division of June and December. Put pegs in for each of the twelve months' divisions.

To find the sun's position at any time of the year, draw a line from the month, and approximate day thereof, to the North-South line. This must parallel the East-West line. Where this line cuts the North-South line is where you place your shadow stick.

To get absolutely reliable time from the sun, two corrections for longitude, and for the "equation of time" are required.

116

The "shadow" reading, with these corrections, will be right to two minutes, if your North-South line has been accurate.

If West of the Meridian of Standard Time, add four minutes to sun clock time for each degree. East, deduct four minutes for each degree.

Draw a figure 8 near the sun clock on the ground, with the top half of the 8 just less than one-third the bottom half. Divide a line across the bottom half into three equal divisions on each side of a centre line.

Each of these divisions represents five minutes of time.

Now mark off the figure 8 into approximate divisions like the sketch. Put pegs in the ground to mark these divisions, and also the five minute divisions on the cross line.

Put a MINUS sign on the right-hand corner, and a plus on the left.

MINUS means that the sun time is behind clock time, and so you must ADD. Plus means that the sun time is ahead of clock time.

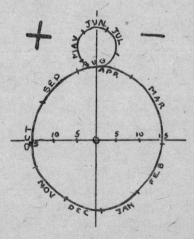

4.

FOOD AND WATER

Many people associate survival with the ability to find food and water. These of course are essential to sustain life.

In all areas, except the most arid, food and water in sufficient quantities are available, but the fear in many people's minds is that the food they find may be poisonous, or the water polluted.

This book establishes safe principles for recognising foods which are edible and safe, and ways to overcome possible contamination of water, no matter how badly it may appear polluted.

The search for, and recognition of edible foods sharpens and develops three of man's senses, sight, taste and smell. On the use of these depends the searcher's success in finding food and water.

Associated with the finding of natural foodstuffs which are edible and safe, is the preparation of these.

Bearing in mind that the person concerned with survival may have no equipment except a knife or machete, the cooking of food and boiling of water may be no less important than the actual finding of these. It is for this reason that these subjects are included in this book.

Food and water are essential to living. Under normal conditions a person cannot live longer than three days without water, but one can live ten days or longer without food.

Food, apart from its vitamins, mineral salts and other minute elements, must contain Proteins and Carbohydrates. Proteins are the flesh builders. Carbohydrates are the energy makers—the fuels for your body's furnace.

Every action calls for work from some of your body's cells, and, although new cells are continually being made in your body tissue, old cells are dying. These body tissue cells require replacing, and it is the digestible protein in your food which is used to build these cells.

PROTEINS are supplied by such foods as meat, cheese, nuts, beans and peas.

CARBOHYDRATES are supplied from the starchy foods such as bread, sugar, potatoes, and roots and tubers, and green vegetables and sweets generally, including honey.

For every action you burn up fuel. The more vigorous your actions the more fuel you require, and the faster your body burns it. This fuel is supplied from the carbohydrates in your food. Your body can no more run without this fuel than can the engine of a car if the petrol tank is empty. Your body stores up in its cells reserves of sugars, so that even if you have no food for your stomach, you can draw on these reserves and keep going for a short period.

Your body also needs other foods such as salt and special minerals and vitamins, but in a natural diet most of these essential specialities are contained in the fruits and meats and vegetables which you would eat.

It is possible to have a full stomach at every meal and at the same time to starve to the point of death. If you

119

tried to live entirely on proteins, you might starve for carbohydrates, and, correspondingly, you could be full of carbohydrates but starved for proteins. There should be a balanced proportion of proteins to carbohydrates, and the proportion is, roughly, one part of protein to six parts of carbohydrates.

Another absolute daily essential is salt. Without sufficient salt there can be serious physical consequences. In tropical areas where there is great loss of body salt through excessive perspiration, it is essential to eat salt, and maintain the salt content of the blood at a safe level.

General rules covering the edible qualities of foods are set out in the succeeding sections. If there is doubt, take no risk. Eat a small quantity of the suspected food, and await results. If there are no ill-effects the food is probably safe.

ALL FLESH IS EDIBLE

Nearly all flesh, if freshly killed, is safe to eat. The flesh of all mammals, all reptiles and all birds is free from any poisonous content and safe. But NOT the flesh of all fish.

By "poisonous" is meant actually toxic, that is, containing a poison. An exception in the reptile world is the Hawksbill turtle, which, in the thorax, contains a sac which more learned authorities class as toxic or poisonous.

PARASITE INFESTATIONS

The words "safe to eat" do not mean that the flesh may be eaten with no ill-consequences. It merely means that the flesh itself contains nothing which will be poisonous to adult human beings.

Many animals are hosts to parasites which can be fatal to man if they are introduced into his body. For instance, the flesh of the rabbit may be infested with hydatids, a worm which, if it finds entry into a human, can often prove fatal. The ancient Jewish law which declared the pig unclean was undoubtedly based on the observation that eaters of pig meat showed a higher death rate than eaters of other meats. Pigs are commonly infested with parasites which can also make man their host. Hence the law forbidding the eating of pig flesh.

In common with the pig and the rabbit there is always the chance that the flesh of almost any animal (particularly animals which graze close to the earth, or which burrow or which frequent fresh water streams) may be infested with parasites dangerous to man, and consequently no flesh is absolutely safe to eat raw, even in emergency. However, the parasites and their eggs are destroyed by heat, and therefore all flesh should be thoroughly cooked before eating.

This particularly applies to all fresh water fish and fresh water shellfish.

BACTERIAL DECAY

Putrefaction and decay are caused by bacterial action. Food is protected commercially by freezing, by salting or pickling, by heating and vacuum sealing, and by many other means. None of these methods which call for equipment are practical in the bush, therefore other methods must be found to preserve meat safely for indefinite periods.

Meat goes bad because of bacterial infection. Bad meat can be fatally poisonous if eaten. When the term "safe to eat" is used it only applies to freshly-killed and fresh meat.

PRESERVING MEAT FOR LONG PERIODS

The preservation of meat for long periods can be done by smoking and sun-drying, by salting and pickling and, for short periods, by cooking in fat. If climate per-

mits, meat can also be preserved indefinitely by freezing.

SUN-DRYING (BILTONG)

The meat to be smoked or sun-dried must be freshly killed. Cut off the fatty portions, and then slice the meat into strips no thicker than half an inch and no wider than one inch. These strips are threaded on to a wire or cane, so that no piece of meat touches another.

There must be free circulation of air round each separate piece.

Hang the canes or wires with the strips of meat above the thin blue smoke of a wood fire until the outer surface is quite dry. This may take from an hour to a day. Do not allow the meat to hang too close to the fire, or in the flame. Smoke alone is sufficient. If the meat is to be sun-dried, the only reason for hanging in the smoke is to protect the moist meat from blowflies while the outer surface is drying.

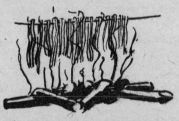

It is also important not to try and build a "smoky" fire by piling on green leaves or wet rubbish. If you do the moisture and essential oils evaporated from the leaves will condense on the strips of meat and make it uneatable.

Many an enthusiastic but inexperienced meat drier has ruined his meat by making a fire of green leaves, and then wondered why the meat was saturated with oil from the leaves.

Blowflies will not lay their eggs, or their larvae, on a dry surface. When the surface is quite dry, take it from the fire and hang it in the sun to complete the drying process.

A single day in a dry atmosphere will complete the drying-out. When carrying dried meat, pack it in a bag of open weave. Do not wrap or pack in cellophane or plastic, otherwise the meat will "sweat" and mildew.

Sun-dried or smoked meat will keep indefinitely and retain its original nutritive food value. You can cook it in a stew, use it for broth, or eat it raw. If well smoked, it is very palatable eaten raw. When using for a stew, it is advisable to soak for an hour or two.

PEMMICAN

This is simply sun-dried meat powdered. It may be mixed with fat in cool climates. Pemmican will keep very well, and can be eaten raw, or soaked and made into hamburgers or stews.

DRYING AND WEIGHT

These simple methods of preserving flesh effect a considerable reduction in weight, simply because the excess moisture has been removed.

This is important to the traveller who goes through

123

the bush on foot. About six ounces of dried fish or meat is equivalent to one pound of fresh meat. There is also a corresponding reduction in volume.

DRIED FISH (*See p. 126 , Edible Fish*)

The fillets of fish which it is known are safe to eat may be sun-dried in a similar manner to meat. With fish it is essential to dry quickly, and, if the day is not hot and dry, then smoke thoroughly over the fire. If the flesh is flaky and cannot be cut into strips, heat flat smooth stones and lay the slices of flesh on these, and place in the sun to dry out thoroughly. Turn the slices frequently. Fish meat is easily powdered into fish pemmican, and can be cooked either by making into fish cakes, or by soaking, if in strips, and then frying in batter.

By keeping the fish strips in the smoke continuously until they are completely dry, you have smoked fish, and very nice too! The best smoke for this is a thin blue smoke, and definitely not a heavy white smoke.

PICKLING

The meat is cut into small joints or pieces of about half a pound each, and put in a strong solution of salt and water (brine). Pickled meat will keep indefinitely in the brine.

COOKING IN FAT

Meat can be preserved up to five or six days in summer by preliminary cooking in fat, and then allowing the meat to remain in the fat in which it was cooked. The heat of cooking sterilises the meat, and the fat seals the meat safely away from bacterial infection. This method is convenient when meat requires to be kept for a short period.

FAT

When sun-drying meat, it is necessary to remove the fatty portions before drying, otherwise the fat will go rancid and taint the dried meat, making it uneatable. The fat should not be thrown away. Fat is food, and the fat cut off the meat should be rendered down and kept, if possible, as dripping for future use.

FREEZING

Freezing as a means of preserving meat is not practical unless in a climate where the temperature can be relied upon to remain below 29 to 30 degrees. Freezing alone is an excellent way to keep meat and is often used during winter skiing trips.

PRELIMINARY COOKING

Meat which has been either boiled or baked has in the boiling or baking been made sterile, that is, the bacteria which cause putrefaction have been destroyed, and therefore the meat will remain safe to eat for a short time. Re-cooking will effect further sterilisation and prolong the period during which the meat can be eaten. The time between cooking and the meat being unsafe to eat depends largely upon the weather; hot humid conditions will make the meat unsafe more rapidly than cool dry conditions.

The presence of blowfly grubs or maggots on meat does not mean that the meat is tainted and unsafe. These maggots do not indicate poisonous properties of decay in the meat. Their presence merely indicates the visit of the female fly, which, seeing suitable conditions for her eggs or larvae, has placed them there where they may have food. Meat which has been blown can be washed and eaten with perfect safety. Admittedly the maggots are repulsive, but they are in themselves quite free from actual poison. The blowfly is no guide to the condition of meat. It will blow any meat, putrefied and poisonous or safe.

EDIBLE—*BUT NOT PALATABLE*

To say that meat is safe to eat does not mean that it is palatable. The flesh from a shag or diver (cormorant) is edible, but so strongly "fishy" and "oily" that it is most unpalatable. Nevertheless, in emergency it can provide the proteins necessary to sustain life, and this flesh is wholly digestible.

The flesh of a cat, dog or rat is edible, and if you did not know the origin of the meat prior to its being cooked, you would eat it without repugnance. Cat tastes almost exactly like hare. Flying-fox, roasted, is as succulent as sucking pig; and snake, roasted in the ashes, has a white meat of delicate flavour. But you would not say they were palatable, simply because the source of the meat to your mind would be repulsive.

The rule is that the flesh of all birds, mammals and reptiles is safe to eat, but not all are palatable.

ALL WATER CREATURES

The flesh of some sea creatures is dangerous to eat

because the flesh contains actual toxins poisonous to your digestive system.

SALTWATER FISH

Provided the fish have the usual appearance of fish, and have scales and the conventional shape of a fish, you can say that it is safe to eat and has no poisons in the flesh.

If the creature does not have the usual "fish shape," and does not have scales, then regard it as poisonous, unless you know for certain that it is safe. An example is the shark, which has no scales. The flesh of the shark is safe to eat, but beware of the "innards." Shark liver has such a high concentration of vitamin D that a feed of shark liver, fried, might be fatal. The eel, which does not have the conventional shape of a fish, nevertheless has minute scales (or so I read somewhere), and the flesh is safe to eat. Properly cooked, it is most palatable, though somewhat rich in flavour.

The puffer or toady, the box fish, the pig fish and the leatherjacket do not have the conventional fish shape, nor do they all have the scales of a fish, and are all poisonous, except the leatherjacket, and I should be doubtful about eating the roe (eggs) or liver.

Colour of the flesh is no indication of the presence of poison in the flesh. Many of the parrot fish, having the fish shape and scales, have green flesh, yet all are edible and very palatable. It is interesting to note that many ancient mariners, including Captains Cook and Bligh, report that their men "*caught a mess of brilliant fish from the sea, and after cooking same were violently ill, being taken with great pains, and they fell a-vomiting, being purged with the poison of the fish they had eaten."*

It has since been noted by many observers that putrefaction of the flesh of many tropical fish sets in a few minutes after the fish has died. Consequently, the poisonous property attributed to the flesh is in reality due to the fish having gone bad in a few minutes. (The author has identified many of these tropical fish once thought to be poisonous; cooked immediately they have been caught, they have been eaten with no ill-effects. At the same time, some of the same catch were kept uncooked; in half an hour they were bad.)

You should reject for food any fish which lacks scales or which is of unusual shape, unless you know for certain it is safe to eat. ('Safe' includes eels, sharks, and rays, the flesh of all of which is edible, but do not under any consideration eat the 'innards'.)

SHELLFISH

All bivalves are free from toxic poisons, except for a reputed poison in the saltwater mussel at certain periods of the year, and the flesh of all is safe to eat, unless taken from contaminated waters.

This particularly applies to freshwater shellfish, which are likely to be hosts for parasite infestations which can be harmful to man.

Pippie   Clam   Cockle

Those taken from freshwater should be well cooked to destroy any possible parasites and their eggs, also the source of the fresh water stream should be known to be reasonably free from sewage contamination.

When the flesh is tough, it can often be made tender enough for eating by beating.

Cooking can be either by boiling, grilling or baking.

BIVALVES

Bivalves are found all along the coastal sea beaches. They make an excellent meal. A dozen to eighteen bivalves are a good feed for one person. To cook, put the bivalves in a billy and pour boiling water on them. The bivalves will open, and the fish itself can be easily removed from the two shells. The fish must be washed several times in water to remove all sand, and then boiled in fresh water, add milk and thickening after boiling (or water and dried milk if desired) for ten minutes. Before cooking, the flesh may be cut into small pieces. After ten minutes' boiling, add thickening and salt to taste. Pippie soup is identical with the famous New Zealand Toheroa soup, only it doesn't cost so much and you get more toheroa!

OYSTERS

Oysters, of course, are eaten raw, or they may be cooked and served as soup. Oysters are edible and safe all the year round.

CLAMS

Clams and most of the other bivalves must be cooked. The big clams of the Barrier Reef are all edible and there are records of captains of ships, long forgotten, sending men ashore to the Reef to collect clams, and detailed accounts of the cooking of them. Practically all these accounts state the clams were boiled before eating.

CONICAL AND SPIRAL SHELLFISH

Abelone   *Whelk*   *Conus*

The flesh of all the conical and spiral shellfish is edible and free from toxic poisons, with one exception, and many are very palatable.

The exception is one family of spiral cone-topped shellfish, the "Conus" family. Many of these have a poison dart or tongue which can inflict a very painful wound (one known fatality was at Hayman Island in 1935). These poisonous "conus" family of shellfish are not usually found out of tropical waters. They can be identified by the spirally-shaped conical top of the shell.

ABALONE

Particularly recommended for food are Abalone (Haliotis). These are a flat spiral up to five or six inches in length and four to five inches across, by about an inch and a half high.

These are invariably found below low tide level and like a position on rock among kelp and long seaweeds. They have some mobility and move sluggishly around the rock. They can be found by feeling gently among the

Shell　　　　Meat (remove shaded portion)

weeds. They feel like a roundish part of the rock and, if taken suddenly, can be pulled free. However, if given a chance to clasp the rock with their myriads of suction cup "feet" they cannot be pulled free with the hand, and a knife must be inserted under the shellfish to lever it loose.

To cook abalone, remove the shellfish from the shell, cutting the muscle at the top of the shell. Remove the intestines, and with a sharp knife trim off the ridge with the suckers, scrape off the blackish lining, and the base of the fish where it is rough from the rock face.

Beat the remaining portion heavily, and then toast on both sides till brown. Eat with salt to taste. Two are an adequate meal for one person.

The flavour is rather sweet, like lobster meat, only very much richer.

Another method of cooking is to cut into small half-inch squares after beating and allow to stand for about half an hour. The abalone "bleeds" with a bluish juice. Boil in this juice for five minutes, add milk and thickening and salt to taste, and boil for a further five minutes. May be eaten hot on bread or toast, or served cold as a savoury. The flavour either way is excellent.

Native people cooked abalone by dashing the fish down sharply on its back immediately it is taken from the water and then tossing the shell and fish on to a fire of hot coals and baking in the shell.

WHELKS

These large shellfish measure up to five or six inches in length and are found in rock pools among kelp and seaweed. The flesh itself is too tough to eat even when beaten. Break the shells open with a rock and remove the shellfish entire. Put these in water and boil for ten

minutes and then strain off the liquid into another billy and add milk, thickening and salt to taste. The result is a really delicious soup. The flavour is identical with crab, very rich, and most palatable.

CRUSTACEANS

All the crustaceans are safe to eat and free from toxic poisons, but freshwater crayfish and yabbies are subject to parasite infestations which may be harmful to man, and therefore the flesh should be extremely well cooked as a safety measure.

Crustaceans are usually boiled, but it is quite practical to simply kill the creature and wrap the shellfish in either an old wet newspaper, a ball of clay or large green leaves, such as banana leaves or palm leaves. The wrapped shellfish is then placed deep in the hot ashes of a fire. Be sure you place it in the ashes, and not the surface coals. Cover the bundle completely and leave for six to twelve hours. The food will not have burnt or dried out, but will be cooked deliciously.

This is an excellent means of cooking all meats. Freshly-killed wild duck, pigeons and all fresh meat is tough. If cooked in the ashes for ten to twelve hours the meat, however tough, will be tender. The meat cannot burn because the temperature of the ashes is slowly reducing all the time. This is an excellent way to cook large fish in camp.

OCTOPODS AND GASTROPODS

The flesh on the tentacles of all the octopods and gastropods (octopus and cuttlefish, etc.) is edible, but many are extremely tough and rubbery. The flesh of octopus tastes exactly like lobster. To cook, beat the octopus tentacles and boil in very hot oil, 10–15 minutes. It is probable that there are other ways of preparing these for food, because they are a favourite delicacy among Mediterranean peoples. *Caution: one small species of ringed octopus —4" to 6" long —has been known to give fatal stings.*

INSECTS

Some of the insects are a valuable source of food. Consider the bee and the food value of its honey.

Honey is so rapidly assimilated by the body that, if given by any means to a person unconscious from exhaustion, it will be almost immediately assimilated and restore consciousness and strength.

Honey is probably the most valuable single natural food for an emergency ration, and certainly the best "energy-giver" for walkers and climbers, except for glucose and proprietary products of a kindred nature.

In addition to the bees, certain species of ants store honey in their bodies, and have marked food value, and the wood grub (the "witchetty grub" of the blacks) is a delicacy when toasted, if one can overcome a natural prejudice. This is simply a matter of mental conditioning.

Vegetable Foods

GRASSES, FERNS AND HERBAGE

Grass Tips   *Fern Fiddles*   *Pig Face*

GRASS TIPS

The young whitish tips of all grasses are edible, and most are very palatable and tender. They can be eaten raw, and have a considerable food value. This applies to bamboo, which is botanically a giant grass. The seeds of all grasses are edible, and a valuable protein source.

FERNS

The young fiddles of many of the ferns are regarded as edible, but only a few are palatable, and many have a tendency to "scour." Bracken tips are edible, but are not recommended for food by this writer.

HERBAGE

Leaves of many forms of herbage are edible and very palatable. The plants specially recommended are Tetragonia, sometimes called New Zealand spinach, and sometimes miscalled "saltbush." This plant grows all along the sub-tropical coastal areas. It may be recognised by its light-green, slightly fleshy leaves (petiole in shape, that is, similar to an ivy leaf), and small yellow flowers. Tetragonia may be eaten raw or boiled. It is very palatable and has fair food value.

Pig Face   *Pig Weed*

PIG FACE (*Mesembryanthemum*)

These are all edible raw and most have a high moisture content and a tendency to act as a mild purgative. Food value is low, but they could sustain life. Baked, they are good food.

PIG WEED

This is edible and good food.

WATERCRESS

This grows in most of the fresh water courses, along the edge of streams. It makes an excellent salad eaten raw, has a slightly "hot" taste, and when freshly picked is crisp and nourishing. A word of warning. This plant may harbour one of the freshwater snails, which is host to some of the flukes or parasitic worms. Do not take a chance; wash the leaves thoroughly before eating.

STINGING NETTLES

These are edible and very palatable, but, of course, they cannot be eaten raw. Boil for ten minutes before serving. Nettles are grown in gardens in France for food. They must be picked with gloves on, and if gloves are not available, pull a sock over one hand and so protect your skin from the poison spines.

Do not confuse these ground nettles with the Nettle Trees or Stinging Trees of tropical areas.

FRUITS, LEAVES AND ROOTS

There are two fairly common poisons in the vegetable world. Fortunately, both are easily identified by taste. One has the taste of a bitter almond or a peach leaf.

This is hydrocyanic or prussic acid, a potent and highly dangerous poison which is often water soluble. When you find this taste in a plant, whether leaf, root, seed or fruit, suspect the plant as a source of food in the raw state, unless you know it is safe to eat.

If this poison is present, try boiling some of the plant, and then taste after boiling. If the "almond" taste is no longer noticeable, then you may regard the plant as probably safe to eat after boiling.

It is unwise to eat a large meal of the plant after this test. It is far safer to eat a small portion, and then wait a half hour. If there are no signs of stomach ache, vomiting or sickness, then you can be quite certain that the food is now safe.

The symptoms are stomach pains, nausea, and vomiting. Poisoning can be serious. Antidotes would be alkalis such as milk or soda (the white ash from a fire is soda ash and would serve as an antidote if mixed with water).

The other poison is recognised by a sharp stinging, burning or hot sensation caused by tiny barbs irritating the tongue, throat, lips and palate. This poison, for example, is found in the stalk of the arum lily. It is an oxylate of lime crystal. It can be exceedingly painful, causing swelling of the tongue, throat and lips. In general, oxylate of lime crystals are not water soluble.

If this poison is detected in a test tasting of a plant, reject the plant out of hand. The poison cannot be removed, and the plant is not edible.

BITTERNESS OR EXTREME ACIDITY

Avoid any plant which is bitter or very acid or very 'hot'. The unpleasant taste is a certain danger signal.

RED IS A DANGER SIGN

The colour RED associated with a plant in tropical or sub-tropical areas can be regarded as a danger signal. Any plant which shows red in any part of its growth, in its fruits, in its leaves, or in its stalks should be regarded with suspicion unless you know for certain that it is absolutely safe.

For example, the strawberry (an alpine fruit originally) is known to be safe to the general run of people, but some unfortunate folk are very sick if they eat strawberries.

RHUBARB
LEAF

Rhubarb has a red stalk, but the leaves are deadly when cooked because they contain a fatal quantity of oxalic acid.

The tomato belongs to the solanum family, the same family of plants as the deadly nightshade. So, in a general way, be suspicious of any plant which shows the danger signal red, unless you are absolutely certain that it is safe to eat. This is particularly applicable to tropical berries and fruits.

Another general sign of probable poison is any fruit which is divided into five divisions. This is a generalisation, but it is better to be cautious than overbold — and poisoned.

LEAVES

The leaves of many trees, shrubs and ground plants are edible, and very palatable, and can comfortably sustain life. The only test is to taste the leaf. If it is tender and pleasant to the palate and the danger tastes of almond, bitter, or extreme acid are not present, then you can eat a small quantity, and if there are no ill-consequences, then the leaves of that particular tree or shrub are safe and will be good food for you.

The leaves of most plants contain oil cells which give the leaf its taste or flavour. This is generally more marked in the young leaves at the end of branchlets.

Beware of all trees which have a coloured sap, white, red or black. Many of these saps are a danger signal, and some, particularly the white saps, can inflict painful burns to the skin or, if allowed in the eye, can cause blindness. Also beware of the ground trefoils, particularly those which have little corms or tubers. These are generally Oxalis, and have a dangerously high content of oxalic acid.

FUNGI

All forms of fungus growth should be avoided. The

food value is negligible, and unless you know for certain that a particular fungus is safe to eat, do not touch it. The fungus plants contain poisons which affect the nerves by causing paralysis. Many are extremely dangerous and to date very little is known of them. The author has had some small experimenting in this field and found a few, apart from the common "mushroom," which are very palatable and quite safe. One of the best of these is the puffball in its very early stage of growth before the ball itself had dried and become puffy.

The writer's advice is: "Leave all the fungus growth severely alone."

ARCTIC BERRIES

In the cold climates most berries are edible. This is in contrast with tropical and sub-tropical areas, where berries generally should be regarded as probably poisonous. In tropical areas the colour red is always a danger signal, and a good rule is to avoid all red berries. This does not apply in the colder climates, where almost all red berries are edible. Poisons are liable to be present in berries and this general rule should be observed in regard to all unknown berries.

SEEDS AND NUTS

A few seeds contain deadly poisons, and these poisons may not always be detected by the palate. In general, a bitter, strongly acid, or burning "hot" taste is a sign of poisonous contents. Any seeds with these tastes should be avoided. The mere act of tasting will not affect you. The poison may be *tasted* but must not be *swallowed*. When you are testing seeds to see if they are edible, you can spit out the portion you have tasted if it is unpalatable, and there will be no ill-effects.

Nuts, of course, are seeds, but for this work have been separated into a different section. Many nuts contain hydrocyanic acid poison. This is always detected by the palate, and in nearly all instances where it occurs it can be dissolved by either boiling or soaking in water for 10 to 12 hours. Other nuts, such as the candle nut—a relative of the tung nut—are violent purgatives. Again, cooking either by boiling or baking may render them harmless. Unless you know for certain that the nuts are safe to eat, regard them with some suspicion and test by first tasting, and if taste indicates no poison, then eat a small quantity. If there are no ill-effects within an hour, the nut will be safe.

ROOTS AND TUBERS

Most of the roots and tubers are safe, but almost all must be either boiled or heat treated in some way before they are digestible. The common potato is almost valueless as a food unless cooked.

Yams are not a particular species of plant. The word "yam" simply means the root of a ground vine. The sweet potato is a yam. They are a prolific source of food among people in tropical and sub-tropical regions. There are many vines which have these ground tubers, and, as far as is known, all such tubers are edible if free from the oxylate of lime crystals. In most yams the hydrocyanic poison is water soluble. Although the bo-

tanical genus of these tuber-yielding plants will vary greatly, there is one factor in common in the veining system of the leaf. This must not be taken as a hard and fast rule, but it is a very good guiding principle. If the leaf shows that the veins radiate from the point of juncture of the leaf with the stalk, rather than from a main vein, then there may be tubers to be dug from the species of plant.

The tubers and bulbs of many plants are edible, and the simple test of tasting for hydrocyanic acid or oxylates of lime crystal can be applied to all with a fair degree of reliability.

Remember that your own body normally provides you with the safeguards. First is the sight of your food. If it looks healthy and clean, it may be all right. The sense of smell is your next safeguard. If the food smells all right, you apply the next safeguard and taste it. If the taste is all right, the food probably is safe.

The principle of edible foods is as simple as that.

Remember to be careful with nuts and seeds; to regard red as a danger signal; and to avoid the fungi. If you remember these three rules you will undoubtedly be quite safe in testing and eating most plants which are palatable.

WATER

Associated directly with food is water. These two are essential to life. Just as there is the problem of finding food in the bush, so too is there the problem of finding water, and many explorers and backwoodsmen died because they did not know how or where to look for water in apparently dry and arid regions.

Many different forms of life are certain indicators of water in the near vicinity. The bees must have water. The mason fly, that big yellow and black hornet-like creature, requires mud and water for the tunnel wherein he stores the spider he has paralysed. Pigeons and all grain eaters need water, but the flesh-eaters such as the crow and the hawks and eagles can go without water for long periods. By knowing something of the nature of the insects, birds, animals and reptiles you can often find their hidden stores of precious water. (See Chapter 7.)

INSECT INDICATORS OF WATER

BEES

Bees in an area are a certain sign of water. Rarely will you find a hive of wild bees more than three or four miles from fresh water. A bee flies a mile in 12 minutes. You can be sure that if you see bees you are not far from fresh water, but you will probably have to look for further indications before you actually find the water supply.

ANTS

Many of the ants require water, and if you see a steady column of small black ants climbing a tree trunk and disappearing into a hole in a crotch it is highly probable that there will be a hidden reservoir of fresh water stored away there. This can be proved by dipping a long straw or thin stick down the hole into which the ants are going. Obviously if it is wet when you draw it out there is water there. To get the water do not on any account chop into the tree. If the hole is only very small, enlarge it with your knife-point at the top. Make a mop by tying grass or rag to a stick. Dip the mop into the water and squeeze into a pannikin. Another method is to take a long hollow straw and suck the water you require from the reservoir. These natural tree reservoirs are very common in dry areas, and are often kept full by the dew which, condensing on the upper branches of the tree, trickles down into the crotch and so into the reservoir inside the tree. Water reservoirs are very common in the she-oaks (casuarinas) and many species of wattle.

MASON FLIES

These large, hornet-like creatures are a certain indicator of water. If you see a mason fly's buildings in an area you can be sure that you are within a few hundred yards of a soak of wet earth. Search around carefully and you will see the mason fly hover and then suddenly drop to the ground. If you examine the place where she landed you will find the soil is moist, and that she is busy rolling a tiny pellet of mud for her building. By digging down a few inches (or at most, a couple of feet) you will assuredly find a spring and clear, fresh, drinkable water.

BIRD INDICATORS

FINCHES

All the finches are grain-eaters and water-drinkers. In the dry belts you may see a colony of finches and you can be certain that you are near water, probably a hidden spring or permanent soak.

WILD PIGEONS

Wild pigeons are a reliable indicator of water. Being grain and seed eaters they spend the day out on the plains feeding, and then, with the approach of dusk, make for a waterhole, drink their fill, and fly slowly back to their nesting places.

Their manner of flight tells the experienced bushman the direction of their water supply. If they are flying low and swift they are flying *to* water, but if their flight is from tree to tree and slow, they are returning *from* drinking. Being heavy with water, they are vulnerable to birds of prey. It is obvious then that the direction of water can be discovered by observing the pigeons' manner of flight.

GRAIN EATERS

All the grain eaters and most of the ground feeders require water, so that if you see their tracks on the ground you can be reasonably certain that there is water within a few miles of your location. An exception to this are parrots and cockatoos, which are not regarded as reliable indicators of water.

The carnivores, being flesh eaters, get most of the moisture they require from the flesh of their prey, and consequently are not reliable water-drinkers. Therefore, do not regard the presence of flesh-eating birds as an indicator of water in the area, nor should you regard the water living birds as indicators of fresh or drinkable water.

MAMMALS

Nearly all mammals require water at regular intervals to keep themselves alive. Even the flesh eaters must drink, but animals can travel long distances between drinks, and therefore, unless there is a regular trail you cannot be confident of finding water where you see animals' trails. This is a general rule. However, certain animals never travel far from water. For example, a fresh track of a wild pig is one sign that there is water in the vicinity, also the fresh track of 'roos and most of the grazing animals, whose habit it is to drink regularly at dawn or dusk. In general, water will be found by following these trails downhill.

REPTILES

Most of the land-living reptiles are independent, to a very large extent, on water. They get what they require from dew and the flesh of their prey, and as a result are not an indicator of water in the area.

WATER FROM VEGETABLE SOURCES

TREE ROOTS

CLIMBING VINES (LIANAS)

The roots and branches of many trees contain sufficient free-flowing fluid to relieve thirst, and this can be collected by breaking into 3 ft. lengths the roots or branches and standing these in a trough (of bark) into which the collected fluid will drain to the pannikin. In some plants the amount of water stored is truly unbelievable, the fluid literally gushing out when the plant is cut.

These vegetable "drinking waters" cannot be kept for more than twenty-four hours. The fluid starts to ferment or go bad if stored, and might be dangerous to drink if in this condition.

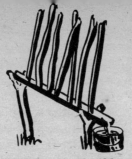

The nature of the plant, if judged by the properties of its foliage, is no guide to the drinkability of the fluids which are its sap. For example, the eucalypts, whose leaves are heavily impregnated with oils of eucalyptus, and in many cases poisonous to human beings, contain a drinkable fluid, easily collected (from the branches or roots). This fluid is entirely free from the essential oils and with no taint of the eucalyptus.

The lianas or monkey ropes found in tropical areas are an example of a prolific source of water.

There are certain precautions, and a few danger signs, with regard to vegetable fluids. If the fluid is milky or coloured in any way, it should be regarded as dangerous, not only to drink but also to the skin. Many of the milky saps, except those of the ficus family, which contain latex, or a natural rubber, are extremely poisonous. The milky sap of many weeds can poison the skin and form bad sores, and if allowed to get into the eye may cause blindness and severe pain.

With all vegetable sources of fluid even though the water itself is clear, taste it first and, if quite, or almost, flavourless, it is safe to drink.

For vegetable sources of water in arid areas the best volume is generally obtained by scratching up the surface roots. They are discovered close to the ground, and if cut close to the tree, may be lifted and pulled, each root yielding a length of from ten to twenty feet. These must be cut into shorter lengths for draining.

Many people who have tried to obtain drinking water

from vegetable sources failed to get the precious liquid to flow because they did not break or cut the stalk or root into lengths. Unless these breaks are made, the fluid cannot flow, and the conclusion is that the root, branch or vine is without moisture.

In general, water is more plentiful from plants in gullies than on ridges, and the flow is wasted if the roots are broken into sections and not cut. Cutting tends to bruise and seal the capillary channels.

DEW COLLECTION

In barren areas where there are no trees, it may be possible to collect sufficient moisture from the grass in the form of dew, to preserve life. One of the easiest ways of dew collection is to tie rags or tufts of fine grass round the ankles and walk through the herbage before the sun has risen, squeezing the moisture collected by the tufts or rags into a container. Many early explorers saved their lives by this simple expedient.

Pig Face *(Mesembryanthemum)* and Ice Plant *(Parakylia)* and Pig Weed contain large proportions of drinkable moisture.

Water on the Sea Coast

Fresh water can always be found along the sea coast by digging behind the wind-blown sandhills which back most ocean beaches. These sandhills trap rain water, and it floats on top of the heavier salt water which filters in from the ocean. Sandhill wells must be only deep enough to uncover the top inch or two of water. If dug deeper, salt water will be encountered and the water from the well may be brackish and undrinkable. It will be noticed, too, that the water in these wells rises and falls slightly with the tides.

These sand wells are a completely reliable source of water all over the world. When digging it is necessary to revet the sides with brushwood, otherwise the sand will fall into the well.

On coastal areas where cliffs fall into a sea a careful search along the lower edges of the cliff will generally disclose soaks or small springs. These in general follow a fault in the rock formation and frequently are evident by a lush growth of ferns and mosses.

MOISTURE FROM FISH FLESH

Another source of liquid sufficient to sustain life at sea, when fresh water has ceased to be available, is from the flesh of fish. The fish are diced, and the small portions of flesh placed in a piece of cotton cloth and the moisture wrung out. This moisture from sea fish is not in itself excessively salty, and can sustain life for a long period.

CONDENSING SALT WATER

It is possible to condense sea water without equipment and obtain sufficient fresh water for drinking purposes. (See moisture condensation.)

A coolamon is made, or alternatively a hole is scraped in the ground and lined, and the salt water is put into this hole. A fire is built, and stones are put in the fire to heat. These when hot are put in the salt water, which soon boils, and the water vapour is soaked up by a towel or thick mat of cloth. In time, this will literally become saturated, and may be wrung out, yielding a fair quantity of fresh drinkable water. Once the cloth is damp and cool, the collection of water vapour is fairly rapid.

Moisture Condensation in Arid Areas

A simple still for water condensation in arid areas can be made from a piece of light plastic sheeting, about 4 ft. square.

A hole is dug or scooped in the ground in a sunny position. The hole should be about 3 ft. across and 15" to 18" deep or deeper if possible.

The site should preferably be in moist ground, a depression in a creek bed is ideal if one can be found. If green material such as shrubs or succulent herbage is in the vicinity, the hole should be lined with this and the material packed down. It may be necessary to weigh the material down with a few flat stones.

In the centre of the hole, and in the deepest part, a billy or container is placed to catch the moisture collected by condensation.

Lay the sheet of plastic to cover the top of the hole, and weigh the edges with stones and use some of the earth scooped from the hole to seal the edges lightly. Place a stone in the centre of the upper side of the plastic sheet above the approximate centre of the water container to weigh it down to just over the container.

Moisture in the soil, and in the greenery placed in the hole will be drawn off by the heat of the sun and condense on the underside of the plastic. Condensation results because the air above the plastic is considerably cooler than the air on the underside of the plastic. The condensed moisture will collect into droplets, coalesce and trickle down the underside to the lowest point where it drops off into the container.

If the underside of the plastic sheet is slightly roughened with fine sandpaper or a similar fine abrasive such as a piece of finely grained stone, the droplets will coalesce and run off more cleanly than if the underside is absolutely smooth. Body waste, such as urine, waste food, moist tea leaves, etc., can be put in the hole. The pure moisture only is condensed. From one to four or five pints of water a day can be collected by this method. If the stay in the area is likely to be of some duration the top few inches of the hole can be removed and fresh green material replaced and the still will continue to work when this is done. Fresh still sites may be necessary every second or third day.

Acknowledgement: This effective method was first

evolved by the Water Conservation Laboratory in Arizona.

Stagnant Water

Stagnant water, or water which has become polluted, can be made drinkable and pure without equipment.

If time permits, such water can be filtered through a sieve of charcoal.

This will both clarify and to a large extent purify the water, but it is always safer to boil it before drinking.

If the water is muddy, the clay particles in flotation in the water can be precipitated by a pinch of alum, which will flocculate and precipitate the particles and so clarify the water. This, however, requires at least 12 hours' wait.

If no artificial means are available, the polluted or dirty water can be filtered by straining through closely woven garments such as a felt hat or a pair of thick drill trousers. The water, if polluted, can be sterilised by

ALUM

adding hot stones to the water in the filter. The water will soon boil and so made sterile and safe for drinking.

In areas where there is a likelihood of water being infected with bacteria, it is always advisable to boil before drinking or, failing this, to chlorinate the water with a pinch of chloride of lime.

5.

FIRE MAKING

The ability to obtain fire is essential in the bush. Fire can provide warmth, comfort, and protection. It is essential for the preparation of food, because heat in one form or another chemically affects the cells of plant foods, making some yield their nourishment, and others release their toxic elements.

Fire enables man to cook flesh and also to preserve it by smoking or drying. Fire is essential to make polluted water safe and drinkable.

The ability to obtain fire under any conditions, provided that combustible material is available, is one of the first essentials in out-of-door living.

The confidence which follows when one masters the skill of lighting fire with no equipment is remarkable.

Making fire by friction and other means is not easy, but when the skill has been mastered, the person acquiring the skill acquires greater knowledge of himself and greater confidence in his ability to overcome obstacles, both valuable characteristics in all avenues of life.

The ability to make fire under almost any condition is essential to the backwoodsman.

It may be important, too, that you know how to make fire that is almost smokeless, or fire that gives little or no flame. In war these two conditions can be of the greatest importance. It is also important to know how to make fire for signals, so that if you are lost, rescuers can be guided to you, and, of course you need fire to cook your food, fire to warm you, and fire to protect you.

THE CORRECT WAY TO LIGHT A FIRE WITH MATCHES

Even if you possess matches, lighting a fire in the bush may not be easy. The wood may be damp, it may be raining heavily, or there may be none of the usual aids, such as paper or kerosene. Therefore it is a good thing to learn how to light your fire with certainty under any condition.

Unless the weather is very dry, and has been so for days on end, do not collect your kindling wood from the ground. It will certainly be damp, and in the morning, after heavy dew, wood picked from the ground will be far too wet to light. Acquire the habit of collecting the thin dead twigs, no thicker than a match, which you will find on almost every bush. Gather a big handful of

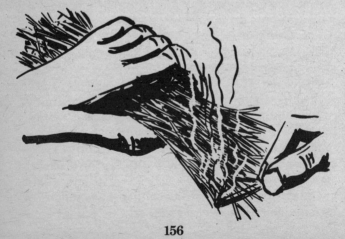

these, and to start your fire hold the bundle in your hand, and apply the flame of your match to the twigs at the end farthest from your hand. They will catch fire easily, and you can turn the bundle in your hand until they are all well alight. Then lay the blazing bundle of twigs in your fireplace and proceed to feed other small twigs on top, gradually increasing the size until your fire is built to adequate proportions.

There will be occasions during very heavy rain when even the twigs are too sodden to catch alight easily. Then you must take a thick piece of wood, preferably from a branch which has not been lying on the ground, and with your knife, machete or tomahawk, split off the wet outer layer until only the dry wood inside remains. Shave this down in curls all round the stick and make four to six such fire sticks. Hold these fire sticks by the butts in one hand and light the other end with your match. The dry curls will catch immediately, and the heat they generate in burning will be sufficient to dry out the thin damp twigs you place on top, so that even during heavy rain you can light your fire with one match. In strong wind or during very heavy rain take your twigs, or fire sticks, inside your tent, and light them in the shelter so provided. Use your billy, carried on its side, to take the burning sticks to your fireplace.

FIRST CUT

These fire sticks, shaved from the inner wood dry after heavy rain, will take flame immediately. Four to six will start a fire for you.

FIRE WITHOUT SMOKE, AND FIRE WITHOUT FLAME

As outlined in the first paragraph, there may be occasions when you desire to have fire without disclosing your position either through smoke or flame.

Smoke is the result of incomplete combustion, and therefore by ensuring that combustion is quickly completed the fire will be nearly all flame, with practically no smoke. This is achieved by feeding the fire with small dry twigs which catch alight almost instantly. By feeding the fire continuously with twigs ⅛-inch thick there will be no 'tell-tale' blue smoke haze. If possible light your smokeless fire under a tree (but not against the trunk); the leaves and branches will completely disperse what tiny amount of smoke is given off by the burning twigs.

Fire without flame calls for the lighting of a small flame fire in the beginning, and then this is fed with charcoal, previously gathered from half-burnt stumps. It may be necessary to fan this continuously if there is no breeze. A charcoal fire needs a lot of air and, though it requires flame for starting, it will burn and give out great heat with a total absence of flame when well alight. An old kerosene tin or 4-gallon drum, pierced to allow plenty of air holes, makes a good brazier for a charcoal fire. By its use there is no visible flame. If a tin is not available, build a stone surround to your fireplace to hide the glow of your charcoal fire.

LIGHTING TWO FIRES WITH ONE MATCH AT DIFFERENT TIMES

To light two fires at different intervals of time with one match may appear to be impossible. But suppose you split one match? You then have two! and therein lies the secret of lighting two different fires with one match. There is a knack in splitting the match, be its stalk of wood, paper, or waxed fibre. There is also a knack in striking the split halves so that they will light, and there is also a knack in lighting your fire when the split match is aflame.

To split wooden matches, push the point of a pin or a sharp knife immediately below the head, and force down sharply—the head will split in two and the wood run off or split. You have two heads and enough wood left on one half to burn for a second or more—long enough to start tinder blazing.

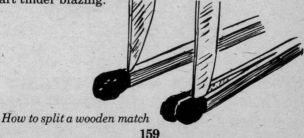

How to split a wooden match

With a paper match simply start to split the match at the end away from the head by peeling the paper towards the head. This will split the head, and so you have two matches, but each has a head on one side only.

How to split a paper match

How to split a wax match

To split a wax match. Treat a wax match similarly. Split the match from the end away from the head and up to the head. It may be necessary to use a knife to split the actual head itself.

HOW TO STRIKE A SPLIT MATCH— DRAW MATCH FLATLY ALONG BOX
In striking all three types of split match the 'stalk' of

the match should be held between the thumb and forefinger, with the tip of the middle finger resting lightly on the head of the match. The match is drawn lightly and 'flat' along the striking surface. Immediately the head starts to burn, the forefinger, which has been holding it gently down to the striking surface, is lifted, and the match allowed to flame.

It requires practice to be certain that you can always split your match and strike both portions. (This splitting of matches reached a high degree of proficiency with prisoners during the war, and many men were able to split a match into six portions, and strike each one of them with certainty.)

BURNT FINGER CURE

In learning how to strike a split match you will probably get a scorched fingertip on a few occasions. The quickest relief is to grab the lobe of your ear with the burnt finger. The natural oil on your ear will seal off the small burn from the air.

PRIMING

How to prepare for lighting fire with a split match.

Lighting a fire with a single portion of a split match calls for extreme care in the preparation of your materials. A bundle of very thin dry twigs should be collected as for fire-lighting with one match, and the bundle should be loosely 'primed' in the centre with tinders of fine dry inflammable material, teased-out dry grass, a bit of teased cotton, fine dry teased-out bark or any of a hundred natural materials will do. Do not pack your tinder tightly or put in too much or you will 'drown' the tiny flame; just a very light priming will catch the flame quickly. When the little flame of the split match is applied to the tinder it must take the flame instantly and set fire to the thinnest of the dry twigs so that the whole bundle will soon be alight.

Lighting a fire with a split match should be practised in order to achieve real proficiency.

KEEPING RESERVE MATCHES DRY

Always keep a reserve of matches in your camp kit. These matches should be specially treated so that they are protected against wet. This can be done with ordinary safety matches by coating the head and stick with

candle grease. Simply light a candle and drip the hot wax on the head, and rub some along the stick. The specially treated matches are best carried in a small screw-top plastic container. The striking side of a match box can also be wrapped in cellophane and enclosed in this container with the matches. By preparing for sudden need through having this reserve of matches available you may save yourself much hardship and difficulty.

LIGHTING FIRE FROM A COAL

Sometimes only a small red coal may be available to start your fire and, unless you know how, you will never get the coal to catch onto tinder, and so give you flame. It is important to know therefore how to make fire from a single tiny coal, no bigger than the pinched-out spark of a cigarette.

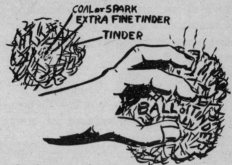

Lighting a fire from a coal.

To light your fire from a coal, collect a bundle of dry tinder (see 'tinders,' page 167), softly tease a large piece, and place the coal in the centre, fold the rest of the tinder over the coal, and with the tinder ball held very loosely between the widespread fingers, whirl the ball round and round at arm's length, or, if there is a strong wind blowing, hold the ball in the air, allowing the wind to blow between the fingers. The ball will commence to smoke as the tinder catches. When there is a dense flow of smoke blow into the ball, loosening it in your hand. These few last puffs will convert the smouldering mass to flame and you will have achieved fire from a coal. This too should be practised frequently.

FIREWOOD

Burning qualities of different woods vary greatly. Some such as pines burn with a clean bright flame and give out considerable heat.

Others char and smoke and give out little warmth.

In general all the pines burn well when dry, and most of the hardwoods are also good fuel, but there are a few species which are unsatisfactory for firewoods.

In tropical and sub-tropical areas, the soft woods of the rain forest are usually poor fuel, as are the trunks of palms, but palm leaves and stalks are good.

Trees which grow in swamp or marshland are rarely good for firewood.

The only way to know which species of wood in a locality are good fuel is to try and burn them. This will soon provide the answer.

In general, the firewood collected will be dead branches. Some of these will be on the ground, others still attached to the parent tree, or others possibly caught in shrubs beneath the tree.

It is better to collect wood from trees or shrubs, rather than wood which is actually lying on the ground. Wood picked up from the ground will usually be damp or even wet, but wood which has not lain on the ground will be comparatively dry, even in rainy weather.

For a fire for cooking, sticks half an inch to an inch in thickness are most suitable because the amount of heat can be controlled more easily.

For a fire for warmth, use thick logs. It will often be easier to burn a long log in half than to try and cut it. For these long logs, start the fire in the centre of the log, and when it burns through, the two halves will be easier to handle. For an all-night fire, occasionally pushing the two burning ends together will keep the fire burning gently, and a fair-sized log can be made to burn all night.

CUTTING FIREWOOD

The cutting of firewood into suitable lengths is always a worthwhile camp chore. Light sticks may be broken across the knee, and stacked in a pile by themselves.

Heavier sticks can be broken in the same manner if they are first nicked deeply on opposite sides.

If the sticks are very thick they may be more easily broken by making deep cuts on opposite sides, and then hitting the stick down sharply on a convenient log or rock with the cut area at the point of impact. One sharp blow will generally break the wood, and you will be able to save yourself the work of cutting right through the wood.

The brittle, dead woods can usually be broken into short lengths by bringing the branch down in the above manner. Unless the wood is brittle enough to break off short it may jar your hands badly, so therefore it is advisable to try each piece lightly at first before you exert a full-strength blow.

SPLITTING FIREWOOD

Blocks of wood are most easily split either around the circular rings (the round markings which show each year's growth), or radially, that is across the circular rings. Some woods will split easily either way. Others will be exceedingly tough.

Breaking dead wood is easier than chopping.

If you try to split the wood the wrong way it will be very hard work and the wood will be 'cranky.' Immediately you try the right way the wood will split fairly easily, unless of course it is knotty. Trial and error is the best way to find out, and use a comparatively light blow to test the grain.

When splitting wood with an axe blade the best results are obtained by driving the blade of the axe into the block of wood, then raising both axe and wood, and by reversing the axe head in the air, bringing the axe head down with the wood uppermost. One blow in this manner will generally open the toughest block, provided it is not knotty.

After wood has been cut for the cooking fire it is good practice to stack it in graded heaps, little, medium, and big sticks separately, beside the fireplace, with fine twigs and thin slivers in a separate stack.

WOODSHED

And finally, you will want to be prepared against a spell of wet weather, and so you'll need a small woodshed. Only then will there be a supply of dry kindling and wood after heavy rain.

The ground dimensions of your woodshed should be at least three feet by four, and about three feet high at the front. It should be to windward of your fireplace, so that windblown sparks will not fall on dry bark or other tinder.

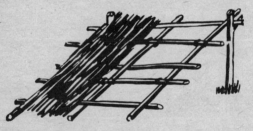

LIGHTING FIRE WITHOUT MATCHES

DIRECT FLAME

Direct flame, using sugar and permanganate of potash (Condy's crystals). Take about one teaspoonful of sugar, and about half this quantity of permanganate of potash (Condy's crystals, probably carried in the first-aid kit), mix together, and place in a hollow cut in a piece of dry wood. This hollow must be big enough to hold the whole of the dry mixture. Round off a straight stick, about ⅜" to ½" thick and 12" long to a shallow point. Place this end of the stick in the powder and rotate the stick rapidly between the two hands. The mixture will burst into a slow flame. Several attempts may be necessary to obtain ignition. This method may not be effective in damp or cold weather.

SPARK

Iron, iron pyrites and steel used with flint and also some of the very hard stones such as quartz will strike a strong spark, from which it is possible to get a spark for fire. The vital spark for fire-making may also be obtained by friction using a drill and bow, by a magnifying glass which concentrates the sun's rays, and by compression of air, which concentrates the heat. In the sequence of fire lighting without matches the first step is to get the spark, then from the spark to a coal and lastly from a coal to flame. The spark must be taken onto a tinder, and therefore the preparation of the tinder is a highly important part of fire-making.

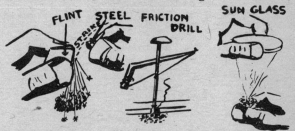

TINDERS AND THEIR PREPARATION

The principle required from a tinder is that it must be readily combustible and finely fibred.

A simple test of natural, that is unprepared, tinder

should be made to discover which materials are suitable. To make the test take a loosely teased handful of the material and blow. If the fire from the coal extends to the tinders it can be regarded as suitable.

Natural tinders are generally found in dry, beaten grass, finely teased bark, and palm fibre. Most of these coarse tinders are improved in their ability to take and hold a spark by being beaten and pounded until the fibres are fine and soft.

Natural fire-catching properties of tinders can be improved by the addition of a light dusting of very finely ground charcoal or, better still, by being thoroughly scorched.

If saltpetre is available a little may be mixed with the charcoal before it is added to the tinder, or the tinder itself can be soaked in a solution of saltpetre and water and allowed to dry out before use.

Tinder impregnated with a solution of saltpetre and later dried must be carried in an airtight container. If carried otherwise the saltpetre will become damp with moisture from the air. With this, or other prepared tinders you always have an emergency means of getting fire.

Note: You will discover that some of the soft inner barks, teased and spun into cord, will smoulder slowly when lighted. This is called a 'slow match.' It is worth while identifying the plants whose bark have this property. Lengths of cord made from such bark can be used to maintain a 'coal' for a long length of time, and so save your precious matches. (See page 170.)

Old cotton or linen rag, scorched black and teased, is among the best of all tinders. A pinch of this, placed where the spark will fall, is certain to take the spark and quickly become a glowing coal.

Using these tinders, lighting fire from spark is comparatively easy.

Striking fire from iron pyrites or quartz.

How to strike fire from flint and steel onto tinder.

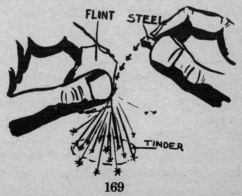

STRIKING A SPARK

Flint and steel, of course, were the common method of lighting a fire before friction matches were perfected and no great skill is needed for their use. The synthetic flint used in a cigarette lighter is a considerable improvement on natural flint. A couple of pieces of synthetic flint pressed into a small piece of 'perspex' make an excellent emergency firelighting outfit (heat the perspex and press the flints in while it is hot. Hold under cold water and the perspex will shrink on the flints and hold them securely).

An alternative to flint and steel are two pieces of iron pyrites, which, when struck together, throw off a shower of hot sparks that will last for at least a second. Iron pyrites is a common crystalline formation, and not difficult to obtain. Iron pyrites and steel will also give a hot spark. Quartz and steel, or two pieces of quartz, will also strike off good sparks, but these latter stones are very much harder to use.

The sparks struck must fall on the tinder, which, in turn, must be blown into a coal, and from the coal to a flame. Only a pinch of tinder is required when you are proficient with striking a spark.

FIRE BY FRICTION

Firelighting by friction consists first in generating a spark or tiny coal, and then nursing this (in the tinder) to flame.

Firelighting by friction is most easily mastered by the rotation of a drill or spindle in a foot piece. The drill, with some native people, is rotated between the hands but this requires considerable skill. Other primitive people rotated the spindle by means of a bow and thong. This last is the easiest method. The components, which should be prepared beforehand, are a bow, headpiece, drill, and footpiece. The dimensions given on page 19 and below are a guide for size.

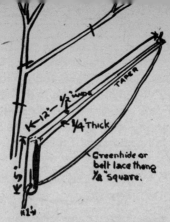

Bow. *Thong is made from a leather lace or a strip of greenhide belt lacing.*

To use a fireset, the drill is put under the thong, and twisted so that *the drill finally is on the outer side of the thong, and with that portion of the thong nearest the handle of the bow on the upper side of the drill.* This is important.

Drill.

If the thong is wrong way on the drill it will cross over itself and cut in a few strokes, also the full length of the stroke cannot be obtained.

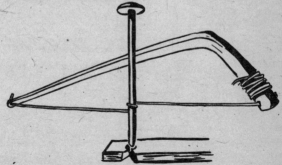

This is how the thong must be round the drill.

171

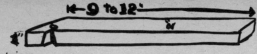

Footpiece.

The foot piece has a shallow hole cut with a knife point into the upper side about half an inch from one edge. In this hole the drill is rotated. Into the edge of this hole from the nearest side, an undercut V is made. This should be at least one-eighth inch into the hole itself.

Headpiece.

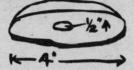

The underside of the headpiece has a shallow hole bored into it, and this is lubricated preferably with lead (graphite) from a pencil. A smear of fat will also serve as a lubricant, or if even this is not obtainable, wax from the ear can be used.

The correct body position for using the bow and drill is

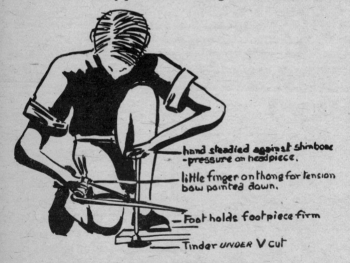

hand steadied against shinbone
-pressure on headpiece.

little finger on thong for tension
bow pointed down.

Foot holds footpiece firm

Tinder *UNDER* V cut

The correct position to hold the various parts of the fireset.

to kneel on the right knee, with the ball of the left foot on the footpiece to hold it firmly to the ground. Place the lower end of the drill in the hole in the footpiece, and the top end of the drill in the hole in the underside of the headpiece.

The left hand holds the headpiece. *The wrist of the left hand must be braced against the shin of the left leg*. This will enable you to hold the headpiece perfectly steady. Actually the headpiece is a 'bearing' for the drill.

The bow is held in the right hand with the little and third finger *outside* the thong so that by squeezing these two fingers the tension of the thong can be increased.

To learn to use a firebow it is advisable to learn first to rotate the drill slowly. This is done by drawing the bow backwards and forwards. The thong round the drill will spin the drill. Only a light pressure is put on the headpiece. Very soon you will see smoke coming from the footpiece, and notice that a fine brown powder is being ground out. This is forming a dark ring round the edge of the hold. This powder is called 'Punk.'

By examining it you can learn whether the woods you are using are suitable for firemaking.

The punk which will produce a glowing coal must feel slightly gritty when gently rubbed between the fingers, and then with more pressure it should rub gradually to a silky smoothness as soft as face powder.

This testing of the punk is extremely important. If you do not know for certain that the woods you are using are suitable for firelighting always make this test first.

When you consider that you have mastered control of the bow and drill you can start trying to get fire. Place a generous bundle of tinder under the V cut. When the drill is smoking freely and you have the 'punk' grinding out easily so that the V cut is full of it, put extra pressure on the headpiece and at the same time give twenty or thirty faster strokes with the bow. Lift the drill cleanly and quickly from the footpiece. Fold some of the tinder over lightly and blow gently into the V cut. If you see a blue thread of smoke continuing to rise, you can be sure you have a coal (you will probably see it glowing red). Fold the tinder completely over the footpiece, and continue blowing into the mass. The volume of smoke will increase, and a few quick puffs will make it burst into flame.

A tip given by some authorities is to put a little charcoal or gritty material into the hole in the footpiece. The claim is made that this enables more punk to be ground out, and the spark to be obtained more quickly.

Suitable woods for footpiece and drill, and this writer recommends that the same wood should be used for both parts, includes the willows and some of the non-resinous pines.

There are a few refinements which are worth knowing when you are making firebow set. These include the boring or burning of a hole for the thong at the tip and also through the handle of the bow. The end of thong at the tip of the bow has a thumb knot tied on the top side. The hole through the handle takes the long end of the thong, which is then wound round the handle in a series of half hitches. This hole in the handle enables you to adjust the 'tension' of the thong with greater accuracy.

A headpiece of shell or smooth grained stone with a hole in it is less liable to 'burn' than a headpiece of wood. Tinder should be carried in a waterproof bag.

FIRE FROM A MAGNIFYING GLASS

Almost everyone at some time or other has focused the sun's rays concentrated by a magnifying glass (sometimes called a burning glass) onto a piece of paper or cloth to make it smoke. Lighting a fire with a magnifying glass calls for a ball of tinder with an inner core of extra fine material (see 'tinders,' page 000). Onto this inner core the sun's rays are focused, and when the finer tinder is smoking freely, it simply requires blowing to

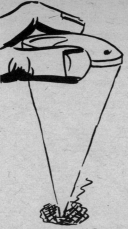

produce flame. A concave mirror is even better than a magnifying glass. Powdered charcoal at the focal point will help the tinder take more easily.

FIRE BY AIR COMPRESSION

In parts of Southeast Asia native people make fire by the ingenious method of suddenly compressing air in a cylinder and thereby concentrating the heat in the air to

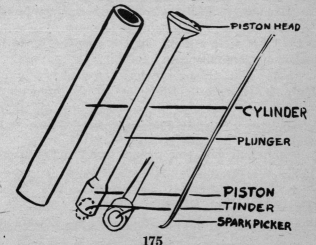

a point when the heat is sufficient to ignite tinder. (They did this hundreds of years before Dr. Diesel thought of the same idea for his engine.)

Their fire-making sets, frequently a cylinder of bone or hollow bamboo, with a bone or wooden piston, are almost museum pieces today.

AIR COMPRESSION

TINDER

In use a small piece of tinder is inserted into a cavity in the lower end of the piston. The piston is placed in the cylinder and the flattened end opposite the piston head struck a smart blow with the palm of the hand, driving it suddenly down the cylinder. Compression of air with concentration of the heat it carries produces a small glowing coal in the tinder placed in the recess of the piston head. Frequently the jar of the blow will shake the tinder loose, so a 'spark remover' is used with the set to pull out the glowing tinder if it lodges in the cylinder.

The dimensions are roughly as follows:

Cylinder. 4″ to 6″ long. Outside diameter ¾″ to 1″. Inside diameter about ½″.

Piston. 4″ to 6″ long, of which the shaft is 3″ to 5″. Piston length ¾″ to 1″. Diameter—to nicely fit the cylinder.

Recess at lower end of piston—about ¼″ wide by ¼″ to 5/16″ deep.

Piston shaft end is smooth and about 1″ to 1½″ diameter for striking with the palm of the hand.

BUILDING A FIRE

Combustion results when temperature is raised sufficiently high for the material to ignite. This is fire. Fire must have air, and you build your fire differently for different purposes.

FOR COOKING

A cooking fire must be a small fire, and one which is easily controlled. Often you need a 'long' fire because there are two or three billy cans, a griller and perhaps a frying pan, all of which must be on the fire at the one time.

Two green logs 6" or 8" thick placed about 12" apart will contain a cooking fire for you and make an excellent overnight fireplace.

A fire for cooking should be 'low,' with the quick heat of small wood. Too big a cooking fire will mean burnt fingers and burnt food. If the fire is too fierce, you will

The ideal way to build an open cooking fire.

not be able to attend properly to the cooking of the food. There is a bush saying about cooking fires — 'The bigger the fire the bigger the fool.' When laying a cooking fire it is a good plan to put a thicker stick in front of the fire. This will serve to rest your frying pan, and keep the heat from your hands; it will also help to contain the fire within the fireplace. A cooking fire should always have a plentiful supply of small wood stacked conveniently near, so that you can feed the fire as the needs of the moment require.

In very windy or cold conditions it is worth making a reflector fireplace for your cooking. A few green logs placed as a windbreak to the windward side of your fire will enable you to do your cooking in comfort.

FIRE IN FLOODED AREAS

Fire can be made in areas totally covered with flood waters. The essential is to build a small platform above water level and on this light your fire.

The easiest way to do this is to cut four forked stakes. These must be straight along the line of drive with the fork projecting from the side. They must be long enough for the fork to be about 6 to 12 inches above the level of water after the stakes are driven into the ground.

Across the forks at either end two cross sticks are laid, and on these two sticks a platform of other sticks is placed, side by side. These are covered with a couple of inches of mud, and on this the fire is built.

By extending the platform a foot or two at one end, you have a storage place for your firewood.

FIRE FOR WARMTH

If sleeping out without sleeping bags or any bedding, select the site for your fire against a dead log. (But make sure the log is not a hiding place for snakes.) Rarely will a single log burn by itself unless there is a strong draught blowing onto it; therefore you must feed the fire with at least one other log. This can be done by selecting a solid, fairly long log, eight or nine inches through if possible and six or seven feet long. By pushing the end of this against the bigger log where you have built your fire, you will ensure continued burning, and as the smaller log burns down during the night you can simply

push it against the big log, and the fire will take fresh heart. An alternative is to lay your logs like a star, and push the ends together during the night.

A small log pushed against a dead fallen tree will give you a good overnight sleeping fire. But be sure to put it out in the morning!

179

THE BUILDING OF A CAMP FIRE

Solid Fire.   *Pyramid fire, lit on top.*

This is the best of all campfires. Three or four logs about 3 ft. to 5 ft. long are laid side by side and across them another layer with, if you desire it, a third layer on top of these. On top of the top layer the starting fire is laid. This is built up finally like a small pyramid. This type of fire is lit at the top. The starter fire ignites the logs below with falling coals and so this fire burns downwards. It radiates heat evenly all round, and requires no attention during the night. Also, because there is no falling in of the fire the risk of sparks spreading and starting a bushfire is greatly minimised.

A common mistake in building a campfire is to make a 'pigsty' construction with heavy logs, on the outside and then pack the inside with light brushwood. Such fires are rarely a success. The light inside wood burns out in a quick blaze of glory, but the heavy outer logs lack sufficient heat to get them properly alight, and also having only small points of contact with each other at the corners do not burn well nor do such fires give out a good radiation of heat. If the 'pigsty' method is to be used, the top two layers should be completely across the top, one layer going in one direction and the other layer crossing it. These top two layers, when alight, get plenty of air from underneath after the brushwood has burnt out and the heat generated will be reflected downwards, giving better radiation than with a simple 'pigsty' construction.

Pigsty fire properly built.

A good camp fire is built if the wood is standing end on, and the fire is built like a pyramid or cone. The centre is fired, and as the core burns away the outside logs fall inwards, constantly feeding the heart of the fire. This type of fire gives good radiation and even with wet wood burns well.

Cone fire.

SLOW MATCH

A slow match is a length of rope or cord which hangs in a smouldering condition to give fire when wanted. (Breech loading guns were fired by touching off the priming with a slow match.)

Today the slow match principle is used by many primitive people as a means of preserving fire and also as a means of carrying it from place to place.

A slow match can be made by making a length of cord or thin rope (from ⅛-inch to ¼-inch diameter) from suitable barks or palm fibres.

Most of the 'silky' soft-fibred barks are ideal. When one end is put in fire or against a glowing coal it will take and hold the spark, smouldering slowly.

A slow match is a safe way when you have no matches or fire-lighting material, to preserve the vital spark for further use after you have doused your fire and left camp for an hour or two. For such a use the slow match should be hung from a branch and exposed to the currents of air.

FIRE IN WET WEATHER

Kerosene-soaked Bandages

The inclusion in your camp gear of firemaking aids such as a few Meta (dried alcohol) tablets is a matter of foresight which you will appreciate if you are overtaken by very bad weather.

One of the really useful fire aids is a kerosene-soaked bandage. The kerosene does not affect the bandage— rather it acts as an antiseptic and helps keep the bandage sterile, and, if need arises, the kerosene-soaked bandage can be used to start a fire in very wet weather.

The best way is to pour kerosene into the roll of bandage until the roll is thoroughly saturated, but not to excess, or the 'dripping' stage. The bandage can then be put back again into the first-aid kit.

FIRE PRECAUTIONS

Observe these campfire rules and you will never start a bushfire.

NEVER LIGHT A FIRE AT THE FOOT OF A STANDING TREE OR TREE STUMP.

NEVER LIGHT A FIRE YOU CANNOT PUT OUT.

NEVER LEAVE A FIRE BURNING WHEN
YOU LEAVE CAMP.

ALWAYS CLEAR AN AREA THREE FEET
WIDE AROUND YOUR FIREPLACE.

Whenever possible, enclose your fire, either with stones, by using a pit fireplace, or by using a couple of green logs.

BUSHFIRE FIGHTING

There are two main types of bushfires. Most frequent is a 'ground' fire in which the fire sweeps along the ground and lower growth, feeding upon the fallen leaves and grass and shrubs. The other type is a 'Tops' or true 'forest' fire, in which the fire sweeps along the tree tops, the leaves of which, because of the intense heat, are rendered highly inflammable. Forest fires move with great speed, and because of terrific air currents which they generate, 'jump' considerable distances.

Most bush fires start as ground fires. When the weather is dry and hot, a ground fire can quickly grow to a forest fire in heavily-timbered country.

GROUND FIRES

A ground fire can be fought either by beating it out or by making a fire break.

If the fire is purely a grass fire, use a green leafy branch to attack the fire by beating the burning edge back towards the burnt portion. When bush and low scrub are alight you may be able to beat the fire out with

184

the green branch, but if possible a length of sacking, thoroughly soaked, will prove a more efficient beater.

Beating out an extensive grass or scrub fire can be hard and difficult work.

If the fire extends along a wide front, too wide for you to attack, or if it is fanned by too high a wind, your best defence is to burn a firebreak between you and the approaching fire.

Select the line for the firebreak where the grass or scrub is thinnest and fire a small area—beating the young fire out on the side farthest from the approaching fire so that it will move away from you towards the main fire.

In the draught created by the heated air, the fire along your firebreak will advance against the wind, feeding upon the inflammable material in its path.

Extend your firebreak in a wide semicircle round the bushfire side of your camp and when the approaching fire reaches the ends of your firebreak be ready to attack it if it starts to burn back against the wind.

Water, if available, can be used to fight a bushfire by playing a jet of water at the heart of the fire. The effect of water on burning wood is to reduce the temperature below combustion point.

FOREST FIRES

There is little that one or two people without firefighting equipment can do against a forest fire. The only really effective way to fight such a fire is by the cutting of firebreaks 100 to 200 yards wide—and this is impossible at short notice.

If a forest fire is approaching, the only safe place to take refuge is in a waterhole. It is no use trying to escape by running away from the fire. Men galloping in front of a forest fire on fear-maddened horses have been overtaken by the racing flames, which, in minutes, have killed both horse and rider.

WATER MUST NOT BE USED ON OIL FIRES

If water is played on burning oil or fat the water particles are exploded and the oxygen and hydrogen of the water feed the fire, increasing its intensity and spreading the danger.

The only way to fight an oil fire is to seal the fire off from the air.

On one occasion the writer saw a forty-gallon drum of high octane petrol catch fire. It was one of a store of several thousand full drums. Everybody panicked and ran for cover except one man, who calmly walked over to the blazing drum, picked up a plug and sealed the opening. The fire went out immediately the air was cut off.

To fight an oil fire, throw sand or dirt on the seat of the fire—that will seal off the air and the fire will die in a few moments.

This particularly applies to the danger of frying pans, where the hot fat catches fire—*never ever throw water in the pan*. Place it in a safe place where the fire can die down or throw dirt or sand or flour on the blaze.

FIRE ON CLOTHING

When clothing catches fire there is a tendency to panic and run. Keep calm—beat the fire out with the hands or roll in the dirt. Better still, grab a blanket or rug and roll in it. You may feel painful skin burns, but if you run, the air will feed the burning clothing and you may be so badly burnt that you will lose your life.

WATER AND OIL FIRE

One of the hottest, most intense fires you can make is to burn water and oil together.

About the easiest method is to place a steel or iron plate on a couple of stones a foot above ground level. Light a fire beneath this plate to make it really hot and while it is heating up arrange a pipe or narrow trough about two or three feet long. One end of this pipe or trough is over the centre of the plate, and the other end is a foot or so higher than the plate. Into this top end of the pipe arrange, by means of a funnel and trough, water and sump oil to be fed down the pipe to the hot plate. The proportion of flow is two or three drops of water to one drop of oil. When the water and oil fall onto the hot plate it burns with a hot white flame of very great heat. The rate of flow can be governed by cutting a channel in corks which plug the bottles holding the water and oil, or if tins are used, pierce holes in the bottoms of the tins and use a plug to control the flow.

This type of fire is excellent for an incinerator when great heat is required to burn out rubbish. It also makes an excellent 'Campfire' where strong flame and light are required and wood is in short supply.

6.

KNOTS
AND LASHINGS

The ability to join two pieces of natural material together, and so increase their length, gives man the ability to make full use of many natural materials found locally.

Sailors probably did more to develop order in the tying of knots, because for them it was necessary not only to tie securely but also to be able to untie, often in the dark and under conditions of bad weather and with rain-tightened ropes.

In bushcraft work probably half a dozen knots would suffice, but knots and knotting have a fascination for many people the world over, and a comprehensive range of knots, plain and fancy, and, with these, splices, whipping, plaits, and net making are included in this book with information of general use.

Knot tying is a useful exercise to obtain better coordination between eyes and fingers. The identification of knots by feel is an excellent means of developing recognition through touch.

In all woodcraft work it is necessary to know how to

tie knots which will hold securely and yet can be untied easily. Many of the materials which you will have to use will be green, some will be slippery with sap, and there are many little tricks and knacks to get the best possible use from the materials available.

Knots and lashings take the place of nails for much bushwork, and when it comes to traps and snares, a thorough knowledge of all running knots is essential.

A brief description of the use to which the knot may be put is given in this book. The diagrams will explain how the knot is tied. The letter "F" means the free or untied end of the rope, and the letter "S" means the standing or secured end.

KNOTS FOR ROPE ENDS OR FOR GRIPS ON THIN ROPE

THUMB KNOT

To make a stop on a rope end, to prevent the end from fraying or to stop the rope slipping through a sheave, etc.

OVERHAND KNOT

Overhand knot may be put to the same use as the thumb knot. It makes a better grip knot, and is easy to undo.

FIGURE EIGHT

This knot is used as the thumb knot. Is easy to undo, and more ornamental.

KNOT FOR JOINING ROPES

SHEET BEND

To join or bend two ropes of unequal thickness together. The thicker rope is the bend.

DOUBLE SHEET BEND

Similar to single sheet bend, but gives greater security, also useful for joining wet ropes.

CROSSOVER SHEET BEND

This holds more securely than either the single or double sheet bend and has occasional real uses such as fastening the eye of a flag to its halyard where the flapping might undo the double sheet bend. (See page 213.)

REEF KNOT

To securely join two ropes of equal thickness together. Notice the difference in position of the free and standing ends between this and the thief knot.

THIEF KNOT

To tie two ropes of equal thickness together so that they will appear to be tied with a reef knot, and will be retied with a true reef knot. This knot was often used by sailors to tie their sea chests, hence the name.

CARRICK BEND

This bend is for the secure fastening of two ropes of even thickness together. It is particularly suitable for hawsers and steel cables. It can be readily undone and does not jam, as do many other bends and knots.

STOPPER HITCH

To fasten a rope to another rope (or to a spar) on which there is already a strain. When the hitch is pulled tight the attached rope will not slip, and the tension on the main rope can be taken on the attached rope. Also useful for a climbing hitch.

FLEMISH KNOT or DOUBLE OVERHAND KNOT

For securing two ropes or cords of equal thickness together.

FISHERMAN'S KNOT

For joining two springy materials together; suitable for wire, fishing gut or vines. Two thumb knots (one on each rope) pulled tight. The knots lock together.

OVERHAND FISHERMAN'S KNOT

Similar to fisherman's knot; for general uses. More positive for gut fishing lines and nylon.

KNOTS TO MAKE LOOPS IN ROPE

BOWLINE

To form a loop that will not slip on a rope end.

BOWLINE ON A BIGHT

To make a double loop that will not slip on a rope end. Also called a bo'sun's chair.

FISHERMAN'S EYE KNOT

This is the best method of making a loop or eye in a fishing line. The strain is divided equally between the two knots.

SLIP KNOT

For fastening a line to a pier or a pole or any other purpose where strain alone on the standing end is sufficient to hold the knot.

OVERHAND EYE KNOT

This method of making an eye or loop is satisfactory and quick, but it sometimes jams and becomes difficult to untie.

FLEMISH EYE KNOT

Used for all purposes where a loop is required, less likely to jam than overhand eye knot.

CRABBINS HITCH

This eye knot, though not very well known, is one of the stoutest eye knots. It has not the tendency to cut itself or pull out common to some of the other eye knots. It also makes a useful running knot.

MANHARNESS KNOT

This is a most useful knot for making a series of non-slip loops in a rope for the purpose of harnessing men for a pull. The marlinspike hitch is made as in lower sketch and then the loop

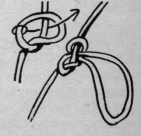

is drawn under and over the other two ropes as indicated. The whole knot is then pulled taut.

MIDSHIPMAN'S HITCH

This is an old-fashioned hitch often used to fasten a block or sheave to a rope's end.

JURY KNOT or TRUE LOVER'S KNOT

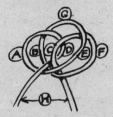

This knot is primarily for a mast head, to form loops by means of which the mast may be stayed. It is called a jury knot because in sailing ship days it was often used to rig a temporary or jury mast. Three hitches as in top sketch are formed. The loop C is pulled under B and over A. D is pulled over E and under F. G is pulled straight up for the third loop. H is made by splicing the two free ends together.

BOW THONG HITCH

Used by New Guinea natives for securing the end of the split cane bow thong to the pointed end of the bow. Also useful for fastening rope over the tapered end of a spar.

KNOTS FOR FASTENING ROPES

SLIPPERY HITCH

Very useful because of the ease with which it can be released in emergency. It holds securely for so long as there is a strain on the standing end.

CLOVE HITCH

For securing a rope to a spar. This hitch, if pulled taut, will not slip up or down on a smooth surface. A useful start for lashings.

BOAT KNOT

This is a method of securing a rope to a thole pin or other small piece of wood on a boat. It is quickly released.

DOUBLE BOAT KNOT

A bight is simply passed through the ring and a marlin spike or other round piece of wood is put between the bight or

the rope. Withdrawal of the
spike quickly releases the knot.

SLIPPERY HITCH

Very useful because of the
ease with which it can be released in emergency. It holds
securely so long as there is a
strain on the standing end.

ROLLING HITCH

To fasten a rope to a spar.
This is a very secure fastening.

TIMBER HITCH

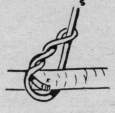

For securing a rope to
squared timber, round logs, etc.
A good starting knot for all
lashings. The standing end
must pull straight through the
loop, not backwards, or the rope
may cut upon itself.

HALLIARD HITCH

For fastening a rope to a spar.
The sketch shows the hitch
open. When pulled taut, and the
hitches closed, it makes a very
neat and secure fastening.

BLACKWALL HITCH

A quick way to secure a rope
to a hook. The strain on the
standing end will hold the rope
secure to the hook.

NOOSE HITCH

This is a quick and easy method of securing a rope to a spar or beam. If desired, the rope can be made more secure by means of the overhand knot shown in Fig. 2.

CAT'S PAW HITCH

For securing a rope to a hook or a spar. It is most useful because it is so easily tied.

LARK'S HEAD

This is an easy method of securing a rope to a ring or hook. If desired to make more secure, it can be stoppered, as shown, with an overhand or thumb knot.

CROSSOVER LARK'S HEAD

Used for purposes above.

DOUBLE LARK'S HEAD

The bight is first made. The ends passed through it. This knot is very secure.

197

TRIPLE LARK'S HEAD

The apparently complicated knot is easily made by taking the bight of the rope through the ring, the ends are passed through the bight and up through the ring, then down through its own bight. Like the double lark's head, this knot is absolutely secure.

SAILOR'S BACKHAND KNOT

Used to secure a rope to a ring or hook. This is very similar to the Rolling Hitch (page 11) and Sailor's Backhand Knot (alternative variation) shown overleaf.

SAILOR'S KNOT

Simply two half hitches round the standing end of the rope.

GUNNER'S KNOT

This is simply a carrick bend and used to hold two shackles or rings together.

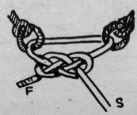

SAILOR'S BACKHAND KNOT

(Alternative variation.) Used to fasten a rope securely to a spar.

CATSPAW

This knot is used for attaching a rope to a hook. The two bights are rolled two or three times and then put over the hook.

KELLICK HITCH

Used for fastening a stone (for a kellick in lieu of an anchor), that will hold in rocky sea bottoms where an anchor might foul. It is a timber hitch finished off with a half hitch.

TOM FOOL'S KNOT

Formed by making a clove hitch as two loops not exactly overlaying each other. The inner half of each hitch or loop is pulled under and through the outer side of the opposite loop, as indicated by arrows.

This knot can be used to improvise a handle for a pitcher by pulling the centre knot tight around the lip of the pitcher and using the loops as handles.

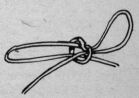

SHEEPSHANK

This is a convenient knot to quickly shorten a rope.

One method of securing the end.

SHEEPSHANK TOGGLED

The insertion of a toggle in the end bights secures the sheepshank against slipping.

DRUM SLING

A slip knot is made as indicated. The drum, can or barrel is placed in the slip knot and the free end is secured with a stopper hitch (see page 7) to the standing end.

200

CHAIN KNOT

When a rope is too long for its purpose one means of shortening it is the chain knot. Remember to put a marlinspike or toggle through the last link before you put a strain on the rope.

DOUBLE CHAIN KNOT

This is the most ornamental of all the rope shortenings. A turn is taken round the standing end and the free end is passed through the loop so formed. In doing this a loop is formed through which the free end is brought. The end is thus passed from one side to the other through the loop preceding. It may be pulled taut when sufficiently shortened and will lock upon the last loop.

TWIST KNOT

This is another easy method of shortening a rope. The rope is laid as in Fig. 1 and then the strands are plaited or braided together. A marlinspike or toggle is placed between the ropes in the centre to secure the hold of the plait.

FANCY KNOTS

WALL KNOT

Unlay the rope a few inches and then pass each strand through the bight of the strand in front. Illustration shows the wall knot ready to be pulled taut.

STOPPER KNOT

Bring the ends of the wall knot round again and up in the centre of the knot and pull each one taut separately.

CROWNING KNOT

Commence the crowning as shown here.

The crowning is now ready to be pulled taut. The strands can be back spliced to permanently secure the end of the rope against ravelling or fraying. Crowning may also be used with other fancy knots such as crowning first, then pulling on a wall knot or a Mathew Walker.

MANROPE KNOT

This is a fancy knot to put a stop on the end of a rope. Top sketch shows the crowning (in the centre), and lower sketch shows the manrope knot pulled taut.

DOUBLE-DOUBLE CROWNING KNOT

This knot is started the same as the manrope, but not pulled taut. The ends are laid for a second crown above the crown (similar to the manrope knot) and with the spike the bends of the lower crown are opened, and the strands brought through these bends and pulled taut.

MATHEW WALKER 1

The strands are laid as in the diagram and then each in turn is pulled taut till the knot is close and tight. The knot itself is rolled up slightly to lay the twist evenly. Pull the strands tight again after this.

MATHEW WALKER 2.

Finished and rolled tight.

The Mathew Walker is reputed to be one of the most difficult of all knots to undo. The

203

Mathew Walker can also be made some distance from the end of the rope and the strands then relaid.

DIAMOND KNOT

Like the Mathew Walker, the diamond knot is ornamental — can be made same distance along the rope. The rope is unlaid carefully. Each strand is brought down alongside the standing end, as illustrated (top). The strands are then put through the loops formed by the other strands in lower sketch. The strands are hauled taut. The rope relaid. Shows the finished diamond knot.

DOUBLE DIAMOND KNOT

This is made as for the single diamond knot, but the strands follow the lead of the single knot through two single loops. The last strand comes through two double loops. The strands come out through the centre when the knot is pulled taut. All these stopper knots can be used for the ends of lanyards, halyards, yoke lines and also as stoppers on cleats, and for rope buckets.

TURK'S HEAD

This is a highly ornamental knot which, instead of being made with the rope strands of the rope itself, is formed with smaller cordage on the rope.

A clovehitch is made as in Fig. 1. This is made slackly to allow the extra strands to be worked through it. Pull the bottom part of the hitch above the top part and put the free end under and up (Fig. 2). The now bottom strand is pulled above the top part and the free end now over and down. This repeat till the circle is complete. The free end follows round three times. The completed Turk's head is shown in Fig. 3.

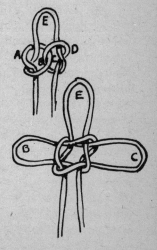

SHAMROCK KNOT

This may be formed the same way as the true lover's knot, but the bottom loop is not spliced. It may also be used to form three loops for stays for a mast. It may also be formed by making a knot as top sketch. The loop C is drawn up through loop D and the loop B is drawn up through the loop at A. These form the side loops and the top loop is formed naturally at E.

BUTTON KNOT

Form two crossover hitches, as Fig. 1. Pass the loop end to the left and with the free end form another loop as shown. Now, with the free end, follow the lay as indicated in Fig. 2 and lay the strands side by side as for the Turk's head. When three to five lays have been put through, work the knot tight and use the free ends to fasten the button to the garment. A bootlace makes an excellent button.

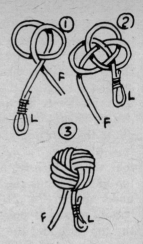

SELVEDGE

To secure a block to a standing spar. The middle of the selvedge is laid on the spar and the two ends are crossed over in turns until the bights at the ends come together. The hook of the block is then put through these two bights.

POINTING A ROPE

The rope is unlaid and a tie put on to prevent it unlaying further. The strands are thinned down gradually, and relaid again. The end may be stiffened with a small stick or piece of wire. The end can be finished off with any of the crown or wall knots.

KNOTTED ROPE LADDER

The length of rope is coiled in a series of half-hitches and the end of the rope is passed through the centre, as in illustration on right (except that the coils are held close together as for a coiled rope when it is to be thrown). The coil of half-hitches with the end passed through the centre is turned inside out, that is, the succeeding coils are pulled over each other. The coil is now thrown, and as it pays out a series of overhand knots are made at fairly equal intervals. In making a knot ladder this is the quickest and most efficient method.

SINGLE ROPE LADDER WITH CHOCKS

This type of ladder has the

advantage of being portable and quickly made. The chocks of hardwood are about 6″ diameter and 2″ deep, and are suitably bored to take the diameter of the rope. Splice an eye at the top end and seize in a thimble to lash the rope head securely. To secure the chocks, put two strands of seizing between the strands of the rope and then work a wall knot.

Alternatively, insert small pegs between the rope strands, and seize the rope with a binding below the pegs.

Lashing

SQUARE LASHING *to join poles at right angles.*

Start with a timber hitch or a clove hitch *below* cross bar. If using a timber hitch see that the pull is straight through the eye and *not* back from it. Pulling back will cut the lashing material.

Put lashing material tightly around upright and cross bar about four complete times.

Frapping turns. — Make about two or three frapping turns. These are turns that go round the lashing and pull it taut. These pull the lashing tight. Secure end of frapping turns either by half-hitches or by passing between lashing at the crossover and secure with a half-hitch.

DIAGONAL LASHING

for bracing or joining spars at irregular angles.

Start with a timber hitch or a clove hitch and take about three or four full turns vertically.

Pass rope under top spar and make about three or four full turns horizontally.

Make two or three frapping turns and either secure by two half-hitches on pole or by passing the end between the lashing and the pole and use half-hitches on the lashing.

SHEER LASHING *to join two poles end to end.*

Start with a clove hitch or timber hitch, lash as in 1 and 2 tightly around the two spars

209

four to six times as in 3. Pass free end under lashings and draw tightly two or three times. Secure by passing it through itself, as in 4.

There should be at least two lashings if spars are being joined together.

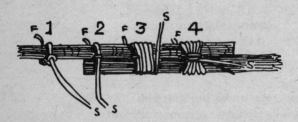

Splices

SHORT SPLICING

Unlay the strands and marry them together; butt hard up to each other. The strand D first goes under the standing end of A, but over strand B and over C on the standing end. Thus each strand at either end goes over one strand of the standing end on the opposite side and under the next strand, so that there is a strand of the standing end between each short side of the splice. Continue working the free strand of each end four or five times into the strands of the standing end.

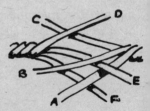

LONG SPLICING

The strands are unlaid for a considerable length and then married as for the short splice. Then the one strand is unlaid and its married counterpart is laid along its place in the rope.

The two centres are simply held with a crossover knot, and the strands thinned down and spliced as for a short splice. The end strands are finished with a crossover knot and again the strands are thinned down and finished as for a short splice. This long splice does not appreciably thicken a rope which may be thus spliced to go through a sheave.

LOOP SPLICE WITHOUT A FREE END

The rope is untwisted to the required place, as in top illustration. The free ends so formed are then spliced back along the rope after the loop has been formed.

EYE SPLICE

A neat eye can be made in a rope end by an ordinary short splice after the loop or eye has been formed.

LOOP SPLICE

The strands are unlaid and laid side by side till the loop is the required length. The strands of the free ends are spliced into the ropes of the standing ends as for a short splice.

Toggle and eye—showing one application of splicing and whipping. Toggle is spliced and eye is whipped in sketch.

Binding or Whipping

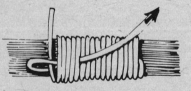

WHIPPING

Before the finish of the binding a loop formed from the end is laid under the binding at the start. This end is bent back to form a loop and the last six to twelve turns bind over this loop.

212

At the last turn of the binding the cord is put through the loop and the free end of the loop is pulled tightly, thus drawing the end of the binding beneath the last turn.

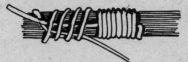

WHIPPING

This is another method. After pulling taut, the two free ends are cut close in and the whole binding is smooth and neat.

To Fold a Flag for "Breaking"

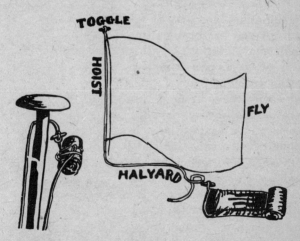

The flag is folded neatly along its length four to eight times, and then the fly is either folded, concertina fashion, or rolled towards the hoist. The toggle is uppermost on the hoist, and the halyard is on the lower side of the hoist.

The halyard is wrapped tightly round the flag, and then bent, and the loop pressed under the last rollings, held by the pressure of the cord against the bunting of the flag.

The toggle is fastened to the eye of the halyard on the mast, and the free end of the flag hoist is fastened to the other end of the mast halyard with a double sheet or crossover bend.

NETTING

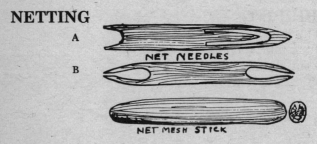

A

NET NEEDLES

B

NET MESH STICK

Hammocks and nets are made by the use of a netting needle and a mesh stick. Either of the two types of netting needle shown in Fig. 1 are suitable and easily made from a thin piece of hardwood or bamboo. The netting needles may be about 8 to 9 inches long and from ¾ inch to 1 inch wide. The mesh stick may be about 5 inches long, oval about ¾ x ¼. The netting cord is put on to the netting needles as for an ordinary shuttle with needle B, and with needle A the cord is looped round the pin in the centre of the eye.

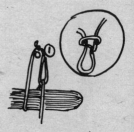

At one end of the string tie a loop and place the knot on a conveniently high nail or hook. The mesh stick is put under the loop and the needle with cord passed through as in Fig. 3. The needle and cord are passed in front of the loop formed in Fig. 3 and under the original loop, while at the same time the other end of the cord is held on to the mesh stick with the thumb of the left hand. The knot is pulled taut.

A succession of these loops are formed until the requisite width is reached, then this first series of loops are placed through a rod or cord, and the loops are netted on to them until the requisite length is reached.

Anchoring a Peg in Sand or Snow

The only way to anchor a rope into soft sand is to attach it to a peg, and bury the peg in the sand.

Scrape a trench in the sand to a depth of between a foot and eighteen inches, deeper if high winds or very stormy weather are expected. Pass the rope round the centre of the peg; scratch a channel for it at right angles to the peg trench.

Fill in the trench and rope channel, and fasten the free end of the rope to the standing end with a stopper hitch (see page 190), and pull taut. The buried peg should hold a tent rope in sand under all normal weather conditions.

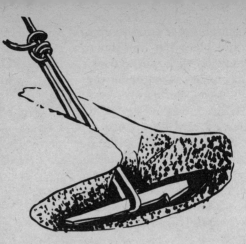

To Anchor a Rope in Open Ground

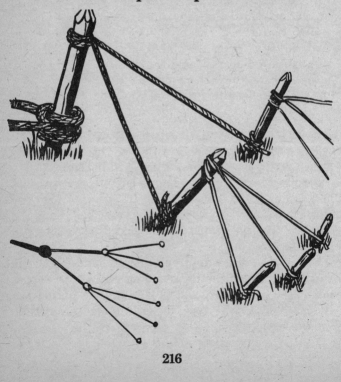

A secure anchor in open ground can be obtained by driving a stout stake well into the ground (see Chapter 3). The rope is later fastened to the base of this stake.

To the head of the stake two ropes are attached, and these are tied back to the ground level of two other stakes driven well into the earth a few yards behind the first stake.

To the heads of these two stakes three ropes are tied and these are fanned out and tied to the bases of three other stakes driven in behind the two stakes.

The main rope is now fastened to the base of the first stake.

This is appropriately called the "ONE-TWO-THREE" anchor and will hold a very great strain if the ground is "solid."

Bush Windlass

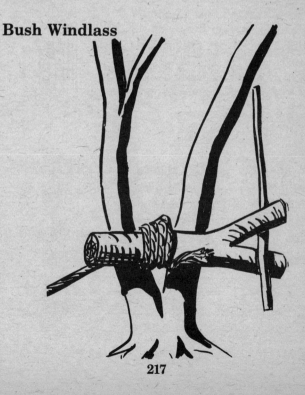

A bush windlass, capable of taking a very heavy strain on a rope can be made by selecting a site where a tree forks low to the ground, with the fork facing the direction in which the pull is required. Alternatively, a stout fork can be driven in and anchored with the "1-2-3" method.

The windlass portion is a forked log. The forks are notched to take the lever (up to seven feet long). The rope is passed round the roller a few times so that it locks upon itself. (If the fork of the roller is long, the rope may pass through the fork.)

This type of bush windlass has many uses.

Lariat or Round Plait

Four strands of equal thickness are tied together at one of their ends.

1. Strand 4 is taken and passed over strands 2 and 3, and then turned behind the strand 2 and brought forward between 2 and 3.

2. Strand 1 (on the opposite side) is taken and passed over strands 2 and 4, and turned and brought forward between 2 and 4.

3. Strand 3 (on the side first worked) is taken and passed over strands 1 and 4, and turned and brought forward between the two.

4. Strand 2 is taken, passed over strands 1 and 3, turned and then brought forward between 1 and 3.

5. This sequence is repeated. Lariat plaiting must be kept "tight," that is, plaited close, and the flat strands *must be turned* as they twist round the two strands they have overlaid.

7.

TRACKS AND LURES

The signs animals leave on the ground can be more revealing than any book written by man, but unfortunately few people are able to see these signs and fewer still can read them.

To understand something of the behaviour of animals one must realise that the development of their senses is markedly different to mankind's, and therefore where we obtain information through our eyes and ears, one animal may obtain the same information through its sense of smell and another through its ability to detect temperature changes, or through vibrations.

Where man communicates with man through speech, some forms of animal life communicate through telepathy. You see this in a flock of pigeons which turn in flight as one bird.

This book broadly deals with some of these special characteristics explaining how knowledge of the 'sensitivity' of the creature is useful, and how the animal's tracks provide a reliable indicator to its habits.

The whole area covered in this book, if practised,

leads to a remarkable development of one's powers of observation and deduction.

Tracks and Their Meaning

SIMPLE DEDUCTION

To be a successful trapper you must learn first to observe, and then to make the correct deduction from your observation. For example, if you see a bird move over the ground in a series of hops it would leave tracks like these.

You agree that these would be the tracks of a hopping bird?

To know that a bird hops on the ground tells you that it is *normally unaccustomed to being on the ground*. This in turn leads to the conclusion that, being unaccustomed to living on the ground, it therefore does not feed on the ground. Where else then might it feed?

Your answer would be that it may find its food either in the air or on shrubs or trees.

But you observe that most birds that look for food in trees *walk* along the branches if they feed on fruit or flower blossoms and that the birds which feed on insects hop from branch to branch. Your final deduction is that birds which leave hopping tracks on the ground are birds which capture their food (in the form of insects) in the air, and so you make a rule, 'hopping birds are insect eaters.'

In a general way this is true, but there are exceptions to all these general rules, and not all insect eating birds are hoppers, and not all ground hopping birds are insect eaters. (Consider your pet canary or the lovely painted finches, both of which are ground hopping, and both of which are grain or seed eaters.)

Now consider tracks which look like this.

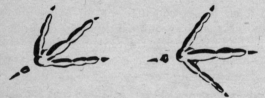

First, these are made by a bird which walks, not hops. Therefore it is accustomed to finding some, or all of its food on the ground. Being a ground feeding bird it may either—

    feed on grain or fallen fruit,

    feed on ground living creatures,

    feed on flesh which it finds on the ground.

If it feeds on grain or fallen fruit it will not have the centre toe development that would be needed by a bird which had to scratch or dig for its food, nor would it have the rear claw development required by a flesh eater.

These, therefore, are the tracks of a ground feeding bird which, not having a digging claw, nor having talons, MUST be a grain or fruit eater.

Notice the development of the centre toe, and powerful claw. This is the mark of a ground feeding bird which scratches or digs for its food. It is a ground insect eater.

Here are four short and powerful toes with strong claws particularly on the hind toe. These are the talon feet of a ground feeder which lives on flesh. The foot tracks of a hawk and eagle, or a crow.

Naturally the place where the tracks are observed has a bearing on reading the correct answer, and if the tracks are found on the edge of a swamp or marsh the answer could be quite different from the answer if the tracks were observed a long way from water.

Tracks read as those of a grain eating ground feeder in forest land could correctly be read, if the same tracks were seen in mud, or by a reedy swamp edge, as tracks of a nonswimming, flesh-eating water bird.

Tracks such as these are easily and correctly read.

The web-footed track of a swimmer such as duck, swan, or geese.

ANIMAL TRACKS

In the animal kingdom the reading of tracks is equally simple. Consider these two—what is the feature you first notice?

It is the single or double thumb, the prehensile digit, which is the mark of every true tree climbing animal. Look at your own hand. Can you climb trees?

There are exceptions to this, as to the other general rules. For instance the tree climbing kangaroo of North Queensland, which has a prehensile tail. (Incidentally the domestic cat is not a true tree climber. It can 'claw' its way up a tree but it cannot 'climb', as, say, a monkey climbs.)

In these tracks the claws of the centre toes are most prominent, and you are correct if your deduction is that these are the tracks of an earth digger, or burrower. The prehensile thumb is undeveloped, you notice.

The digging claws may be on fore or hind feet. Generally the fore feet show them most sharply, but whether on front or hind feet, they are the invariable mark of the digger.

These tracks show neither the prehensile thumb or the digging claw.

If you deduce that they are the tracks of flesh eating animals you would be correct, but why?

The answer is that the tracks show pronounced 'toes,' and that toes, when not used for climbing or digging, both of which call for special development, have another special use in that they give the foot a 'springboard' when running, and so you make the deduction that these are the tracks of fast running animals, and they are not grazing animals because no grazing animal shows 'toes,' unless you recognise the hoof of a cow or horse, sheep, etc., as 'tips' of toes or 'toenails,' which they really are.

These tracks are made by the grass and herbage eaters. Having neither climbing thumbs, to escape from enemies by climbing, nor digging tools, to escape by burrowing, their only means of escape is by running. Therefore you may decide that animals which have cloven hoofs are very fast running.

TRACKS INDICATE HABITS

Tracks made by animals on the ground, when read correctly, show the pattern of the animal's habits. This calls for continuous and careful observation. It is important to recognise the fact that animals, and all living creatures, are as much creatures of habit as human beings. A particular animal will follow the same track to and from water day after day. It will hunt in the same area continually, and only leave the area when driven out by fire, flood or drought. Even then the move is only temporary, and it will return when conditions once again are favourable.

This 'habit-forming' characteristic of animals makes it possible for the experienced trapper to predict the animal's movements, and so he selects the sites for his traps or snares, certain that they will be visited.

In the bush you will find many animal trails. These are the 'roads' of the bush creatures. They travel over them continually backwards and forwards, to and from their resting places to their feeding grounds and favourite waterholes.

By observation of the number and newness of the tracks and droppings on these trails you can gauge the extent of animal traffic.

If you put an obstacle across one of these animal trails the animals will make a detour around the obstacle, always following the line of least resistance, and come back to the road again beyond the obstacle.

A very good example of these roads are the trails radiating from a meat ants' nest. Exactly the same pattern is repeated in jungle, forest and grassland by all animals. Examine the upward side of a leaning gum tree, and if you see scratch marks of varying ages then the tree is a 'tree road' of possums or koalas, which either live in dead hollows or come to the tree nightly to feed on the young leaves or mistletoe berries. By looking up at a tree you can quickly tell if it is a feeding tree, or a living-quarters-tree. (The latter will show many dead limbs which are hollow, and therefore comfortable living quarters for possums and phalangers.)

ANIMAL WORLD'S 10 SENSES

As human beings we experience five senses. These are: Sight, Sound, Touch, Taste, Smell. These senses are the result of very highly specialised cells. One group of these cells in our eyes are stimulated by light and colour. As a result we 'see.' So it is with all our other senses.

As human beings our eyes tell us more than any of our other senses, and all senses are directed to one end . . . LIVING. By living is meant, first the finding of food which it is safe for us to eat, and then keeping ourselves out of danger, and so keeping our race or species perpetuated.

In these end purposes of the senses the whole animal and vegetable kingdom differs in no way from us. It appears to this writer that some forms of life have developed senses which are quite beyond our human experience, and therefore rather difficult for us to understand.

The full list of these senses (sensitivities) might be as follows:

Light sensitivity ⎫
Sound sensitivity ⎪
Taste sensitivity ⎬ experienced by humans
Touch sensitivity ⎪
Scent sensitivity ⎭
Temperature sensitivity
Vibration sensitivity
Supersonic sensitivity
Telepathetic sensitivity
Directional sensitivity.

Note: These are purely the author's observations, and not backed by scientific proof; consequently readers are advised not to accept these or the following remarks without reservation.

These sensitivities vary in their development between one creature and another. Here are a few examples of their existence which you can establish for yourself.

Sound Sensitivity

BANG

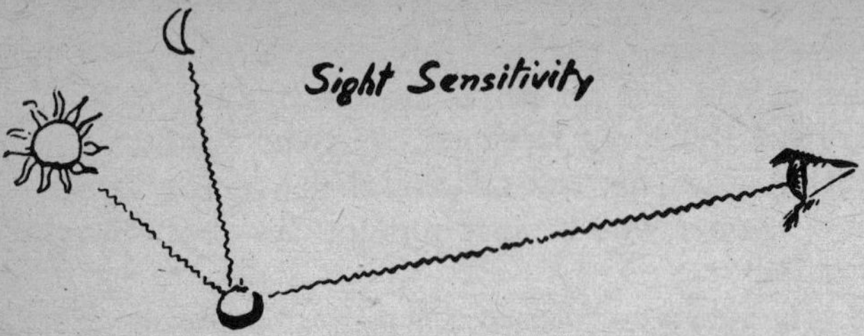

Sight Sensitivity

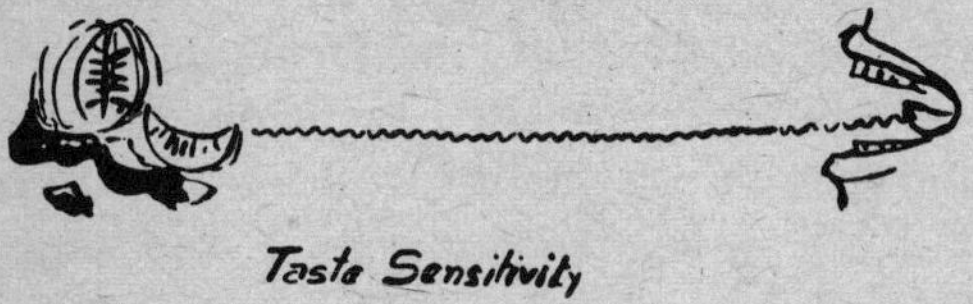

Taste Sensitivity

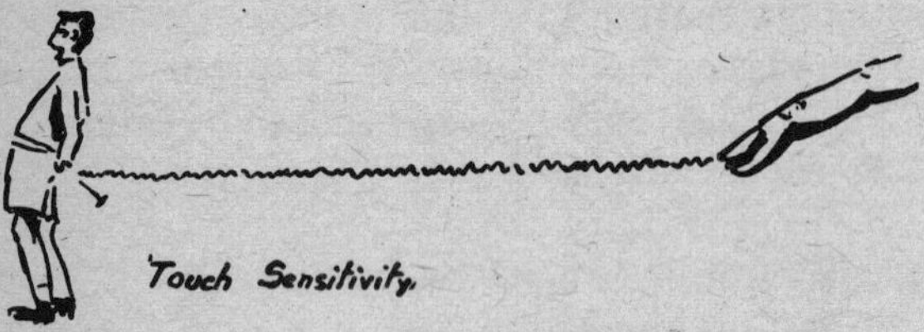

Touch Sensitivity

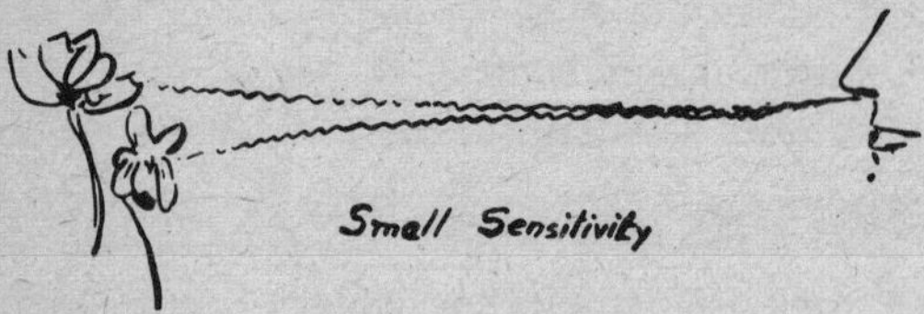

Smell Sensitivity

TEMPERATURE SENSITIVITY

Temperature Sensitivity

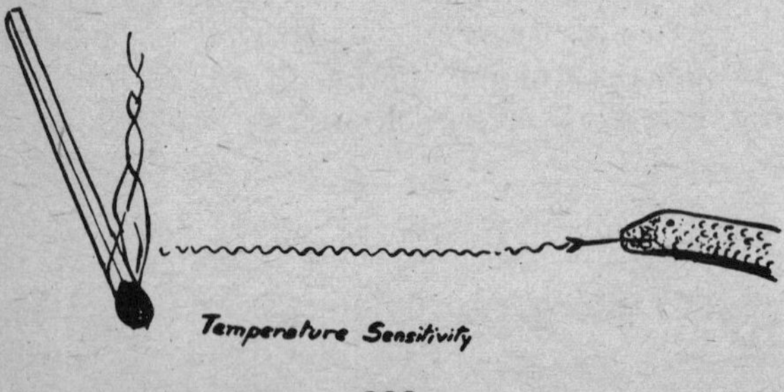

Temperature sensitivity can be observed if you put a leech in a screw-top covered glass jar, and cover the sides with thick paper. If you look down into the glass jar you will see the leech standing on its tail in the centre of the jar, weaving his upper end around. Put a burning stick a foot away from one side of the jar and he will loop towards it. Move the stick to the other side and he will change direction at once.

The leech cannot smell the stick, he cannot see it, nor can he hear it, but he is so sensitive to temperature that he can feel it. Because leeches feed on the blood of animals you can understand that their 'temperature sensitivity' will lead them to sources of food.

Snakes also have a highly-developed temperature sensitivity. A snake's action of continually putting out its tongue is to guide it to warmer temperature, which to a snake may mean food (very much as if your eyes were habitually closed, but by flicking them open frequently you would be 'guided' towards light, and the light would in turn let you find food).

VIBRATION SENSITIVITY

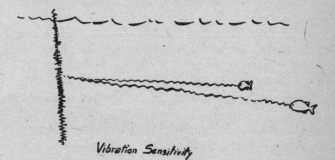

Vibration Sensitivity

Vibration sensitivity seems to be most highly developed by water living creatures. It becomes evident by the actions of fish which show themselves to be attracted to the centre of small vibrations. This can be proven by throwing fine sand into still water. Small fish will instantly dart towards the sand, but if a heavy stone is thrown, they will scatter. A thread, fastened to a stone lowered beneath the water, if pulled taut, and lightly vibrated by rubbing, will also attract small fish. Cease the rubbing, which causes the vibration in the water and the fish will disperse. Rub, and they will be attracted again.

SUPERSONIC SENSITIVITY

Supersonic Sensitivity

Throw a small pebble high into the air at dusk any summer evening, and watch its flight. Suddenly you will see a bat flash towards it, and then turn and fly away.

The bat sends out high pitched sound waves (beyond the pitch to which the human ear is tuned, but you may be fortunate enough to hear the 'Chirp' almost like a tightly-strung wire being plucked). These sound waves which the bat sends out in flight rebound when they meet any obstacle, even a tiny flying insect. The bat's acute ears detect and follow the 'echo' which tells it "an insect for food is over there," and so the bat turns in its flight, all the time sending out its high-pitched sound-waves, and following up the echo till it finds the insect. This is 'supersonic sensitivity.'

No doubt the echo from the pebble becomes too strong and the flying bat sheers off to avoid a collision.

Bats, which have low power vision, can fly through a maze of crossed wires unerringly because of this supersonic sense. With fruit eating bats, or flying foxes, there appears to be an extremely acute sense of smell, and the supersonic sense does not seem to have been highly developed.

Group Sensitivity

TELEPATHETIC OR 'GROUP' SENSITIVITY

This sense is seen when you watch a flight of birds, pigeons are particularly good examples. The flight, moving in one direction, turns, all together, and changes direction. The movement is not made by one bird who acts first as a leader but simultaneously by all the birds in the flight. The only feasible explanation is that they have a 'group sensitivity,' which, shared by all the birds in the flight, tells them to change direction.

DIRECTIONAL SENSITIVITY

Directional Sensitivity

Directional sensitivity is fairly well spread over the animal world. Many humans have this sense, which may have been acquired by training, but whatever the explanation they show a strongly marked sense of direction. Birds show it in their ability to 'home,' and in their migratory habits. Many species of fish show it in their breeding habits, returning to spawn in the same rivers in which they themselves were hatched.

SCENT SENSITIVITY HIGH
WITH ANIMALS

Humans learn more through sight than through any other sense and as a result our sense of sight is more highly developed than any of our other senses.

As humans, we say, "There's a savage dog; look out he doesn't see you." This is because we think all animals like ourselves depend on sight.

The savage dog will not see you at first, but he will scent you, because his nose tells him more than his eyes. This high development of 'smell sensitivity' is more common with wild creatures than their development of sight.

It is difficult for us, as humans, to think as the wild animals think. For instance, if we saw a 'snare' or trap we would be cautious. For the trap to be effective it would have to be concealed from our sight, so that we could not see it.

An animal would smell your scent on the same trap. The sight of the trap would mean nothing to it, but the man scent attached to it, and lingering possibly for weeks after it was set up, would warn the wild animal, and your trap or snare would be quite ineffective.

Until you can realise that scent (of which you are completely unaware, because you have very poor 'smell sensitivity') tells an animal more than sight, your traps will catch nothing. This of course does not apply to all creatures. Birds and fishes are an exception, but it does apply to nearly all wild animals in their natural bush conditions.

Whilst the 'man scent' may spell 'danger' under some conditions, under other conditions where the animals have been accustomed to man and live on their leavings (as rats, dogs and cats often do), the man scent, instead of being a warning signal, becomes a lure. Under true bush conditions, however, the 'man scent' is invariably a danger signal to all wild animals.

The man scent can be killed either by hiding it beneath a stronger smell, or by allowing it to weather off the trap or by removing it.

To 'kill' man scent you can either use a stronger scent of which the animal will not be suspicious, or you can use a scent which for one reason or another will attract the animal to your trap or snare.

This last is called a lure.

In the bush you will find many plants whose leaves

when crushed have a strong perfume. If you crush these in your hands before, during, and after you have made your trap, you will leave the scent of the leaves on the trap, and this will be so much stronger than your man scent that it will drown the latter. Of course your scent will remain all round the area, and the animal will be suspicious.

FIRE REMOVES SCENT

Fire is a good destroyer of man scent, and if you scorch the trap or snare by making a torch of dry grass or dead leaves, you will cleanse it to the animal's nose, and he will be less suspicious.

LURES

The use of a lure is undoubtedly the most effective way to kill man scent.

Urine of the species of animal you want to trap is an excellent scent killer, and urine of a female of the species taken when she is 'on heat' or 'in season' is an infallible lure for males of that species. The urine should be taken from the bladder of a newly killed female, and bottled for future use.

Another fairly good lure is oil of aniseed, or oil of rhodiun. A very light touch of one of these lures on the bait is all that is required.

Salt is also a very effective lure in areas away from the coast, but salt is not in itself a scent killer.

Noise lures are often highly effective. These may take the form of special whistles, or may be in the form of squeaking or friction instruments. Noise lures are not commonly used in conjunction with traps or snares.

Food lures are always highly effective; small particles of food are scattered lightly around the area of the traps or snares, and the animal, scenting this food, finds it plentiful in the area, and scavenges round looking for more till finally he finds the bait in the trap, and is caught.

Obviously some of the man scent will be on the food lure particles, and, although the animal may be suspicious at first, finding that no harm comes to him, his suspicions will decrease.

An excellent use for food lure particles is to scatter them thinly along an animal trail, and then fairly thickly on either side of a simple noose snare.

BAITS

In the section of this book dealing with animal tracks you saw that there were broadly four different divisions of animal feeding pattern. These were:

Tree feeding animals,
Earth digging and feeding animals,
Flesh eating animals,
Grazing animals.

Baits for tree feeding animals must be fruits,

Baits for earth digging animals must be roots, or insects,

Baits for flesh eaters must be flesh,

Baits for grazing animals must be herbage.

236

TEST BAITING

Test baiting an area will show what animals are in the locality, and what baits they will take. To test bait an area select a site which is on light dusty clean soil that will clearly show all tracks. The area should be three or four yards square.

1 PUMPKIN SEED
2 CARROT
3 S. Potato
4 BREAD
5 MAIZE
6 APPLE
7 BREAD + HONEY
8 BREAD—ANISEED
9 CABBAGE
10 S. Potato ANISEED
11 MEAT
12 FISH HEAD
13 SORGHUM SEED

Drive ten or a dozen short stakes, each about a foot long, into the ground. There should be at least three feet between each stake. Tie different baits, some with lures and some without to the stakes. Make a sketch map of the position of the stakes and notes of the bait each carried.

This work should be done in the afternoon. The following morning you must visit the area, and on the soft dust you will see the tracks of all the creatures which visited the area during the night, and what baits they took.

You will see bird tracks at the seeds, and tied up worm (if you put one there). You will see the tracks of tree climbing animals around the stakes where you had a piece of apple, and you will see the digging claw tracks of earth burrowers around a piece of sweet potato or a

237

carrot, while a pumpkin seed will have attracted both a bush rat and a bird.

You will notice, too, that some baits, possibly those with lures, have been untouched, while others have been taken.

This work of test baiting is an essential preliminary to successful trapping. Salt is a good addition to all baits.

Suggested test baits for Australian conditions are as follows:

Roots:
   Sweet potato
   Carrot
   Parsnip
   Dandelion root
   Yam or other
      ground tuber.

Seeds and Grains:
   Pumpkin seed
   Melon seed
   Corn
   Wheat
   Sorghum seed
   Peanut
   Nut.

Flesh:
   Meat
   Fish head
   Worm
   Cheese.

Fruits:
   Apple
   Banana
   Fig and local
      fruit baits.

Herbage:
   Cabbage leaf
   Lettuce leaf
   Celery stalk
   Carrot top.

These should be used both with and without lures.

DEVELOPMENT OF SENSE ORGANS INDICATES DEGREE OF SENSITIVITY

In a general way high development of sense organs indicates degree of sense dependence of the animal.

For example, animals which have large ears have acute hearing, and animals with pronounced nasal development have a sharp alertness to scent.

238

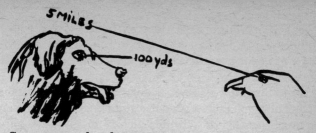

Sense organ development is not a mere matter of size of the organ.

A human eye, or an eagle's eye, are not as large as a dog's but the development of both the human eye and the eagle's eye far exceed the development of the dog's, they both have a far greater range of adaptability to varying conditions of light, and, something the dog's eye lacks, they are both sensitive to colour.

In the act of seeing there is first a rapid scanning of the area with the eyes. In this scanning, something, it may be movement or any departure from the normal pattern, cries 'stop' to the eyes. This is 'selection,' the second part of seeing. Having selected an object for attention, the third stage, 'recognition,' commences, and only when this is completed do we 'perceive' or 'see.'

The eye does this continually, and is adapted for 'seeing' under a wide range of light conditions. It also has the ability to see colour and can discern and perceive over a wide range of distances.

In contrast to the human eye with its high state of development, compare the human nose. Its development is so poor that it is of little use as an aid to living. If the meat on your fork is bad your nose might possibly detect the odour, or if cloth is burning you might smell

it, but when you consider the scent sensitivity of a deer or a dog which can smell you half a mile downwind, it is apparent that the human nose tells its owner literally nothing.

Since size alone is not a definite indication of the extent of development of a sense organ, you must rely on your observation to tell you which of an animal's sense organs are most highly developed.

For instance, a dog's nose does not appear to be extremely well developed physically. It is not unduly large, as is the nose of an elephant (its trunk), or the nose and nostrils of a deer, horse or cow.

But by observation, that is 'seeing' and deduction you will learn that a dog's nose is its most highly developed organ, and therefore its most important sense for 'living,' with 'hearing' as the next sense, and 'sight' last on the list.

Watch a dog looking for a stone which you have thrown. His eyes follow it in flight, but when he is seeking where he thinks it has fallen you see him running round with his nose to the ground, and it is his nose, and not his eyes which find the stone for him, and he selects the stone from among hundreds of others solely because it has your scent on it.

Watch a horse when you hold a carrot out to him on the palm of your hand. First he puts his nostrils to it, rarely if ever his eyes, then he takes it in his lips.

WHEN A SENSE ORGAN IS HIGHLY DEVELOPED THE ANIMAL MAKES USE OF THAT SENSE ORGAN IN PREFERENCE TO ITS OTHER SENSES

In a general way an animal's feeding habits tell you much about its sense development. For instance all digging animals must have a strong scent development in order to find food hidden in the earth.

All flesh eating animals must have good near sight development to stalk and find their food. They must also have a good distant scent development to be aware of food which may be hidden and out of direct sight.

All grazing animals must have very good scent development to select the choice morsels of herbage for their food, and also to warn them of an approaching enemy. They also must have good hearing development, and finally they must have good sight development to recognise an enemy and to see which is the best direction

241

for escape. Since many grazing animals feed by night as well as by day, the eye must be very large in size in order to take in more light at night, but this is purely a matter of size and not necessarily of actual development or high sensitivity.

SIMILARITY OF FORM DOES NOT MEAN SIMILARITY OF HABIT

Animals which appear similar in shape and form do not necessarily have similar habits. Rabbits and hares are similar in shape and form and feeding habits, but very different in habits.

Rabbits, as you know, live in colonies underground, but hares live singly in a 'form,' or nest, on the surface.

When a rabbit is alarmed it seeks safety in the warren.

When a hare is alarmed it seeks its safety in running

at speed. A rabbit is attracted by newly dug earth. A hare prefers grassland and avoids new ground.

This dissimilarity of animal habits within their own family group or species exists throughout the whole animal kingdom. One type of wild dog will hunt in packs, and another will hunt singly, as does the fox. One member of the cat family will climb trees, and pounce on its prey from overhead; another species will stalk its prey at a drinking pool and make its kill there.

One species of kangaroo or deer will live on open plains, and another species will avoid open country, and live only in forest land, while yet another species prefers hilly or rocky country. One type of pigeon feeds solely on fruits growing on trees and another type will prefer ground feeding, selecting fruits which have fallen to the ground, and ground growing seeds and grain.

THE BALANCE OF NATURE

Over countless ages a balance between the different forms of life has been attained.

As a simple example, if all the animals of a country were grass eating, there would be no check on their population growth, the grass which is their food would eventually be destroyed, and as a species the grass eating animals would die out in a couple of generations. There would be no balance.

Introduce flesh-eating animals into these conditions. They live on the grass eaters, and also on one another,

243

and the population of all is kept at a lower level. Further, the weaker animals are killed off, and the stronger alone survive to breed. In a short time a balance between grass eaters and flesh eaters has been achieved.

This is the balance of nature.

Continuous destruction of wild life can easily upset this balance, and, like a chain reaction, the unbalance spreads. The uneven balance of nature can also be caused by the introduction of either a plant or animal foreign to the country.

In one part of New Zealand domestic cats gone wild become a plague. The cat plague was finally traced to the introduction of red clover.

It happened this way. The red clover is very deep throated, and only one species of bee could extract the nectar. This species of bee made its hive in the earth. With the plentiful supply of honey, this type of bee increased rapidly. A certain type of field mice liked the honey of this bee, and they too increased in population, feeding on the earth hives of the red clover bees. With the increase of mouse population the cat population flourished until finally the cats assumed plague proportions.

Excessive trapping also can upset this balance of nature, but trapping used intelligently can help nature to restore its balance. Trapping can also be extremely valuable as an aid to the extermination of pests.

TRAPPING AND CHARACTER TRAINING

It has been shown that TRAPPING calls not only for an extensive knowledge of the mechanics of bush-made traps, but also for a thorough study of the habits and ways of life of all wild creatures.

The person who undertakes the work of trapping, whether for a livelihood or as a means of studying wild creatures at close quarters (as the artist and the zoologist must do) must be a person of wide understanding and great tolerance.

Trapping naturally brings about a love of wild animals, because it effects a full and complete understanding of their ways of life.

No true trapper could be cruel to wild creatures. His sympathies are too large to endure cruelty. The best way in the world to engender a love of wild animals is to be a trapper. Only then can you realise how intelligent and lovable all the wild creatures are.

This does not apply to the average professional rabbit-trapper, who is a trapper solely because it provides him with an easy means of making money quickly.

There are exceptions, too, among wild dog hunters, or 'doggers.' Many doggers relish the challenge which is put up to them by a savagely intelligent 'killer' dog with a big reward on its scalp. For these, the dogger has to use all his skill and cunning to match that of the wild dog.

To be efficient in trapping work the trapper must possess infinite patience, he must be able to stalk a wild animal in order to observe it at close quarters. He must learn about its sensitivities. In this and all the other work called for in trapping his own sensitivities are sharpened, and his intelligence and observation developed to a remarkable degree.

No people equal the native in powers of observation and deduction. This is due to the single fact that the native depends solely upon his hunting for his food.

What hunting has done for the native in perfection of his powers of observation, trapping can do for the white man to a lesser degree.

This development of observation and cultivation of the powers of deduction, coupled to the painstaking care which is necessary to all trapping work, play a major part of character development of an individual.

For example, in stalking an animal to observe it at

reasonably close quarters, the would-be trapper soon learns that he must approach up wind, he learns to take advantage of every scrap of cover, and to avoid showing himself on the skyline. He learns that he can approach the animal more easily if he keeps still when the wind is still, and moves when gusts of wind move the bushes, stirring them into action. Only then will his movements pass unseen by the animal he is stalking. With the development of his observation, and aided by his intelligence he soon finds out that he can place an obvious object such as a piece of white rag on a distant bush where it will constantly attract the animal's suspicious attention, and, taking advantage of this, he can circle and approach from the opposite direction.

The making of a trap out of bush materials calls for a ready eye to see the right sticks quickly, and requires cunning, and co-ordination of head and hand to cut and shape the sticks correctly. Having made the trap, it must be sited in the right place, and then watched. All this calls for observation and infinite patience. Once the animal is caught there comes with its capture an appreciation of its apparent helplessness, and a sympathy with its predicament. This in turn leads to a genuine love of all wild life.

IS TRAPPING CRUEL?

Nature lovers will contend that trapping is cruel and unnecessary.

Undoubtedly this is true of much of the trapping which takes place now, and has taken place in the past. Trapping for the skins is cruel, wasteful and not in any way productive of good. Similarly in other countries trapping of animals for the pelts threatened whole species of wildlife with extinction.

The general run of mechanical trapping is extremely cruel. Most animal traps are similar to the common rabbit trap. A device with two steel jaws that clamp onto an animal's leg generally breaks it, and holds the creature in agony until it is killed, possibly hours later, by the trapper.

These traps are not discriminatory. Protected animals and even birds are caught in rabbit traps set near warrens by river banks. Pets, too, are caught and their legs broken so they either have to be destroyed or left maimed for life. Trapping of this nature is cruel and wasteful.

Trapping can be humane, and need not in any way cause suffering or extreme distress to the wild animal. Pen and box type traps can be used to catch animals alive. These type of traps cause the animals no discomfort or pain. Other types of traps such as logfalls kill instantly. The wild creature is not left in lingering agony for hours. When it touches the bait, death is merciful, and instant.

It is vitally important in all trapping work that you should never leave the trap, if set, unattended for more than a few hours.

A set but unattended trap may catch and hold an animal captive. The animal in the trap may either perish through lack of water or food, or may dig its way out, if the pen of the trap is made of stakes driven into the ground.

The trapping of small birds such as painted finches, larks, thrushes, lovebirds and parrots, where it is desired to capture them for sale into captivity, is cruel. It may be argued that these creatures' lives are more secure when caged, and have freedom equal to their wild life if under proper conditions.

The trouble is that they rarely are under proper natural conditions when in captivity, and except for the 'lure' type of cage trap, the trapping methods are cruel, and very destructive of life. (The method of trapping small birds for pets usually makes use of snares on a stick set in a bush or tree which the birds frequent.)

This writer recommends to every bush-lover that if they ever see a snare stick they should destroy it immediately, without any regard for the feelings of the person who made it and placed it.

It will be argued also by many bush-lovers that it is not in the best interest of the community to make information about trapping or traps public. These people will delude themselves into the belief that small boys will set up traps and snares indiscriminately, to the immediate peril and destruction of all wild life. They will argue too that all trapping is cruel, and unnecessary. No bush-bred boy will trap unnecessarily, and no city-bred boy would have the essential knowledge of the wild to be able to trap anything with effect. Trapping is not effective unless the trapper completely understands the habits and life of the wild creatures. This is something completely foreign to the city-bred boy.

REASONS FOR TRAPPING

The trapping of wild creatures, whether bird or animal, can only be justified on the grounds of 'Preservation.' Some wild animals prey on other less-aggressive species—particularly is this true of the domestic cat, which, having gone bush, becomes the No. 1 killer of wild life. Cats are difficult to poison. They regurgitate the bait and continue their destruction unaffected. Fortunately they are comparatively easy to trap and when captured can be destroyed. Dogs which have gone bush, or which have mated with wild dogs, and also foxes, rank with cats as destroyers of native life.

8.

SNARES AND TRAPS

The ability to pick up a couple of dead sticks from the
ground, and with a sharp knife and a little know-how
produce a practical and workable release for a snare or
trap is a valuable exercise in improvisation and inven-
tiveness. As far as is known this is the first time a
collection of improvised releases and with this snares
and traps has ever been published. Some of these are
potential man-killers, developed by soldiers in jungle
warfare to protect themselves. The knowledge of these
possible man-killers must be treated with as much re-
spect as a loaded firearm.

They are included because they could be lifesavers for
man stranded in hostile country.

The snares and traps shown are far more humane
than the vicious steel-jawed devices which clamp onto a
wild creature's leg, inflicting severe pain, creating
panic in the captured animal, and hold it prisoner until
it finally dies from pain, hunger or exhaustion.

Conservationists may condemn releasing the knowledge of how to make the mechanics for these snares and

traps, implying that this will inevitably mean the destruction of local wild life.

This is not correct, in practice the opposite is the truth.

None of the traps are killers. The wild animal is caught alive and unharmed. Most people, after examining the captive, feel that it is too interesting to destroy (unless it is itself a destroyer), and will release it unharmed. More often than not the snares and deadfall, which are humane killers, will be used to capture the "pest" creatures, dogs and cats which have gone wild and are the biggest killers of local bird life, rabbits, foxes, and other "vermin" animals. These are the "scavengers" which are the real destroyers upsetting the balance of nature in a locality.

Two cardinal rules are: never set a trap which might injure anyone without first putting up warning signs in the area, and never leave a trap or snare set, and then forget about it. Some wild creature may be caught in it, and if it is a trap, suffer hunger needlessly.

The following traps and snares are but a few of the many which you can improvise with a little ingenuity. The releases and principles are comparatively few in number, but the variations are infinite. When making your trap or snare, make it sufficiently strong to hold the animal when it is caught. You must put good workmanship into traps or they are likely to be ineffective. It is far better to spend an extra hour in work to make the trap secure and strong, rather than try and save an hour by thinking that a flimsy erection will suffice.

Knowing the animal which you are hoping to trap will enable you to decide whether to set the release 'fine' or whether to set it 'tough,' so that the animal will have to tug and worry the bait, and thereby become bold and unsuspicious.

Included in these traps are a few which could be exceedingly dangerous to man. These are given because they are very little known, and could possibly be of great value to explorers or others. Several of these man-killers were devised during the War in the Pacific by men who were adrift in the jungle and used these 'automatic sentries' to make their camps safe from attack by hostile natives or enemy forces.

Some of the traps are illegal in certain countries, and the trapper should acquaint himself with the local game and trapping laws.

The type of trap you must make depends largely upon the animal for which it is being set, and the local conditions. Only experience can guide you in deciding which trap or snare will serve you best.

SIMPLE SNARE
Snare set over rabbit burrow.

Snare set in path, held in position with twigs.

This is merely a running noose set either in the entrance to a burrow or other hiding place of the animal, or else set across one of its paths. The noose should be of some strong material; fine brass wire (picture wire) is probably about the best. The brass is stiff enough to bend easily into shape, the noose will stand by itself, and being very thin it will probably not be seen by the animal, and yet it is strong enough to hold the snared creature captive. One end must be very securely fastened to a peg or other reliable anchor.

If fine wire is not available for noose snares, cord can be used, or if this is not available it can be spun, plaited, or twisted from local fibrous material.

Generally when cord is being used it will be necessary to hold the noose spread open. Very thin twigs can be used for this purpose. They should be set lightly in the ground, and have just enough strength to hold the noose open. Remember that the snared animal has sharp teeth and therefore the ability to chew its way out of the snare if given time. Wire obviously is difficult for the animal to bite, but with cord there is no difficulty, and an animal can release itself in a few minutes if it does not panic and struggle forward into the noose, as so often happens. When you set the noose snare it must be visited regularly at short intervals.

Snare set in animal path.

GROUND SNARE

TOGGLE AND BAIT STICK RELEASE

Select a site where there is a springy sapling. Lop the sapling of its branches and top. Bend the sapling over, and make a mark on the ground under the head of the bent sapling. This is the place where you will set the sticks for the snare. Cut two hooked stakes. These should be sharpened at the point, and bevelled at the head so they will drive easily into the ground. They

252

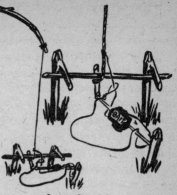

must be straight and strong, and preferably cut from dead wood. The hooks should be about two to three inches above ground level. Between the two hooks, and about twelve inches in front of them an anchor peg is driven into the ground. Three straight sticks for the release are selected. One must be long enough to go between the two forks and lie under them. The other is only about three inches long and is the toggle stick, and the third, which is about twelve inches long, is the bait stick. A stout cord is tied to the head of the lopped sapling, and the sapling itself is bent so that the head is over the two hooked stakes. Where the cord from the head of the sapling touches the cross stick, the toggle stick is tied securely, and above it another cord is tied and formed into a running noose.

The toggle stick is passed in front of the stick between the two hooked sticks, and under, so that the cord lies hard against the front side cross stick.

The lower end of the toggle stick presses against the bait stick, which in turn presses against the anchor peg. The noose is laid over the bait stick.

When the animal touches the bait stick, it frees the toggle stick, and the upward spring of the sapling, acting swiftly, draws the noose round the captive bird or animal.

This snare should not be left set for more than twelve hours at a time. If the sapling is kept bent for too long it will lose its springiness, and render the snare ineffective.

An alternative release may be effected by using two forks driven in at such an angle that the cross stick is pulled against the lower side of the fork.

The setting of the noose may be varied for certain types of ground feeding creatures so that the noose, instead of lying flat on the ground, over the bait stick, is held vertically so that the animal or bird must put its head *through* the noose to reach the bait.

GROUND SNARE

TOGGLED BAIT STICK RELEASE

In this snare a springy sapling is lopped of its top and branches. Two strong hooked stakes are cut, and one with a shorter hook is driven into the ground directly beneath where the head of the sapling comes when it is bent over. At right angles to the hook of this stake, the other hooked stake is driven into the ground. It should be about one foot distant. The cord for the snare is tied to the head of the sapling, and the noose made in another cord tied just above the free end. The free end is tied to the bait stick, which held beneath the fork of one stake, is pulled upwards against the prong of the hook of the

other stake. Setting can be varied in sensitivity by narrowing down the edge of the hook against which the bait stick is pulled. Noose, or nooses should be vertical and spread a few inches away from the bait, so that the animal must put its head or forequarters inside the noose to reach the bait.

This snare should be released after about twelve hours of setting to restore the springiness to the sapling.

GROUND SNARE

REVERSED TOGGLE BAIT STICK RELEASE

A whippy sapling, trimmed of its top and branches to reduce the weight, is bent over, and directly beneath its head a very stout hooked stake is driven into the ground.

A strong cord is tied to the head of the sapling, and the other end of the cord is tied an inch or so from one end of a toggle stick some eight to ten inches long. This long end of the toggle stick is passed *under* the fork of the hooked stick (see sketch). The bait may either be placed on this toggle stick, or alternatively on the stick which it presses to the ground.

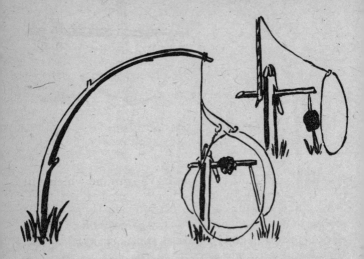

A noose is tied to the cord *above* the tie of the toggle stick, and brought forward, and held in position by thin twigs (not shown) so that it is a few inches in front of the bait stick. If the toggle stick is used to carry the bait it is advisable to put out two nooses, one on either side of the bait.

Care must be taken to see that the long end of the toggle stick is short enough to pass freely under the hooked stick. If the toggle stick is too long it will simply smack down on the ground and jam the release. It must be short enough to swing completely free under the hook.

GROUND SNARE

STEPPED BAIT STICK RELEASE

A whippy sapling is trimmed of its branches and head,

and bent over. Note the point on the ground which will be directly under the head when the snare is set.

Two strong hooked stakes are driven into the ground about nine inches apart. A cross stick is roughly squared in the centre and placed beneath the two hooks with one of its squared faces directly facing the ground. The bait stick is cut with a cleanly cut faced step, the bottom of the step is on the lower end of the cut. To the top end of the stick the cord from the sapling is tied securely (a clove hitch or stopper hitch is good for this purpose).

One, or better still, two, nooses are run out from the main cord, and held vertically a few inches from the baited end of the stick by thin twigs (not shown). An animal touching the bait disturbs the seated faces, and releases the stepped bait stick which holds the bent sapling. Sensitivity of the release is effected by the 'grip' of the seated face of the bait stick.

GROUND SNARE

NICKED BAIT STICK RELEASE

A whippy sapling, lopped of top and branches, has a stout cord tied to its head. The sapling is bent over, and directly beneath the lopped head, a strong hooked stick is driven into the ground. The end of the hooked side is sharpened to a chisel point.

The bait stick is cut with a square nick so that this will engage the chisel edge of the hook. The cord from the head of the sapling is tied to the top end of the nicked bait stick, and the bait is secured on the lower end.

From this cord the noose is tied, and spread a few inches in front of the baited stick.

Fine setting is obtained by making the nick shallow, or for a stubborn release cut the nick deeply.

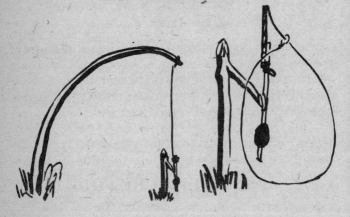

GROUND SNARE

CROSSBAR BAIT SNARE

Two stout straight stakes are cut. On the upper end of each a nick is cut, with the straight step on the top end of the stake. The cross bar is now cut, with a side branch so that the end of the side branch is a few inches away from the cross bar. The side farthest away from the side branch is squared on top and sides to fit the squared faces of the stakes. A whippy sapling, lopped of its branches and top, is bent over so that it comes directly above the head of the two stakes driven into the ground.

A cord from the head of the sapling is tied to the centre of the cross bar. The side branch is baited, and two nooses are spread either side of the baited crossbar.

Depth of cuts into the two stakes affects the degree of sensitivity of release.

GROUND SNARE

DOUBLE ENDED FIGURE FOUR SNARE

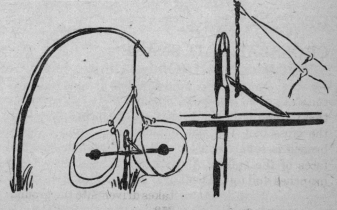

A whippy sapling, trimmed of its branches and head, is bent over and the site directly beneath the head marked on the ground. Before releasing the sapling a stout cord is tied to the head. The three sticks for the release are now cut. One of these is a stake. It must be sharpened at the point, and bevelled at the head. About eight inches from the head two sides are squared off at right angles to each other, and about three inches below the head an undercut nick is made in one of the sides opposite to one of the squared sides.

The crossbar bait stick is now cut. This may be two feet long. In the centre it is nicked or cut to provide a squared step less than one-quarter inch deep. On the end farthest from this step, and at right angles to it, an undercut nick is made. The toggle release stick is now cut. One end is sharpened to a chisel edge, and put in the undercut nick in the stake. The crossbar is placed with its step against the squared edge of the stake, and the undercut nick facing to the top. Mark on the toggle stick where the end should be cut to sit in the upper nick of the crossbar, and sharpen the toggle stick to a chisel point. Tie the free end of the cord from the sapling head to the toggle stick, and then tie on cord for four nooses, and set same in position with forked twigs.

GROUND SNARE

A DOUBLE SPRING SNARE

Two saplings are trimmed and bent towards each other. At their heads two interlocking sticks are tied. These sticks are cut so that they step into each other. The bait stick is lashed to one of these, and four cords for the nooses (two onto each sapling head) are lashed.

The snare is set bending the two saplings over, locking the two sticks together, and then setting the nooses, two on each side of the bait, and a few inches distant.

When the animal disturbs the bait, it twists the inter-locking sticks, and so releases the two saplings. In springing apart they pull the nooses against each other, and hold the captured animal securely.

GROUND SNARE

TRACK SPRING SNARE

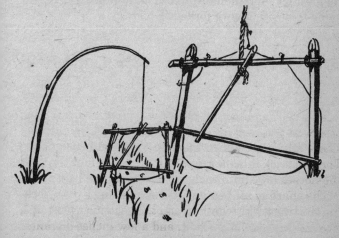

261

A site is selected on an animal trail where a tall sapling is available a few feet to one side of the track. The sapling is lopped of its branches and top, and a stout cord is tied to the head. Where the bent sapling crosses the trail tall stout pegs are driven well into the ground on either side of the track. To the tops of these stakes a cross bar is securely lashed. There may be occasions when convenient trees will serve instead of stakes.

A stout cord or rope is tied to the head of the sapling and a few feet along the cord a thin strong stick is tied. This stick should nearly reach from the crossbar to the ground. The cord from the sapling is tied a few inches below one end. This end is placed under the crossbar, and the lower end which will now pull forward strongly with the pressure of the bent sapling's spring, is laid against a thin cross-stick. The noose of the snare is lightly tied to the top crossbar and the stakes to keep it spread open. Release is effected when the animal touches either the bottom stick, knocking it down, or the toggle stick with the cord. Either action will release the holding down of the sapling, and it will spring upright, tightening the noose around the animal's neck.

TREE SNARE

SIMPLE NOOSE FOR TREE CLIMBING ANIMALS

Note.—This snare is prohibited in many areas, and should not be used unless absolutely necessary, and only where its use is permitted.

A site is selected by examining a tree which shows the claw marks of tree climbing animals on its bark. The 'lean' of the tree is carefully examined, and on the upper side of the 'lean' a stout straight pole eight to ten feet

long, and at least three or four inches thick is placed to make a 'path' for the animal from the ground to well up the tree trunk. The animal will use this pole to climb the tree on its nightly excursions. Onto the upper end of the pole set a simple wire noose, fastened securely to the pole itself.

The animal in climbing or descending the pole will put its head or paw into the noose, and so ensnare itself.

Note. —A point of interest is that most tree living animals will descend a tree if the base of the tree is consistently beaten with a heavy instrument such as the back of an axe or a heavy club. Nocturnal animals will descend a tree in broad daylight, but the blows must be continued and fairly heavy. It is probable that the animal feels the shock through the tree and, obeying an impulse to quit before the tree falls, leaves its hiding place. This is an excellent method of getting night feeding animals into daylight for photographing.

TREE SNARE

NOOSE SNARE STICKS FOR SMALL BIRDS

Note.—This is a prohibited snare, illegal in many districts. It should not be used except to catch pests.

A straight stick three to four feet long is selected. Onto this many fine nooses, each between ½″ and 1″ in size, of horse hair are tied securely and the stick is then tied with the nooses uppermost to a shrub or small tree which is a favourite resting place for small birds. They alight on the stick, and their feet become entangled in the snares. One or two birds so caught will call others to them, and in a short time seven or eight birds will be all snared on the noose stick.

This type of snare stick is condemned for general use. It has a place for the orchardist to clear starling and fruit eaters from his orchard, but it should not be used to snare small birds such as finches and wrens for the purpose of putting them into captivity. If you see such a stick, obviously set for such a purpose, take it and destroy it. You will be doing the birds a good turn by this action.

LOGFALL

SLIP RELEASE OF BAIT STICK

This logfall is suitable for ground living animals, and depends for its action upon the turning or twisting of a forked bait stick, one end of which is sharpened to a point which in turn supports the smoothly cut face of the cross bar on which the logs are lying. Select a site where the animals feed. Cut your bait stick with a widely forked prong. The lower end should be roughly sharpened, and the top end brought to a sharp point. A stout

stake is sharpened and bevelled at the head so that it is
nearly flat. This stake is driven securely into the
ground. The two or three heavy logs for the fall are
selected and trimmed so they will lie together on the
cross bar. The cross bar is cut with a squared side at one
end, and the other end is trimmed off with a smoothly
inclined face. The squared side is laid on the top of the
bevelled stake. The logs are laid on the cross bar, and
the sharpened point of the bait stick is put under the
inclined cut on the end of the cross bar at such an angle
that it will slip off if the bait stick is twisted. The lower
end of the bait stick rests on a chip of bark or a smooth
flat stone so that it will not sink into the ground. Sensitivity is adjusted by the angle of the bait stick on the
cut at the end of the cross bar.

LOGFALL

SQUARED FACE RELEASE OF
BAIT STICK

The general construction of this logfall release is
similar to the slip release. A stout stake is sharpened
and driven into the ground as for the preceding trap.
The cross bar, except for two squared sides in place of the

smoothly cut inclined end is exactly the same. The bait stick is forked and at the upper end a square seated cut is made to take the squared side of the cross bar, so that when the weight of the logs is resting on the cross bar the squared side is securely resting on the square cut at the top end of the bait stick. When the prong with the bait is disturbed the bait stick is twisted, and the crossbar unseated so that the logs fall on the animal beneath, either breaking its back instantly or crushing its head so that death is immediate.

LOGFALL

FIGURE FOUR RELEASE

In this type of logfall the two or three heavy logs are bound to cross pieces at head and foot so that they will lie together. Alternatively a platform of light sticks weighted with heavy stones can be made. Release is effected by the Figure 4 method. For this release three strong sticks are selected, one about two feet high for the upright, one about three or four feet long for the bait stick, and one about eighteen inches for the release stick.

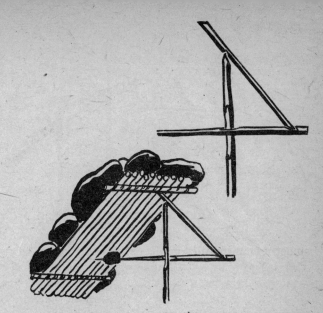

The upright is sharpened to a chisel edge at the top, and twelve inches below this and facing the same direction as the straight edge of the chisel end the stick is squared off on two adjacent sides. The bait stick is cut with a nick sloping backwards a couple of inches from the thickest end, and about twelve inches further along with a squared step, the squared side of which is farthest away from the nick. The bait is at the far end of the bait stick. The release stick is sharpened to a chisel edge at either end, and a nick parallel to the chisel edge is cut some few inches from one end. Setting of the trap is effected by standing the upright stick a few inches from the end of the logs. Lifting the logs and putting the release stick under the cross bar, with the chisel cut of the upright in the nick in the release stick. The far end of the release stick is seated in the nick at the end of the bait stick so that it draws the square face of the cut against the squared face of the upright stick. Any disturbance of the bait releases the logfall.

LOGFALL

TOGGLE RELEASE

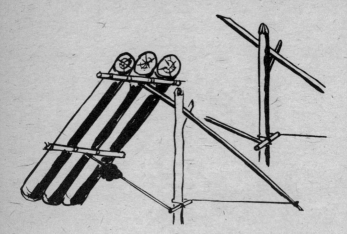

Two or three logs are secured to a cross bar as for the figure 4 release. The release sticks consist of a forked stick about two feet long for the upright, a support stick about three feet long, a toggle stick of four or five inches, and a bait stick, long enough to reach from the upright stick to the lower cross bar holding the logs together.

The trap is set by standing the upright with the fork uppermost a few inches in front of the logs. The support stick is laid over the fork, and to its farthest end a cord is tied. The length of the cord should reach from the end of the support stick to the upright stick. The end of the cord is fastened to a toggle stick and this is passed around the upright. Against one end of the toggle stick the bait stick is placed so that its farthest end presses against the lowest cross bar. Release is effected when an animal disturbs the bait stick, and so releases the toggle, allowing the logfall to drop.

In place of a group of logs for any of these traps, a

platform of stakes, heavily weighted with big stones, may be used with equal efficiency.

LOGFALL

TREE LOGFALL

Note.—This is an exceedingly dangerous trap. It is so absolutely unsuspected and sudden that it should only be used either to guard against surprise from attack if in a country of hostile natives, or if set to kill large animals. Notices of warning should be placed at either end of the path. This trap is a man-killer.

A site is selected along a trail which the animals use regularly. The site must have a branch of a large living tree overhanging the path. A heavy line is thrown over the branch so that when allowed to hang free its end will lie on the path. To this line a stout rope is tied and the rope hauled up and over the branch. To one end of the rope a heavy log is slung so that it hangs horizontally.

269

The log is hoisted to the branch, and the rope brought back so that it is concealed by the tree trunk; a toggle is tied where the rope touches the ground. At this place two very strong hooked stakes are driven into the ground, and a release similar to any of the noose releases (toggle and bait or reversed toggle) are used to hold the rope.

To what would be the bait stick in the snare release, lengths of cord or ground vine are tied for a trip cord and by means of hooked sticks the trip cord is led through the bush parallel to the animal's path to positions on either side of the place where the log will drop when it falls. This distance can be calculated by allowing for the log to fall at the rate of 28 feet the first second, 56 the second, and 28 feet more for each further second, and so on. (Drag on the cord reduces the log's rate of fall to this figure.) If the animal travels at three miles an hour, it moves forward 4 feet 6 inches a second. Thus, if the log is 100 feet above the path it will take two and a half seconds to fall and the animal will have moved 11 feet 6 inches after it has pulled the trip with its feet.

After setting this trap it should be given a test drop and, if satisfactory, reset only after placing warning notices several yards either side telling people to pass around the area, and not under any consideration to pass along the track. Failure to provide these notices might easily lead a careless person into gaol for manslaughter.

Remember this trap is a potential man-killer.

BOW TRAP FOR GUARDING A PATH

This is an extremely dangerous trap, and a certain man-killer if the bow is strong and the trap properly set. It should not be used except in cases of emergency.

A bow of considerable strength is made, and lashed to two stakes driven securely into the ground. The two stakes are set an inch or so apart. At right angles to the bow, and at the position where the bow string will come

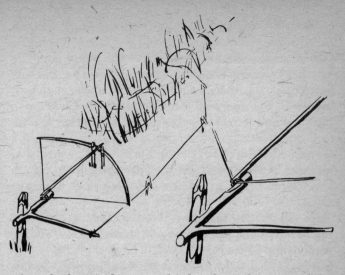

when the bow is drawn, a third stake is driven into the ground. The horizontal angle between the lower end of this peg and the place where the bow is lashed to the twin pegs should be such that the arrow will be given correct elevation to catch the man or animal at a vulnerable height when the trip cord is touched. The site should be at the bend of a trail or path.

Release can be effected by a hooked stick which has a square nick cut on the outside edge of one side, and at right angles to this cut a reversed nick is cut to take the

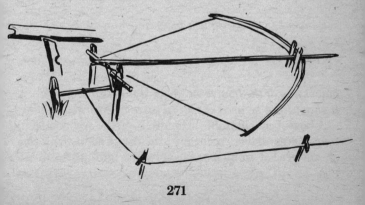

bow string. The rear peg is squared at its rear and on one side to form a right angle. The squared cut of the release stick engages the squared face of the stake, and the thong is hooked over the undercut nick, so that the bow is held drawn back to the rear peg. The arrow notch is in the thong. Release is effected by tying the release cord to the other end of the hooked stick and leading the release cord through the grass or bush to a position at the edge of the path. Guiding of the cord is effected by means of inverted hooked sticks. At the path the release cord is tied to convenient growing material such as a wisp of grass, a ground vine, or even a casual stick.

An alternative release is effected by deeply nicking with a square face the underside of the arrow. Into this nick a chisel edge release toggle stick is engaged. The release stick passes in the rear of a short cross bar so that the forward pull of the bow pulls the lower end of the release stick to the rear. This lower end is pressed against a trigger stick which is pushed against an anchor peg. To this trigger stick the trip cord is tied and from here it is led through the bush to the path, and set as a trip cord across the trail in the same manner as the hooked stick release.

A WORD OF WARNING . . . remember that this trap is a man-killer. Never ever leave it set and ungarded unless to defend yourself. Place warning signs on the path.

THROWER

There may be occasions when it is desired to create a diversion on one side of a path in order to frighten animals or people moving along the path away from it and into an ambush. For this purpose a thrower can be set up at a convenient distance from the path so that when a trip cord is touched the thrower will hurl a stone or other missile onto the path, and so drive the animal off the path and towards the hunter.

A forked springy sapling is lashed between two trees as for the stabber. The end of the sapling is forked, and in the forked end a shallow pouch is woven between the forked sticks. These forked sticks should be at an angle of about 45 degrees from the horizontal towards the path. The sapling is bent back and down and secured as for the stabber, and about four feet short of the place where the head came when it was at rest a very stout stake is driven into the ground to act as a 'stop' to the forward thrust. The sapling must be lashed fairly high up the two trees and bent downwards to the securing release, so that when it is tripped the movement is upwards. When the sapling is released and swings upwards it carries the stone in the pouch, and coming suddenly to the stop the stone is thrown from the forks forward to the path

PIG STABBER

Note. —This is a very dangerous trap to leave set where it might injure anyone walking along the path. Warning

A site is selected where two trees grow close together near the path the animal uses. A very springy sapling is cut, and lashed between the two trees so that when unbent it reaches to the centre of the track. To the end of this sapling a sharp dagger-like knife, or failing that, a pointed spear of hardwood is lashed. If wood is used, make sure that it is straight grained, and harden the end by scorching over fire. Sharpen to a good point.

The sapling is bent back as far as your strength will permit and note where the bent back of the sapling comes to above the ground. A few feet back from this point set the sticks for the release given in the snare. 'Toggle and Bait Stick' (page 252). To the bait stick of this release tie the trip cord, and run this along the ground to the position at which the bent sapling came when the head was straight over the path. The trip here should be very light and raised a few inches above the ground. The animal passing along the trap in either direction releases the trip, and the sapling is released with the spear.

Caution. Remember that this is a very dangerous trap and if used, warning notices must be placed either side.

BOX TRAP TO CATCH ANIMALS ALIVE

DOUBLE-ENDED PEN WITH SELF-LOCKING DOORS

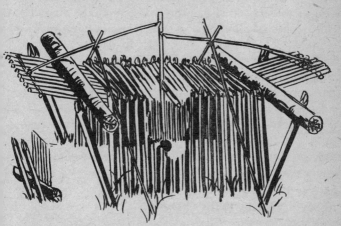

A strong pen of the size required is constructed with both ends left open. The pen is completely roofed over, and in the centre, one of the cross sticks across the roof is squared on one side and on its under surface. The cross pieces at the extreme ends are secured extra strongly to take two drop doors. A couple of inches beyond the line of the side walls, and about three inches from the end uprights very strong stakes are driven into the ground at an angle leaning away from the line of the pen. The two doors are made and hinged with loops of rope or strong vine to the end crossbars, across either end of the pen. On the outside, two support sticks are crossed about seven to ten inches above the roof of the pen. The release sticks are sharpened at one end to a chisel edge, and the bait stick is cut with a squared step about eighteen inches below its top (the square face at the lower end). Ten to twelve inches above this and parallel to the first cut, two square-nicked cuts are made with the squared face on the top side of the cut. The trap is set by putting the bait stick between the crossbars and engaging the squared cut of the bait stick with the squared face of the cross bar. The chisel end of one of the release sticks is placed in one of the top nicks of the bait stick, and the other end between two of the crossbars of the door. The release stick sits on the support sticks as a fulcrum. This is repeated at the other door. Both doors are now raised, and any disturbance of the bait stick will release the support sticks and the doors will drop. The locking device is effected by cutting two heavy poles about eight to ten inches longer than the trap is wide. These are laid across the top end of either door. When the doors start to drop the logs roll down the falling doors, and jam against the outward leaning stakes, thus wedging the doors tight.

PORTABLE BOX TRAP

BOX TRAP TO CATCH ANIMALS ALIVE EXTERNAL RELEASE

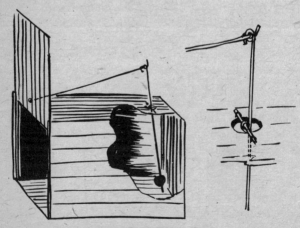

A box is made exactly similar to the box trap on the following page. A hole is bored in the roof 3 inches from the closed-in end. The bait wire is made with an eye at the top, and about four inches below this another eye, and the hooked portion for the bait some eight or ten inches below this lower eye. With this release the cross wire is placed through the lower eye, with the top eye above the roof of the box. The bait is fastened to the hook inside the box, and the release wire secured with its own eye to the top eye, and its farther end lying longways along the roof with the end itself in a small hole through the bottom of the drop door, and in such a position that it holds the door up. When the animal takes the bait, and drags backward with it, the top end of the bait wire is forced to the rear, and so withdraws the wire at the door from the hole and allows the door to stop, imprisoning the animal.

PORTABLE BOX TRAP

BOX TRAPS TO CATCH ANIMALS
ALIVE
INTERNAL RELEASE

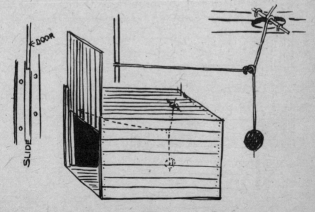

277

A stout box of a size suitable for the animal to be trapped is made. To one end a sliding door is fitted. This door must slide up and down easily between two grooves. On the inside of the door, and near the lower end a small hole is bored for about a quarter of an inch in depth.

On the roof of the box, about three inches from the closed-in end a hole about one inch diameter is bored right through the wood. The release mechanism is made by taking a piece of stiff wire (8 gauge), bending an eye in it at the head, and another eye about six inches lower down, and immediately below this lower eye bending the wire in a wide hook, and cutting it off at the end of the hook. Through the top eye another short piece of wire is passed (with the eye in the centre of the hole in the roof) and the short piece of wire lying parallel to the end of the box, it is secured in position with a staple at either end. Another piece of wire is fastened to the lower eye, now inside the box. This piece of wire must be just so long that when the hook is slightly forward, the piece of wire will engage in the hole which was bored in a short distance in the foot of the door.

The trap is baited by securing the bait to the U-shaped hook on the lower end of the wire inside the trap. The free end of the inner piece of wire is placed inside the hole at the lower end of the door. When the animal disturbs the bait the wire holding up the door is withdrawn, and the door drops, imprisoning the animal.

PORTABLE BOX WITH INSIDE STICK RELEASE

BOX TRAP TO CATCH ANIMALS ALIVE

There are occasions when a piece of wire may be unobtainable, then this internal stick release can be

improvised. The box is made as for the preceding portable box traps, complete with sliding door. For the release three forked sticks are used with the bait stick, which should have a fork at one end. The length of the three forked sticks should be such that two of them are equal and about three-quarters the height of the inside of the box, and the third should be about half the height. The fork at the end of the bait stick is so trimmed that one end of the fork is about an inch shorter than the other. Setting is effected by placing the bottom of the door on the longer of the two arms of the fork bait stick with the shorter arm in the inside of the door. The two longer forks are set near the end of the box, their forks holding the far end of the bait stick a few inches from its very end. The shorter forked stick is placed with its fork over the farthest end of the bait stick, and its other end against the roof. The bait is secured to the bait stick near the first pair of forks. When the animal takes the bait, it either disturbs the setting of the forked sticks which hold the slide door up, or it pushes the forked end of the bait stick inwards and allows the door to drop.

LOG ROOFED PEN

BOX TYPE BAITED TRAP FOR CATCHING ANIMALS ALIVE

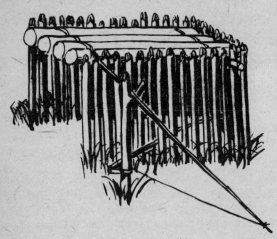

A pen of adequate size for the animal to be trapped is strongly constructed. The pen is built with two sides and one end only. Across the closed end a strong cross bar is secured. Release of the log weighted roof is by means of a toggle and bait stick almost exactly similar to the toggle release of the logfall. A forked stick is stood upright a few inches from one side of the trap at the open end. Across the fork a supporting stick is placed with the end of the roof logs resting on it. To the far end of this supporting stick a length of cord is fastened, and to the end of this a short toggle stick is tied. The end of the toggle stick is pressed against the bait stick, which in turn is pressed against the stakes opposite and at the far end of the pen. Disturbance of the bait stick releases its engagement with the toggle stick, which in turn releases the support stick and the roof falls heavily, imprisoning the animal in the pen.

BOX TRAP FOR CATCHING ANIMALS ALIVE

FALLING CAGE, FIGURE 4 RELEASE

A cage, either of sticks lashed to a pyramidal or other suitable shape, or of boxwood, or netting is made of adequate size. Release is effected by means of the figure 4 release. This is an excellent trap for ground feeding birds, and if the ground is baited with grain, or small fruits it is a certain trap for pigeons. The upright stick is cut with a chisel edge at the top, and a few inches from the bottom end it is squared on all four sides. The support stick is sharpened to a chisel edge at one end, and where it will cross the top of the upright, a nick is cut parallel to the chisel edge. The bait stick has a nick undercut at the thickest end, and at the place where it will cross the upright it has a cut made with a square face at the end of the cut farthest from the undercut nick. Setting is effective by standing the upright in front of the trap, and placing the support stick with its nick on the chisel edge of the upright, and the upper end supporting the raised edge of the box. The chisel end of the support stick is placed in the undercut nick at the end of the bait stick. The squared cut in the bait stick should now engage with a squared face of the support stick, and with the baited end of the stick well under the trap.

WIRE CAGE TRAP FOR RABBITS

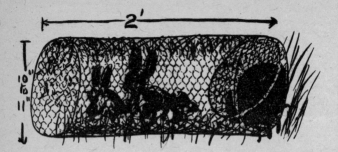

One of the most effective methods of catching rabbits is by means of a wire netting cage trap set at the entrance to one of the burrows of the warren. The warren itself is carefully examined, and a suitable burrow selected for the site of the trap. All the other burrows are covered with a layer of paper stuffed into the hole and packed for a few inches with earth. At the selected burrow the trap, simply made in the form of a long cage of wire netting with one end closed and with the other end as a wire door suspended from the top of the cage and falling so that it can be pushed easily into the trap but when it falls cannot be pushed outwards.

The rabbits in the warren coming to the burrows stuffed with paper are disturbed and suspicious of the rustle of the paper, and come finally to the burrow which has the wire cage in front of it. They push forward into the opening and the door lifting inwards permits them to enter the cage. When they are inside the cage the door drops behind them, and there is no escape back into the safety of the burrow. Ten or twelve rabbits a night can be taken from a warren with this trap, which is far preferable on humanitarian grounds to the steel-jawed commercial trap so commonly used.

NET TRAP FOR CATCHING ANIMALS ALIVE

An alternative to the box type traps for catching animals alive and without injury can be devised by using many of the releases shown, in combination with the pull of a springy sapling. For purposes of demonstration in these pages one such arrangement is shown above. The net, of suitable size and strength, is spread on the ground and the centre is baited, as for any of the spring snares. When the release is effected the four corners of the net, being tied to the main rope holding down the sapling, are suddenly pulled upwards, enfolding the captured animal in the net without injuring it in any way. The animal in its struggles gets its legs through the mesh of the net, and so cannot climb out or tear the net to escape. It may chew its way out if the net is left unattended for any length of time.

USE OF A RAT TRAP OR A FISH-HOOK FOR DUCKS OR GEESE

Select an area where, by the tracks and droppings, you know wild duck or geese feed. An ordinary rat trap, baited with a frog, and securely tied to a convenient log

or stake is set either on a stone, or some place where it will lie flat and secure. The bird, in taking the bait, springs the trap, which cutting into its skull kills instantly. The fish-hook baited with a frog is tied to a stake by a short length of line. When the bird takes the bait it is hooked and held for killing. Alternatively, the cord from the fish-hook can be tied to a heavy stone, which, dislodged when the bird takes the bait, falls into the water and drowns the bird.

These two methods of catching wild birds are illegal in many countries, and are decidedly unsporting. They would be a legitimate method of getting game for food only in emergency. Another method frequently used by poachers for killing pheasants, pigeons and grain-eating birds is to soak split peas and then put thin wire through them, leaving about ⅛-inch of wire projecting from either side of the peas. The birds pick up the peas. The wire pierces their crops and they die quickly. This method is strictly illegal and destructive, and should never be used. You may find such 'doctored' peas or grain in an area and, if so, immediately inform the nearest game warden or ranger. Vandals who destroy bird life by such means as this are severely punished in most civilised countries.

BLIND ROLLER FOR AN AUTOMATIC FISHERMAN

A discarded blind roller is fixed, with its bracket to either a pole or the convenient branch of a tree. The

fishing line is secured to the roller, and then, with the roller pawl engaged, the line is pulled so that it touches the water, or until the tension on the line is considered to be adequate. The roller is removed from the brackets and rewound by hand. This will give tension to the line to play the fish. The baited hook is lowered into the water, making sure that the pawls are engaged. When the fish strikes it will disengage the pawls, and the tension of the wound-up roller will play the fish, finally bringing it almost to the surface of the water. The lazy fisherman simply has to unhook his catch, rebait the line and cast in for his second catch.

In general it is better to set the blind roller on to a pole which can be set horizontally above the water, and lashed to a convenient tree or stake, than to set the roller onto a branch. It is easier to remove the catch and reset, and also the pole with the roller blind can be moved to other locations.

FISH TRAP

ARROWHEAD TIDAL FISH TRAP SUITABLE FOR AREAS OF FOUR TO SIX FEET TIDES

This is a permanent trap and will always ensure a plentiful supply of fish at all seasons. Select a site on an estuary or sheltered cove where the beach slopes fairly

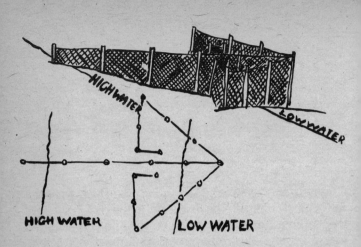

evenly. At this site run a fence of wire netting out at low
tide so that the top of the fence will be a few inches above
high water level, and the lower end will have a foot to
eighteen inches of water at low tide. From the low water
end of the fence run back two wing fences each at an
angle of about forty-five degrees. These two wing fences
should come halfway up to the high level water mark,
and from the shore end of these two wing fences run two
short fences parallel to the beach and stopping with a
turnback to the arrowhead about two yards short of the
centre fence.

The fish come in to the beach on the rising tide and
feed swimming along the beach. They come to the central fence, and turn along it to the deep water, reach the
corner at the deep water end and are turned by the wing
fence, and again by the fence parallel to the beach. You
can clear the trap at low tide, taking from it only those
fish which you need. This trap has the advantage of only
catching fish of good size, and not killing anything
which may not be required for food. There will always be
fish left in the pool at low water, and some of these are
bound to find their way out to deep water at the next rise
of the tide.

TIDAL ROCK POOL TRAP

A site is selected where there are a number of rock pools well covered at high tide, and barely dry at low tide. One such rock pool is selected, and heavily baited with such food as crushed up shell fish, small portions of freshly killed fish, crushed up rock crabs and the like. Across the normal opening of the rock pool a wall of rocks is built so that the top of the wall will be a few inches below the water at high tide.

This should be done at a time when there is a low tide at dusk and dawn.

The fish, feeding at night on the rising tide, come to the rock pool, drawn there by the lures and baits lying on the bottom. With the fall of the tide they are trapped until the next full tide and if the rock pool you have selected is not too large at low tide you can easily collect your catch with a scoop net.

CRAB OR LOBSTER NET

Make a circular wire hoop, three or four feet in diameter, and sew a piece of net or thin bagging around the edges so that there is a foot or so sag. To the wire hoop, tie three or four short lengths of rope, and join these together about three feet above the hoop. These cords from the hoop are tied to the hoisting rope, which can

either be buoyed or tied to a convenient post or piece of rock, depending upon the location where the trap is being used. The bottom of the net is weighted with a piece of rock, and baited with a few fish-heads or portions of small fish. These must be securely tied to the bottom of the net.

The net is lowered into the sea, and left for about two hours. Pull it up swiftly, and any crabs or lobsters which have been feeding on the bait will be caught in the sag.

For lobsters, set the net on a rocky weedy bottom, or for crabs, on a sandy bottom, preferably not far from an underwater reef.

FISH TRAP

DRUMMET

A drummet is simply a wire cage with inverted cone shaped entrance at either end. These doors lead inwards and the fish swimming in through the cones are held securely inside the trap. A drummet can either be set in mid-stream, or dropped down into a deep pool of a nearby river, or set off a rocky ledge at the seaside.

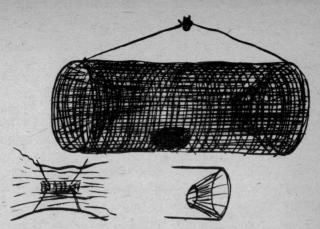

A drummet must be baited to be effective, and almost any old bait will do, fish-heads, inedible varieties of fish, large shellfish or other bait will all attract fish to the feast.

Make your drummet large and weight the bottom with a couple of heavy stones, also use a large-size mesh so that small fish can swim out freely. A drummet is an ideal way to ensure a regular supply of fresh fish.

SNARE FOR LOBSTERS OR YABBIES

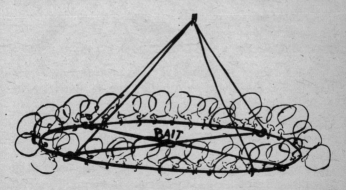

A circle of heavy gauge wire (8 g.) is made. The circle should be from 12″ to 15″ across. To support its shape two cross wires are secured.

Around the circle of wire a series of running nooses are tied. The noose need be no more than 2 inches across. Heavy nylon fishing line is excellent for this. These nooses should be about 1″ to 1½″ apart around the circle.

The bait is tied in the centre where the supporting cross wires pass each other.

Three or four cords tied to the circle are joined to a central rope which is buoyed to mark its position.

This is an excellent lobster snare.

HOLLOW LOG TRAP FOR FRESH WATER FISH

The fact that fish cannot swim backwards is made use of in this hollow log trap. A hollow log, not too large in diameter is covered at one end with a piece of wire netting or other material which will allow a free flow of water. A sling is made in such a manner that when the rope is pulled to lift the trap to the surface it will tilt the hollow log so that the wired-in end is lowest. The bait is put in a few inches from this closed end and the trap lowered into a convenient pool or off a rock ledge.

The fish swimming about in the stream will scent the

bait, and eventually find their way into the hollow log
by means of the open end. If the hollow in the log is not
too large the fish will be unable to turn around to swim
out, and as a result will be trapped in the hollow. The
open end of the hollow log should always be upstream,
otherwise the current may wash the fish free.

A similar method of catching smaller fish is possible
with an open-necked pickle bottle. The bait, such as a
piece of dough, or other food, is stuck at the lower end of
the bottle. The bottle is placed in shallow water, taking
care to see that all air is first removed before setting the
bottle in position. Small fish such as sand mullet, whit-
ing, etc., will swim into the bottle, and cannot return.
This is a good way to catch small fish for bait.

LOBSTER OR CRAYPOT

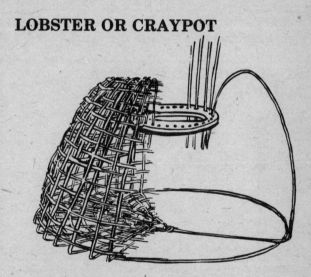

A board about one foot square, by one inch thick, has a
circle drawn on one side. The diameter of the circle is
about eight inches. Quarter-inch holes are bored around
the circle. These holes are about an inch apart. Five-foot
lengths of cane are put into each of these holes, and
about three or four inches above the board start weaving

split cane, so that the shape is like a wide funnel. The upright canes are gradually bent further and further with this weaving till they come right over and down, when the whole working is turned upside down for greater convenience. At the base, which should be about two feet from the top and about three feet across the circle, turn the canes sharply in to the centre of the circle. This, when the lobster pot is turned right way up in the water, is the bottom of the trap.

Weight the bottom with a heavy stone, and bait with old fish heads or other fish bait, and lower the lobster pot into a rocky weedy position. Lobsters live in caves in the rocks, and generally in colonies. The hoisting rope for the pot must be buoyed with a marker so that you can find it again. The pot may take a few days to 'weather' after you have first made it. Several such pots will secure you a fair supply of lobsters or crayfish.

IMPROVISED FISH-HOOK MADE FROM THORNS

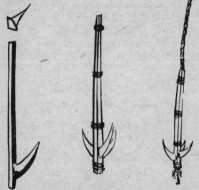

Three long and strong thorns are cut with about two inches of wood left above the upward curve of the thorn, and about a quarter inch below the end of the wood of the thorn. Make sure the thorns are long, hard and sharp. The wood section is pared down with a sharp knife so that the angle is about 120 degrees. If this is done correctly the three pieces of wood with the thorns can be fitted together to make a three-pronged hook. The wood is strongly bound with tough fibre thread at least twice on the shank, and once below. If possible it is advisable to bring the line, or at least a short length (for a cast) down the centre where the three pieces of wood join. This cast should be finished off with a thumb knot at the butt of the hook so that it cannot be pulled through.

Such hooks as this are quite as efficient as the steel hook, and can be easily made by anyone with careful fingers.

FISHING SPEARS

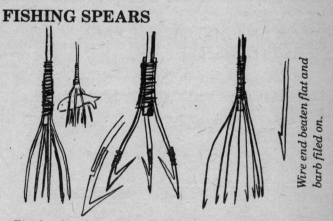

Wire end beaten flat and barb filed on.

Fire-hardened sticks. Barbed trident. Barbed heavy wire.

The best spearing is over shallow sandy shallows at night with an acetylene torch or very powerful five or six cell electric torch. With fish spearing the aim is to pin the fish down with the spear rather than thrust at the fish. Move the spear slowly till it is over the fish and then jab suddenly in the strike. Fish spearing by day can be either done from a boat or raft or coracle, or from a rocky ledge. In any case you will need a sea glass or underwater goggles so that you can see clearly without any interruption by surface ripple. A sea glass can be made by cutting the bottom out of a tin and simply looking through the hole the tin provides. This will protect the water within the tin from surface ripple. Or, better still, you can put a glass bottom to the tin and secure it with sticking plaster or scotch tape. When fishing from a boat, spear as nearly vertical as possible. In spearing for fish move slowly and quietly, and allow for the angle of distortion of the water. Remember that fish have a natural protective colouring and at first they will be difficult to see. They are easiest to detect when they move, or by their shadow against the sea bottom. Fish spears should be multi-pronged for greater efficiency, and, if made of wire, are more certain if barbed.

STICK SNARE FOR SURFACE FEEDING FISH

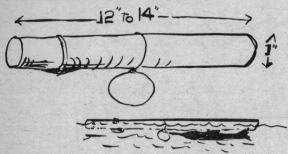

Surface feeding fish may be snared by means of a noose set on the underside of a weighted stick. The stick should be ten to twelve inches long, and on one side a small chip of stone is secured, either by tying or by slightly splitting the stick and driving the chip of stone into the split. A noose of gut, horsehair, or other thin material is tied so that the noose is on the same side as the stone chip. A number of these noose sticks are made and thrown into the sea from a rocky promontory. Surface feeding fish such as Long Toms and Garfish take cover beneath any debris floating on the surface of the sea. This is their protection against sea birds from above, and other bigger fish from deeper water. They will hide under the noose sticks, and in time either their bills or tails will become caught in the noose. Their struggles against the noose tire them out, and the wash of the surf takes them in to the beach. A couple of hours after you have thrown the noose sticks into the sea they will have drifted in to the wash at the beach and you can recover the sticks and any fish which have become snared in the nooses.

BAITED FLOAT STICK

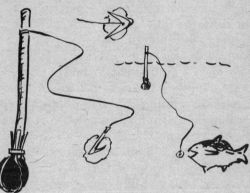

An effective method of fishing with float sticks in fairly calm water or off beaches where there is a set inshore to the beach is possible by constructing a number of 'float sticks' to which a stout short length of fishing line is attached, with either a baited hook or a boomerang-shaped piece of bone or shell baited as for a hook. These float sticks are made about two feet long, and on one end a fairly heavy stone is attached by means of a couple of straps of bark strips of cane enclosing the stone, and bound to the stick. This weight will make the stick stand upright in the water. To the top end of the stick the line is attached, and this should be about two to three yards in length. The farthest end of the cord carries the baited hook or piece of bone. These sticks are thrown into the water and allowed to drift. The fish taking the bait is hooked either by the hook or by the boomerang, and struggling against the drag of the bait stick, exhausts itself so that the drift or current takes it in its course. It is necessary if you are using this method of fishing to watch the direction of drift or current and know whereabouts to look for the sticks some hours after you have cast them into the water.

TRACKS, BAITS AND LURES

Trapping calls not only for a knowledge of the mechanics and construction of a particular trap or snare, but also for an intelligent knowledge of the habits of the animal to be captured.

This knowledge can be gained by observation of its movements and its feeding habits, and of course by its tracks. For example, you know that all animals with cloven hooves are grazing (ground feeding) animals, but did you realise that all animals which leave the track of a thumb, or even two thumbs, are all tree-climbing animals, or that all animals which burrow show the track of their digging claws quite clearly? Similarly all animals which leave pad-like tracks are carnivorous, that is, flesh eaters.

The same principle can be read into birds' tracks. Hopping birds are generally insect eaters, tracks of walking birds show they may be grain, insect or flesh eaters, and when you learn to recognise the talons of the tracks of a hawk or crow from the insect-digging toe of a lyre bird or an ibis you are well on the way to being able to read correctly the story book of tracks and trails.

All the traps given in this book are ineffective unless they are sited correctly and baited properly.

As a human being you regard siting as a matter only for your eyes. You SEE things. You must remember when trapping that wild animals rely much more upon their sense of scent than upon their sense of sight. They 'see' things with their noses, not with their eyes. Your scent if left on a trap will warn an animal of danger. You can destroy this scent by either drowning it, or by scorching the trap to burn it clean, or by allowing it to stand for a long time to 'weather' and so lose the human scent.

Human scent on a trap or snare can be drowned by the use of a stronger scent which is also a 'lure.' A lure is a smell which will attract an animal. Two excellent lures are oil of aniseed and oil of rhodium. Both will attract most bush animals.

Before setting up any trap you would be wise to test bait the locality to find out which baits will attract the animals, and also to find out what creatures are in the locality.

To test bait, select your site on a piece of clean dusty ground. Drive fifteen to twenty small stakes into the ground, and attach to each a different bait, some with lures, and some without. Mark each peg with a number, and make a note of the number and the bait which each carried. This work should be done in the afternoon. When you have all the baits fastened to the pegs, brush the ground clean. When you visit the test baited area next morning you will see the tracks of all the creatures that came to it in the evening, during the night and in the early morning. These are the times when all wild animals feed.

The tracks will tell you which animals took the baits, and also what baits were taken, and then, if you make your traps and bait them with the correct baits, they will be effective for you.

In general, tree climbing animals will take fruits as a bait, digging animals will take sweet potato or carrot or any of our edible roots, while flesh eating animals of course will only take flesh. Herbage eaters will often take a cabbage or lettuce leaf as a delicacy and, in many civilised areas, bread will be an effective bait.

9.

TRAVEL AND GEAR

It may be necessary to travel through unknown country, and this, without map, compass or any equipment. Under some conditions the traveller may have been totally unprepared and on his ability to travel and arrive may depend his ultimate survival.

In this book a little known or used ability of the eyes to stereoscope aerial or other pairs of photographs, and view the subject in true three dimensions, unaided by any optical equipment, has been included. Under some conditions this knowledge may be useful.

Apart from this, the exercise itself is a valuable and exciting experience in the use of the eyes.

There are many suggestions in this book that will provide real opportunities for adventure, which could be simply doing ordinary things differently.

Travel and gear is of necessity directly associated with "Time and Direction," Chapter 10.

MAPS

Before you set out on any journey through the bush

you must have a map of the area or else you must make one as you go along.

A map is a plan of a section of country. Being a plan it is drawn to a scale or proportion, and thus is nearly always shown prominently, generally at the foot of the map. As a plan it should also show either TRUE North, MAGNETIC North, or both, which by convention is generally at the top of the map. Unfortunately this useful convention is not always followed, and therefore you must check your map if the North is not shown. If it is not marked you must add this essential information. Show TRUE North as a strong line and MAGNETIC as a dotted line and mark each, so that anyone else using your map will know the difference.

Being a plan of a section of the country, your map will show ground features such as rivers and mountain ranges in relation to one another, and it may show man-made features such as buildings, roads and railways.

AERIAL PHOTOS

An alternative to a map is an aerial photograph of the country, or better still, aerial pairs of photographs. To read either an aerial photograph or aerial pairs you must learn to hold them correctly.

With aerial photographs but not necessarily with aerial pairs, the shadows must fall towards you as you look at the photograph.

If you hold an aerial photograph upside down, that is with the shadows falling away from you, you will almost certainly read hills as valleys, and vice versa.

Aerial pairs if looked at stereoscopically must be looked at in a special manner, but if a single one of an aerial pair is being studied, it must be viewed with the shadows falling towards you. This is important.

In this aerial the shadows fall towards you, and you can "see" the mountain ranges. Turn it upside down, now the hills become valleys, and the valleys hills.

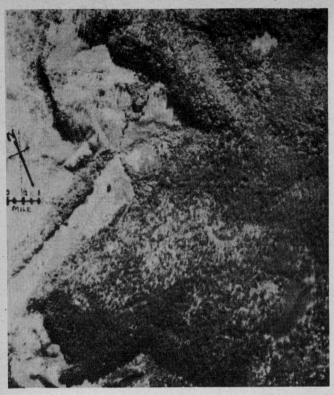

An aerial photo can give more information than is commonly given on a map, but you must be specially skilled in reading the photograph, and it takes a real expert to look at a photo and say, "That is ploughed land, and that is forest land, while that is grass country."

The texture of the earth's surface photographed tells the story to the eye of the expert.

STEREOSCOPIC VIEWING OF AERIAL PHOTOS

This is true too of aerial pairs. These are photos taken

hundreds of feet apart while the plane is flying several thousand feet above the ground. When looked at stereoscopically the mountains and the valleys show form in full three dimension. You can stereoscope these pairs with your eyes alone, unaided by any mechanical means, provided you have two points of vision, that is provided that there is equal or nearly equal vision in both your eyes. The stereoscopic effect is obtained by making each eye see a different image.

The easiest way for you to do this at first is to roll two pieces of paper into tubes about ten inches long and one inch diameter. The exact size is not critical.

Put one tube to your left eye, and place it a few inches over the left eye picture (see last paras. of this section to know how to recognise left eye picture and right eye picture). Now place the other tube to your right eye, with the other end of the tube a few inches above the right eye picture. The two pictures must be side by side, and identical spots on each picture must not be more than three inches apart.

Each eye will see a different image, and with a slight exercise that feels rather like "crossing your eyes" you will see the two pictures merge together, and by concentrating on the single image when they come together you will suddenly see it become fully stereoscopic. (Try

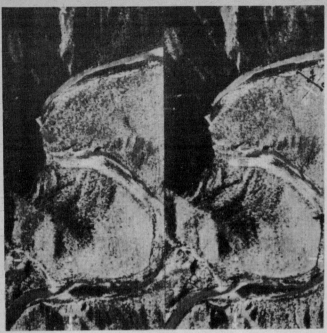

Photo U.S.A.A.F.

Correctly paired.

and bring the two black dots on each picture together.)

This is an eye exercise which at first will make your eyes rather tired, but keep it up. The exercise is good for your eyes, and soon you will be able to look at a pair without tubes and fuse the two images instantly. Try it with tubes on these two pictures. The photo is of a mountain gorge in Dutch New Guinea.

When you have trained your eyes to see each image through the paper tubes you can take the tubes away, and hold the stereoscoped image in your vision.

In stereoscopic use of aerial pairs you must know how to recognise right eye from left eye pictures. If by chance you reverse the images the mountain crests will be deep craters, and the valleys will be ranges. Here is the same stereoscopic pair reversed, viewed stereoscopically you will see this happen.

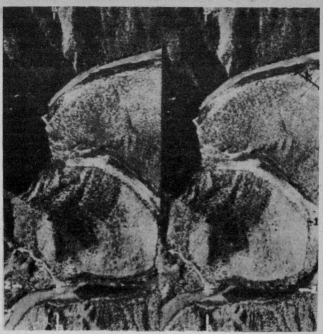

Incorrectly paired.

Photo U.S.A.A.F.

Note to that in reading stereoscopic pairs it is not necessary for the shadow to fall towards you.

RECOGNITION OF RIGHT AND LEFT STEREOSCOPIC PICTURES

To discover which is the left eye image select two identifiable points similar in each photo of the pair. One is the black spot on the line YY crossline 1 on the end of the mountain range, and the other is the white spot to the right where the little river joins the main stream on the line XX crossline 2.

One of these points must be on what would be one of the points of highest elevation of the land, and the other on one of the lowest elevations. The two points must be as close to a vertical line as practical. The parallax will

303

show you which is the right and left eye image. In the left image Y and X are closer than in the right image.

Explanation: The parallax is the angle between the point nearest to and the point farthest from the camera. Compare this with same photos reversed on page 302. Notice the space between A and B in both photos. In the left image A and B are further apart than in the right image.

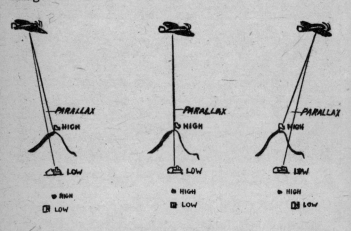

The two pictures must be equal in density of print, and must be placed side by side to be viewed. The maximum distance between two points for comfortable stereoscopic viewing with unaided eyes should not be more than three inches; by straining you may be able to fuse separations four inches apart.

NOTE: You can make three dimensional pictures with an ordinary single lens camera by taking two pictures from different positions with exactly the same exposure and aperture. The distance between the two positions is governed by the distance of the nearest object in the foreground from the camera. For every thirty feet the nearest part of the foreground is distant there should be not less than nine inches, and not more than one foot separation in position.

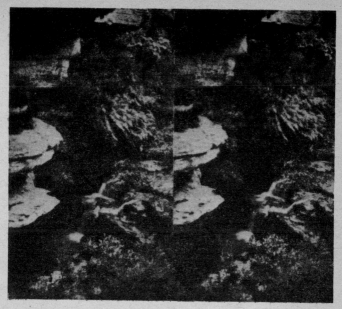

ROUTE FROM AERIAL PHOTO

When deciding a route from an aerial photo, or from an aerial stereoscopic pair which you have stereoscoped it is essential that you mark the TRUE North on the photo and also determine a scale. The scale will probably be approximate, but it should be sufficiently close to give you not more than half a mile error per five miles of travel.

It is also advisable to prepare a route or sketch map based on your study of the aerial photo or pair. If you do this you will work to your sketch map, and only refer to your aerial when some point of doubt arises.

LOGGING YOUR ROUTE, AND MAKING A CHART

A log is a record of the essential information of your

journey. This information must include distances and bearings, and may include any other information which the log writer considers helpful to himself or others.

Distances for log making in cross-country travel are calculated from the factors of rate of travel, and time.

Rate of travel varies. On open undulating country with short grass underfoot a walker will average a mile in between seventeen and twenty minutes, but in steep rocky country overgrown with scrub and thick growth underfoot a mile in sixty minutes might be good speed, and I have known places in New Guinea where one had to cut one's path through thick pit-pit (a giant grass up to 12 feet high) and there a mile forward would not be made in eight hours.

The following table may be considered a fair guide to walking paces. Remember there is a tendency to overestimate rate of travel.

COUNTRY	Time to walk one mile	
	Minimum	Maximum
Open country, firm underfoot, level or slightly undulating	15 minutes	20 minutes
Scrubby country, rocky underfoot, 50 to 100 ft. ascents and descents	24 "	30 "
Scrub and jungle. Steep ascents and descents (1-10 to 1-3 grade), rocky or bad underfoot	30 "	40 "
Long steep ascents and descents of 800 to 1000 ft. or more, rocky or uneven underfoot	60 "	90 "

These figures are for an active man laden with a 30 to 40 lb. pack. With heavier loads the maximum time would apply. Rate of progress can be checked by each individual walker for himself. He can assume that 110 paces equal 100 yards, on level walking, and by multi-plying the time to walk 100 yards by 17½ he will have a very accurate indication of his walking speed per mile.

In climbing or descending rocky or broken ground his pace will be very much shorter and slower, and the walker will take about 150 to 170 paces (depending upon slope) to equal 100 yards. On very steep slopes there may be 200 paces or more per 100 yards of lateral distance.

Time of course can be obtained from your watch, or, failing that, from your sun clock-sun compass (previously drawn on your map) or drawn on the piece of paper on which you are keeping your log.

A log is kept most easily by recording the information in vertical colums.

Time	Rate of Travel	Distance Miles	True Bearing	Observation
8.30	3½	3	84	Open grassland very good walking. High ranges to east about 4 miles. River 1 mile south.
9.30	2	1	197	Climbed steep saddle to range crest. Very rough and stony. Grade on top 1-8. River ½ mile south at foot of range.
10.00	2½	3¾	110	Range crest stony underfoot. Many small crests to be climbed. Sides too steep to detour. River going southeast along foot of range. Range rising to east.

This information is later plotted, and in this form it becomes a chart of your route.

With this chart plotted you are never lost, because you always know where you are *in relation to the point from which you started.* It was in this manner that early explorers recorded their routes into unknown lands.

CHOICE OF ROUTE

Given a free choice it is always advisable in cross-country travel to choose a route *up* spurs and ranges and *down* streams, unless in very mountainous country. By following this principle there is less likelihood of getting lost for the simple reason that all spurs lead to the main range crest, and all streams lead to the main river course. By travelling *down* spurs, or *up* rivers it is very easy to take the wrong spur; or follow the wrong water-course and so in a few miles to find oneself hopelessly bushed.

This applies to country which is sparsely populated. Therefore before setting out across country it is advisable to carefully study your map, and plan your route, remembering all the time the general rule to choose if possible, a route up spurs and down rivers.

This sketch map will show you how very easy it is to get "bushed" by either travelling down a series of spurs, or up a watershed. The wise bushman, wishing to go

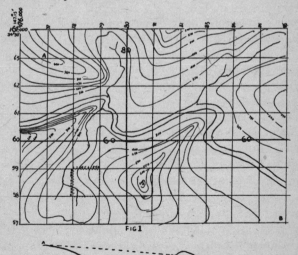

from A to B, will go by the route C rather than by the route D.

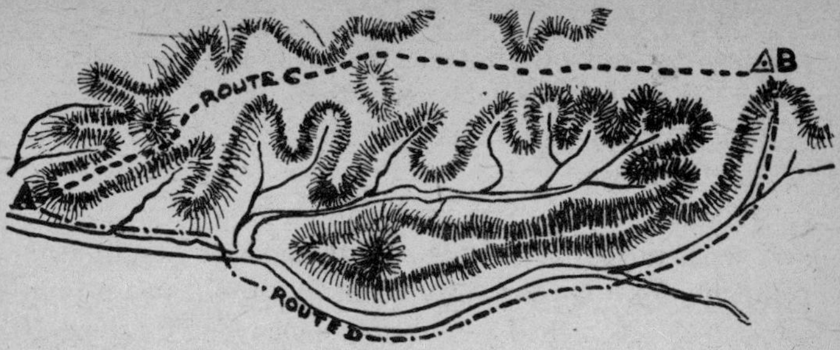

You will find these alternatives are often presented to you in cross-country travel.

MAP READING

While many maps show man-made features such as prominent buildings, roads, railways, and canals, it is advisable to read the ground shape of the land and not place too much reliance on man-made works. The surface of the land will never change, but man-made construction may vanish.

FIG 1

FIG 2

The most obvious natural features are ranges and rivers. The ranges may be very steep, or gently sloping, and to show this map makers either use 'contour' lines or hatchuring.

Contour lines are imaginary lines parallel in height and with an equal height separating one height line from the next. By correctly reading contours on a map you can tell if one hill is convex or concave in its slope. If concave, you can see the bottom of the hill from the top, unless of course intervening vegetation limits your visibility. With convex slopes you cannot see the lower grades because the curvature of the slope cuts off your field of vision.

The end of the spur in top left position of the map shown is a convex slope, and the slope east from the hill bottom centre is a concave slope.

A convex slope shows the contour lines closer together at the foot of the hill, and wider apart at the top, while a concave slope shows the contour lines farther apart toward the lower slopes.

Position on a map is always given by a 'map reference.' These are a series of numbers which indicate the square referred to. You will see in the top left corner of the map (Fig. 1) numbers reading vertically and also other numbers reading horizontally. These numbers are always shown on military maps, which you are more likely to use than others.

The vertical figures indicate the longitude (shown as 147 degrees 15 minutes), and the other figures 976,000 are the number of yards from the 'base line' of that section of country. Reading to the right from the top left corner each smaller square is indicated by the last two THOUSAND numbers, 77, 78, etc. Each square is 1000 yards (unless marked otherwise—see the map scale for this information). The same rule applies to the horizontal numbering; on this column is shown the latitude of the line in this case 34 degrees 50 minutes south of the equator). Map references are read from west to east first and from south to north, so that the figures 78.58 mean that you look along the grid line 78 until you find the square starting 58, and the reference is within that 1000 yard square. Each thousand yard square is divided again into ten smaller squares, each of which is 100 yards. This gives a six-figure reference 782.583. and you will find that this is the fork of the creek in the third square second row from the bottom.

Now see if 806.584 is the top of a hill?

Map reading when done correctly allows you to build up in your mind a picture of what you could see from any given position. If you were on the spur at A 768.632, could you see the position B at 858.572? In the lower diagram (Fig. 2) the elevations between A and B have been plotted. The tongue of hill running north-east through 81.59 and 82.60 would interrupt your view of B from A.

A military map also shows you a 'legend,' which are symbols indicating vegetation, water, and roads, etc. This is generally given at the foot of the map, and assists you in building up in your mind a complete picture of the country.

Hatchuring, instead of contour lines, is used by some

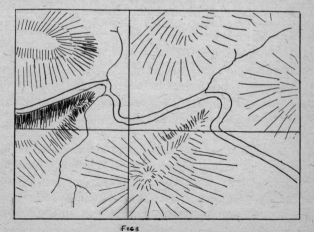

FIG 3

311

map makers to give an indication of the nature of the country. Fig. 3 would be a hatchured map of the same country shown in Fig. 1. In hatchuring thick strokes close together indicate very steep grades, while thin strokes far apart indicate gentle slopes. In many European maps the hatchurings are definite, thick strokes very close together might mean a slope of 1 in 2, to 1 in 3; thick strokes farther apart a slope of 1 in 4 to 1 in 6; thin strokes close together 1 in 8 to 1 in 10. These of course may be also expressed in degree of slope (1 in 56 grade equals a one degree slope).

THE SUN COMPASS-SUN CLOCK

Direction and time can both be obtained by drawing a sun compass-sun clock on your map. Trace off overleaf for the latitude line nearest to your map, and it will be both a compass and a clock for you. With a sun compass-sun clock, when you have any one of the following you can discover the other two.

1. A watch to get correct time.
2. A reliable compass.
3. A map correctly oriented (that is laid in the ground so that the features drawn on the map correspond exactly with the recognisable ground features).

WHEN YOU ARE ABLE TO ORIENT YOUR MAP CORRECTLY

The north-south line of your sun compass will correspond with the north-south of your map, and your time is read and corrected as explained in the preceding instructions.

To orient your map select two, or better, three, recognisable land features, and identify these on your map. Turn your map until the identified features exactly correspond in direction with the ground features. When this is done your map should exactly fit all the ground plan visible from your position.

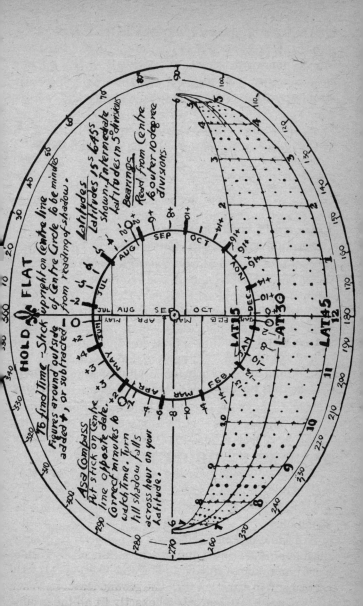

WHEN YOU HAVE A WATCH SET
TO CORRECT TIME

Place a thin shadow stick on the centre line of the sun compass which must be held flat, opposite the appropriate date, and turn the map until the shadow falls across the adjusted time on the latitude line.

When you have done this your map will be set to TRUE north, and oriented with the ground features.

WHEN YOU HAVE A COMPASS

Place your compass on the map with its axis along TRUE north line, and turn both map and compass *till the compass needle is pointing to the MAGNETIC north of your map.* (This may be east or west of TRUE north depending where you are.) The magnetic variation is shown on ALL Ordinance Survey (Military) maps.

When you have done this, hold the shadow stick on the north-south line of the sun clock opposite the appropriate date and where the shadow of the stick falls across the latitude line is local sun time. To correct to STANDARD or CLOCK time make the correction for the equation of time shown opposite the date, and also the correction for longitude by deducting four minutes for each degree you are east of the longitude of standard time, or adding four minutes for each degree you are west. (When east of the longitude or standard time the sun is earlier, and when west the sun is later.)

When the magnetic of your compass exactly points to the magnetic north of your map, then your map is correctly oriented.

WEATHER LORE

An infallible weather forecast, if a change of weather is coming up, is in the nautical couplet:

"When the rain is before the wind, your topsail
    halyards better mind,

But when the wind is before the rain, then hoist
your topsails up again."

In plain words this says that when rain comes first
without wind then expect a long period of bad weather
with high winds and heavy rain. But when wind comes
first and is followed immediately by rain, then fine
weather will follow at short notice.

Many people are trapped by bad weather in the bush
every year, and if they but knew of this simple weather
sign they could be prepared, and get out to a position of
safety before really bad weather sets in.

Another infallible weather signal is the appearance of
cumulus nimbus cloud, a foreteller of thunderstorms.
While a greenish light in the sky preceding a thun-
derstorm is an almost certain sign of heavy hail.

CLOUDS AND THEIR READING

CIRRUS

CIRRO-CUMULUS

CUMULUS

CUMULUS-NIMBUS

Cirrus, this is the "mare's tail" sky of the landsman,
shows as long threads or wisps of cloud. This is the
highest of all cloud formations, and is a sign of a "high"
barometrical pressure, which means fine weather.

Cirro Stratus, and Cirro Cumulus. In these clouds the
former is long wispy cloud, and in the latter rounded
small cloud the typical "mackerel" sky. Both are indicators of a high barometric pressure, and fine weather.

Cumulus and Cumulus Nimbus. Cumulus is the high
white piled-up masses of cloud seen in summer. When
streaked with horizontal bands it is Cumulus Nimbus,
or thunder cloud, a sign of coming storms, which may be
of short duration, or may indicate a change in the
weather generally.

Nimbus. This is the grey ragged cloud which uniformly covers the sky. It is the true rain cloud, and an indication of low barometric pressure and rainy weather.

Storm Scud. This is formless masses of very low cloud driven fast before the wind. It is a sign of very low barometric pressure, and continuing bad weather.

CARRYING GEAR

The first thing in travel is the method of carrying your gear. The conventional pack or rucksack need not be described in this column, which concerns itself with improvisation, and therefore only those methods which call for no "shop-made" gear will be given.

THE SWAG

The swag, proverbial Australian means of carrying a heavy load, is one of the best methods in existence. It is simply made and very easily carried. It has the advantage of being extremely well balanced, two-thirds of the weight being carried behind the body, and about one-third in front. The result is that the carrier walks completely upright. Clothes, tent, bedding and the gear not wanted for the day's walk are carried in the swag at the back, while the food and cooking utensils and day's needs are in the "dilly" bag in front. Because of this the swag is not opened during the day but the dilly bag, attached to the front and right at your hand, is immediately accessible.

The only components for a swag are a swag strap, two binding straps and a dilly bag. The swag strap, preferably of soft leather, should be about two feet six inches long and a couple of inches wide; the two binding straps can be of any strong material such as rope, or a plaited cord, or a narrow leather strap. The dilly bag can be a sugar or flour bag, some two feet long, and twelve to fifteen inches wide.

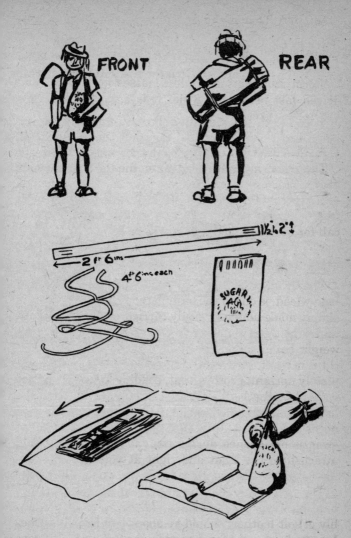

Laying out the gear for a swag, and rolling it and tying on the dilly bag.

These are the components for a swag. The swag strap should be soft and, if need arises, can be easily woven or plaited from strong grass, vines, bark strips or other material as indicated in Chapter 1. A soft leather strap is ideal.

Half the knack of carrying a swag consists in knowing how to "swing" it. Lay the roll, with the dilly bag extended in front of you, and then put the arm farthest away from the dilly bag through the swag strap. Heave the roll towards your back, and swing the body towards

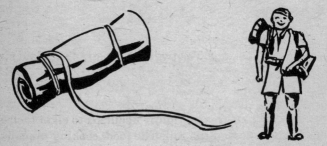

The alternative swag. Note the long strap and the position when the swag is "swung."

the swag, so that the dilly bag flies up and out. Duck the opposite shoulder, and catch the swinging dilly bag on it. The swag strap will then lie over one shoulder and the dilly bag over the other, with the swag roll carried at an angle across the back.

An alternative method of carrying the swag is to use two straps, one about 3 ft. 6 ins. long and the other about six ft. long. Both straps should be about an inch and a quarter wide and of strong soft material. The roll is made as for the swag, and the long strap is tied securely about five inches from one end of the roll. Five inches from the other end of the roll the other strap is fastened with the dilly bag held in position by the strap.

The swag is lifted to the left shoulder with the dilly bag in front and the roll at the back, the neck of the dilly bag hanging over the left shoulder. The long strap is passed on top of the right shoulder, and then under the armpit and around the back, and tied to a loop at the bottom corner of the dilly bag. This type of swag prevents the dilly bag from swaying, and is preferred by some "bushmen."

To roll the swag, lay your groundsheet or swag cover flat on the ground, and then fold your blankets to a width of about thirty inches by about fifteen to twenty. Spare clothes are laid lengthways on top, with your other gear. The sides of the groundsheet are folded in, and the whole is rolled from the blanket end to the free side, into a tight roll. If a tent is being taken this in turn is rolled in the tent. The two binding straps are laid six to eight inches from either end, that is 18 inches to 24 inches apart.

The two binding cords pass through the loops of the swag strap and are tied tightly about six to eight inches from either end of the roll. The food, cooking utensils, and daily needs are put in the dilly bag, and the neck of this is tied right at the junction of the binding strap with the swag strap, or alternatively a series of cuts in the neck of the bag can be made and the binding cord passed through these so that the bag is tight to the roll. If this is done it is a good idea to make a cut down the side of the bag for about twelve inches so that the contents can be taken out without removing the bag itself from the binding straps.

THE ADIRONDACK PACK

This is an easily improvised method of carrying heavy loads and an Adirondack pack can be made in less than half an hour. Select two light widely splayed hooks, with the arm of the hook 1 ft. 6 inches to 2 ft. long, and the shank portion three or four feet in length. It is better to use dead wood, which is well seasoned. This is lighter. A number of short straight sticks are lashed to the inside edge of the shanks above the arms, and two straps are woven or plaited, and tied to the lower end of the shank and again about eighteen inches from the lower end. The two shanks should be about fifteen inches apart where the straps are at the upper end.

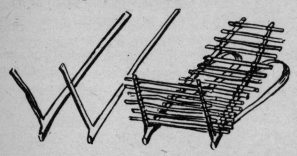

Showing an Adirondack pack, and how the load is carried high on the shoulders. If desired a head band can be used to steady the load.

PANNIER PACK

A pannier, eighteen inches square at the mouth, and two feet to two feet six inches deep, is woven from canes, rushes or any convenient pliable material. To this two straps woven from some pliable material are secured at the top, and eighteen inches below. The gear to be carried is loaded into the pannier.

RIVER CROSSINGS

One of the principal hazards in cross-country travel are river crossings.

For the crossing of rivers, and if the walker is a swimmer, the pack can be wrapped in a groundsheet which has its corners and loose-folds tied together. This will support the traveller who holds the pack in his hands and by kicking with his legs he can cross safely with his pack. It is advisable to tie a short length of cord to the wrist so that if the pack slips from the hands it can be recovered.

It is inadvisable to try to swim a river while wearing walking boots. These should be taken off and placed with the pack in the groundsheet. If a party of four or more are crossing, tie two or three packs together after each has been put in its groundsheet. One party stands by on the bank while the other party crosses.

Always place a layer of fern or grass or small brush beneath your pack before folding the groundsheet on it. If your groundsheet leaks slightly, this precaution will give your pack an inch or two clearance and keep it dry. With a frame rucksack, lay your frame uppermost—with a swag, place your swag roll and dilly bag side by side before folding the groundsheet.

A method of improvised water travel for poor swimmers or non-swimmers is by the use of two calico ration bags inflated, and used as water wings. These will easily support a human body in the water, and the non-swimmer can be taken across the river with absolute safety.

A pair of long drill pants can also be used to support a nonswimmer. The trousers are wetted, and the cuffs tied in a thumb knot, and then, holding the fly to the front with the legs hanging behind the back, the trousers are swung up, forward and then suddenly down into the water, so that air is trapped in the legs. The crutch is put across the chest, and the two legs under the arms. By this means any nonswimmer can be taken across a river with safety. The experienced swimmer who may have to travel for some distance along a river will find his trousers or long-sleeved shirt a veritable life-saver if used in this manner. He can tread water while inflating the legs, and they will remain buoyant for from ten minutes to a couple of hours, depending on the material from which they are made. One aircrew man who bailed out into the sea kept himself afloat for more than thirty-eight hours by this means.

RAFTS

Small bolsters made of ground sheets can be rolled up and lashed together if there is a party travelling together. These make an excellent raft, stable and buoyant, for either ferrying the party over the river or for actual travel along the river itself.

Showing how to make a bolster, and how the bolsters are lashed together into a raft.

Rafting is a practical means of water travel. The raft is built up from dry driftwood, and can be secured and made tight by lashing. In still water the raft can be poled along if the water is shallow. In travelling upstream it must be towed if the current is strong, or if travelling downstream, a "kellick" made either from a log of hardwood or a heavy stone is dragged astern in rapids. A sweep or long paddle ahead enables the raft to be steered because the water sweeping past the structure travels faster than the raft and this provides "steerageway" in reverse.

A raft, with kellick and sweep.

CORACLE

When a canvas or heavy duck fly, or waterproof tent,

or Japara or Willesden cloth tent is available, an excellent Coracle or boat can be made easily and quickly. The dimensions of the coracle are determined by the size of cover when laid flat. This is first measured and an allowance of at least eighteen inches for "turn up" is deducted from each of the two sides and the ends.

To these dimensions an oval is drawn on the ground, and nine inches inside this oval a second line is drawn. A number of straight sticks each about two feet long are cut and these are driven into the ground every six or eight inches around the two ovals.

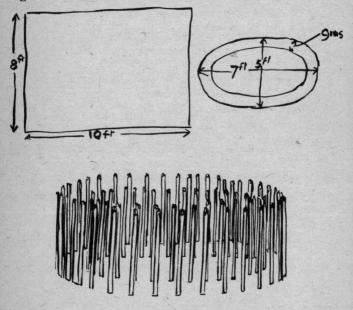

Sticks in double row around the two ovals. This is the appearance of the frame structure for coracle building.

Between these double rows of stakes green or half-dead fern, light branches and other waste bush material is packed to a height of about fifteen inches. This material does not need to be packed very tightly, but should be firm. When the required height is reached the wall is

324

bound with vines, strips of bark, or other available material. A few long sticks, just a few inches shorter than the length of the wall, are placed lengthways, with a number of shorter cross sticks on top. These are tied to the top lines around the wall.

This is the wall of the coracle complete, but without the floor sticks.

The canvas which is to be the cover for the coracle is laid flat alongside the structure. It is necessary to put a six-inch (unpacked) layer of fern, grass or other soft material over the whole of the centre area. The coracle wall is lifted straight up from the double wall of sticks, turned over, and laid on the centre of the canvas. It may be found desirable to lay it diagonally rather than square. The sides are turned up, and tied over the wall to the floor sticks, and when this is done the coracle is ready for launching.

This is a completed coracle launched. A coracle six feet by four wide with fifteen-inch walls will easily support four men.

Care must be taken to sit inside the walls and not on them. Any weight pressing on the walls will tend to break them down, and allow water to flow over the sides.

A coracle is perfectly stable, and when poling or paddling along a shallow river it will be found more convenient to stand. For long trips paddles, as for a canoe, can be used, or even oars lashed to the top of the wall in place of rowlocks will enable good progress to be made.

Long river journeys can be made by coracle—travelling in it by day, and at night removing the coracle cover from the walls and pitching it as a tent.

BARK CANOE

Where timber is plentiful, and the destruction of a green tree is permissible, a bark canoe can be made. The essential quality is that the bark must not be brittle, that it shall be reasonably pliable (considering its thickness), and that it be fibrous, and easily stripped from the tree. Also the barrel of the tree must be straight and free from branches and knot holes. The bark is cut around the lower portion of the tree, and then a ladder is made and it is ringed again fifteen or more feet above the lowest ring. The two rings are joined with a series of zig-zag cuts running straight along the barrel from one ring to the other.

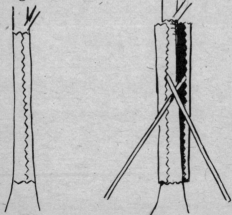

A tree ringed and ready for the bark to be removed.

The entire sheet of bark is carefully removed in one piece by means of two long poles chisel shaped at one end which is inserted (one on either side) in the vertical cut. By working these poles up and down under the bark, it will gradually be lifted and spread, coming off the tree in one sheet. This is spread with the opening on the lower side, and a quick fire of leaves is lit inside. The heat from this fire will drive the sap, in the form of steam, through the dry outer bark, and make the sheet more pliable. When it is flexible, the whole sheet if possible should be turned inside out after the fire treatment. Do not attempt this if there is any sign that the sheet of bark will split; instead allow the rough outside to be outside of your canoe.

The two ends are drawn together as closely as possible, and six inches to fifteen inches from the ends a series of holes are cut with a sharp knife. These holes should be cut in a zig-zag pattern. Vine, or very tough bark strips or other strong tying material is laced through these holes and the lacing pulled tight to draw the ends together. Inside, the ends are packed with clay which will make them completely watertight.

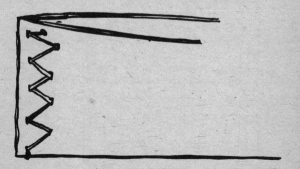

The first stage in the construction of a bark canoe. The ends have been drawn together, and the inside is packed with clay.

Spreaders are required across the centre of the canoe, and to fit these, two split pieces of round timber about two feet long and at least four inches across are cut. Holes are cut in the bark near the centre of the canoe at the top and through these the lashing material for the spreader ends are lashed. These two spreader ends are nicked in the centre to provide a seating for the spreader itself. The spreader is simply a straight strong stick wide enough to keep the centre of the bark canoe spread open; the ends are seated against the two nicks cut in the spreader ends.

Except for paddles the canoe is now ready for launching. Paddles are shaped out of any convenient straight-grained dead timber with the blade about six inches wide if possible.

A bark canoe must be kept in the water all the time. If taken out or allowed to dry it will almost certainly split or crack and be unserviceable. If left in the water it should remain in serviceable condition for two or three years.

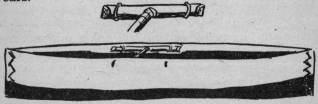

The finished canoe. Note how the spreader ends are secured in position, and how the spreader sits in the nicked cuts.

HEALTH

CARE OF FEET

It is vitally important to take proper care of your feet on a walking trip. A small blister can rub away and become a raw spot, and you will be immobilised and your progress both painful and slow.

If the feet show signs of being tender, the skin can be toughened up by urinating on the feet. When blisters threaten or develop, sticking plaster will prevent their further development, and offer immediate relief. The best treatment for a blister when it has already formed is to thread a piece of clean cotton through the blistered skin, cutting off the thread a quarter inch on either side of its point of entry. This will drain the fluid from the blister but prevent the air from entering. Cover the blister with sticking plaster or a bandage.

Ingrowing toenails are another cause of foot trouble. Immediate relief can be obtained by scraping the top of the toenail either with a file, rasp, the sharp edge of a knife, or even a piece of broken glass. The top of the nail should be scraped until it is sufficiently thin to be easily depressed with the tip of your finger.

Corns, of course, can be pared down, but a reputable make of corn plaster, and avoiding tight-fitting shoes, is the best way to keep free from these troubles.

Twisted ankles are a common ailment in rocky country.

If the twist is not too severe the best thing is to keep on the move, gradually getting the ankle into working order through exercise. If the twist is severe, sufficient to make the walker completely immobile, alternate bathings with very hot water and cold water will stimulate the blood flow, and give the patient some relief. After this treatment apply a tight bandage and the patient should be able to limp along.

When walking along river courses it is not advisable to remove your boots. Most riverbeds are stony, and frequently the stones are slippery with algae and other slimy growths, so that when walking barefooted one is likely to take a sudden fall. Also the water-rounded stones on the sole of the foot can become extremely tiring after a short distance.

Water will not damage your boots, but drying them

out by a fire later will, so never, never put your boots by a fire to dry. Far better to leave them wet. They will be wet again after five minutes walking through damp bush in any case. When you try to dry boots out before a fire you also dry out the natural oils in the leather, and your boots become stiff and hard. If they are put too close to the fire they will burn.

If your boots become too severely damaged to use, you can walk barefooted on grass and sandy earth, but if you try barefooted walking on stony roads your feet will soon go to pieces and you may be badly crippled. Improvised moccasins can be made from the soft inner bark of several species of trees.

BUSH REMEDY FOR STOMACH AND BOWEL UPSETS

A very simple remedy for many abdominal troubles is to chew and swallow a piece of charcoal every two or three hours. A lump about the size of a threepenny piece should give some relief if the trouble is similar to a gastric or bilious upset. A frequent cause of stomach ache is the drinking of very cold water while hot through walking. It is a good precaution under such conditions to drink very slowly, and warm each mouthful of water in the mouth before swallowing it.

CLEANLINESS AND FOOD

Cleanliness of eating utensils is very important. These should be washed immediately after a meal, and left exposed if possible to the sunlight after washing. If there is any doubt about your meat being safe to eat, then assume it is bad, rather than take the chance. The safest way to carry meat is to partly cook it while you know it is still fresh and safe. Cooking will destroy the harmful bacteria of decay, for a period. Such items of mixed meat as sausages are best cooked before you leave home, and then carried in the fat in which they were cooked. This will preserve them for four days to a week, depending upon the weather.

Butter can be carried in the hottest weather if packed in a container which in turn is put in the middle of your flour. The flour will act as an insulator, and keep the butter at whatever temperature you packed it.

CARE OF THE EYES

Nature has provided your eyes with a most effective germ killer, your tears. A tear will kill most bacteria and is a defence for your eyes.

Despite this natural protection, your eyes may suffer from glare or from entry of a particle of dust or sand. To protect your eyes from glare, tie a bootlace, or a thin strip of bark or some dark-coloured material, across your face just below your eyes. This will break the glare from the ground and give you almost immediate eye relief.

If a particle of dust or sand enters the eye do not rub the particular eye affected. Rub the opposite eye. Rubbing will stimulate the flow of tears and these will help to wash out the irritating matter. If this is not effective, try cupping water in your hands and immerse your sore eye in the cupped water. This will generally prove effective.

10.

TIME
AND DIRECTION

The measurement of time, and the obtaining of accurate direction (from North) are not primitive skills. Of the two, direction is the more recent development, although to the Polynesians it is older than their awareness of time.

Obtaining time and direction without equipment is practical, and in general can be more accurate than the average person's watch or compass.

Both words, "time" and "direction", are inter-related because if one has accurate time, accurate direction is obtained in a matter of seconds, or if one has accurate direction (from north) then accurate time is immediately practical without a watch.

The methods given in this book have been proved in jungle and desert and are applicable anywhere on the earth's surface.

The subject of navigation has been surrounded by many technical words, necessary to the science, but in this work the author has attempted to simplify the whole subject, and endeavoured to avoid words which would have no meaning to the average reader.

INTRODUCTION

Although a compass is the accepted method of obtaining direction, it is not always reliable, nor is it of very great value in dense bush, or areas where deposits of iron affect its needle. A watch is the accepted means of measuring time, but the watch may be out of action, and therefore it is necessary to have other methods to obtain both time and direction.

DEFINITIONS

'*Time*' is our method of measuring the intervals between events. The most regular event in our daily lives is the movement of the sun, and therefore for everyday purposes time is measured by the sun's movement. The stars provide a more accurate method of measurement and are used by navigators and astronomers. '*Direction*' is the line or course to be taken, and in this case can be considered as from North or one of the cardinal points of the compass.

SUN MOVEMENT

As you know, the sun crosses the imaginary North-South line (Meridian) every day when it reaches its highest point (Zenith) above the horizon.

Therefore when the sun is at its highest point in the sky it is North or South of you, depending upon your position on the earth's surface, and the sun's position relative to the earth's equator.

For all practical purposes there are twenty-four hours between each sun crossing of your North-South line, or Meridian. During the twenty-four hours the earth will have revolved apparently 360 degrees; therefore it will

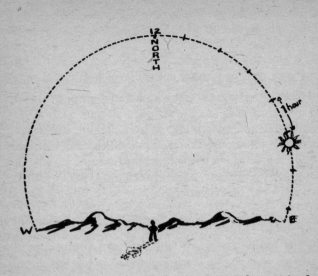

move 15 degrees for each hour, or one degree in four minutes. This is very convenient to know, because if you know the North or South accurately, you can easily measure off the number of degrees the sun is from the North-South line, and this will give you the number of hours and minutes before, or after noon. These measurements must be made along the curved path of the sun, and not on a horizontal or flat plane.

TIME FROM THE SUN WITH COMPASS

A means of measuring degrees—arms must be fully extended.

Hand at full arm's length, fingers widely spread	22 degrees
Thumb turned in	15 degrees
Closed fist	8 degrees
From second knuckle to edge of fist	3 degrees
Between two centre knuckles	2 degrees

These vary slightly like your personal dimensions and for accuracy should be accurately checked by each individual with a compass.

By this means, if you have a compass, time can be easily read from the sun's position. This should be possible to within four or five minutes. Decide from your compass your true North-South line and remember to make allowance for the magnetic variation from True North. Measure the number of degrees the sun is from this imaginary line, and multiply the number of degrees by four to obtain the number of minutes.

For example:

Here the sun is 34 degrees from the North-South line. It is morning, because the sun is on the eastern side of the North-South line, 34 x 4 = 136 minutes before noon; therefore it is sixteen minutes to ten in the morning *local sun time*.

This does not mean that it will be 16 minutes to ten by

the local clock, because there are two corrections to be made before local standard (or clock) time can be determined. These two corrections are dealt with under the headings of EQUATION OF TIME, and LONGITUDE CORRECTIONS (see pages 349 and 351).

It is sufficient for the moment that you can measure time accurately from the sun.

ACCURATE DIRECTION FROM SUN WITH A WATCH

The method of obtaining direction from a watch by pointing the hour hand (or 'twelve o'clock' depending upon which hemisphere you live in) is not accurate, but only approximate.

The accurate method, knowing the time, is to calculate the number of degrees changed to minutes in time, before or after noon, and then to measure from the sun's position along the curved path of the sun through the sky. Even if you make no allowance for the two corrections (see section Equation of Time and Longitude Corrections of Time pages 349, 351), you will be accurate within five to eight degrees and if you make the two corrections for time you will be accurate to less than one degree.

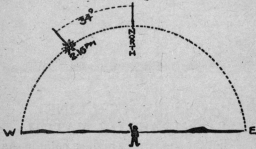

Example: It is 2.16 p.m. by your watch, therefore the sun is to the west of the North-South line. 2.16 p.m. means that the sun has travelled 136 minutes of time past the North-South line. It travels one degree along its curved path in the sky every four minutes of time, so that it is 34 degrees along its path past noon. Measure this back along the sun's path and you will have true North. (For Northern Hemisphere read South for North and reverse all other cardinal points.)

CARDINAL POINTS AND BEARINGS

Having found the true North, you can find any bearing from true North very easily and within five degrees of error. If the bearing you want is less than 180°, face East, and stretch out your left arm to true North. Raise your right arm along your side till there is a perfectly straight line along both arms. Your right arm is now pointing to South or 180 degrees True. Bring the two arms together evenly, and you are pointing to East or 90 degrees True, and you can then measure the number of degrees from these cardinal points to the bearing you require. By facing West, and pointing your right arm to the North and your left to South you can get bearings greater than 180 degrees.

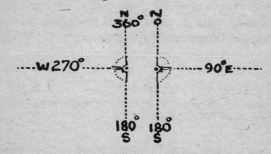

FINDING NORTH-SOUTH LINE WITHOUT COMPASS OR WATCH

Knowing that the sun is at its highest point in the sky at midday, and that this point is on the North-South line means that by finding where this position will be, will give you true North.

You can do this by measuring the points of shadow made by the top of a fixed stake. These points of shadow may give you a curved line either concave or convex to the stake. Continue the curve made by the points of shadow, and then draw a circle on the ground round the base of the stake. Where the curved line cuts the circle will be accurate East and West, and a right angle from these two points will be an accurate North and South line.

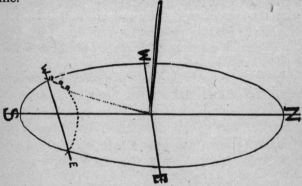

Here you see the stake, and points of shadow recorded over an hour in the morning. The dotted line is a continuation of the curve made by the points, and the intersection of this curved line with the circle gives you East and West. If North of the Equator the cardinal points will be reversed.

This Shadow-stick method is very accurate, if done over a period of an hour or two.

EAST-WEST LINE—DURING EQUINOCTIAL PERIODS

You will find from the foregoing that it is actually easier to find the true East-west line than the North-south. The idea of always working from, or to, North is largely conventional. The top of every map is assumed, unless marked otherwise, to be North. All bearings are measured clockwise from true North, but in actual practice it is often easier to find one or other of the cardinal points, rather than concentrate on finding the North Point. An instance is the ease with which the East-West line can be discovered.

There are two days in the year when the points of shadow will form an accurate East-west line throughout the whole day. These two days are the 21st March, and the 21st September, the days when the sun is over the

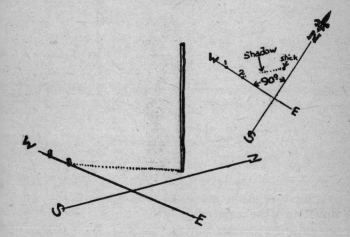

Equator. On these two days the sun is at right angles to the axis of the earth, and therefore directly over the Equator, and no matter where you are on the earth's surface the shadows will move true East and West on these two days. Because of this if you mark a point of shadow by putting a peg into the ground, and then, five minutes later, mark the new position of the same shadow you will have a perfect East-West line. For general purposes if less than 40° North or South latitude this method will serve you for about two or three weeks either side of the Equinoctial periods with reasonable accuracy, so that on any day between March 1st and

April 14th or September 1st and October 14th you can assume that the shadow line is very nearly a true East-west line. At all other periods or when you want greater accuracy you will have to work out the curve and extend it to the edges of the circle as in the preceding section.

The points of shadow move accurately true East and West on March 21st and September 21st.

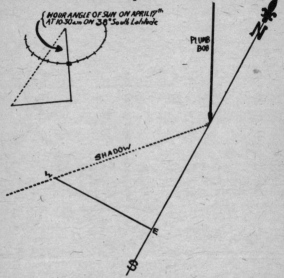

An extremely accurate method of finding true North is to work out the hour angle of the sun and transfer this hour angle to the shadow thrown onto the ground from the string of a plumb bob.

To find the hour angle, use the method given in the section on the sun compass (see pages 362-367) and extend from the shadow of the stick, the hour angle correct for your Latitude and date.

The sun compass diagram does not require to be set correctly to work out the hour angle. Any direction will serve for the imaginary North-south line.

When the triangle has been worked out, a corresponding triangle is made on the correct side of the shadow from the cord of the plumb bob.

You should work out the hour angle on the sun compass on the ground about fifteen minutes ahead of the watch time, so that when you have worked on the diagram and made the necessary time and longitude corrections, you will be able to plot the hour angle at precisely the right moment on the shadow. This method, if done accurately and corrections of time for longitude and Equation worked out, should be correct to within less than a quarter of a degree, or one minute of time.

FINDING LOCAL TIME WITHOUT COMPASS

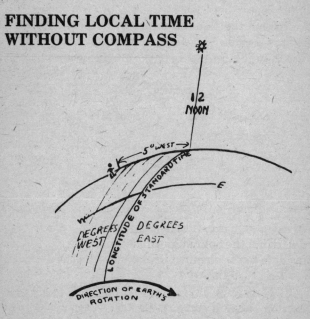

It is apparent that if you can find North-south by the method given from the shadow of the stick that you can then work out the number of degrees the sun is off the North-south line and thereby discover the correct local time, provided you know the longitude of standard time, and the longitude of your position.

341

THE SUN'S PATH THROUGH THE SKY, AND TO FIND THE SUN'S HEIGHT IN THE SKY FOR ANY PERIOD

To be able to accurately measure the sun's path along the sky you must know how high it is at its highest point (Zenith), and to find this out, you should be able to discover the sun's position North or South of the Equator for any day of the year.

This position of the sun is called 'Declination.' As you know, the sun is farthest North on June 21st, crosses the Equator September 21st, farthest South December 21st and recrosses the Equator on its way North on March 21st. This is caused by the inclined angle of the axis of the earth in relation to its path round the sun.

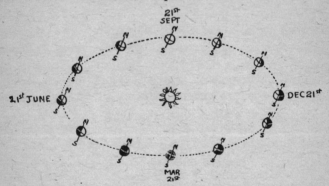

TO FIND THE SUN'S POSITION NORTH OR SOUTH OF THE EQUATOR

The degree, or slope of the inclined path is approximately 23½ degrees, so that when the sun is farthest North it is overhead 23½ degrees North of the Equator, and when farthest South it is overhead 23½ degrees South of the Equator.

It is possible to work a circle of 'Declination' showing you the path of the earth round the sun, and the reason.

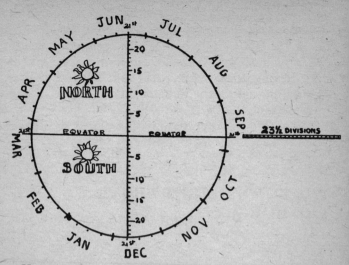

You can draw this diagram on the ground. Take a straight stick and cut 23½ divisions along its length. The size of the divisions must be absolutely equal.

If you use the width of your knife blade, or some equally simple measure, it will serve. With this stick as a radius, draw a circle on the ground, and divide the circle into four quarters with straight lines that cross the centre of the circle.

Now divide each quarter of the circumference of the circle into three equal divisions. Mark these June, December, March and September as shown. Now divide each month into four smaller equal divisions. These represent the four weeks of the average month.

Draw a thick line from the start of the fourth division of June to the start of the fourth division of December, and from the start of the fourth Division of September to the start of fourth division of March.

These lines should intersect each other in the centre of the circle. The lines from June to December represent the North-south line, and the line from March to September the Equator.

For any day of the year find the approximate day on

343

the outer circle and draw a line parallel to the Equator line to the North-south line, and then simply measure off with your stick the number of nicks from the Equator line, starting in the centre, to the date line. If the sun is on the June side of the Equator line it is North of the Equator; if on the December side it is South.

You should be accurate to within a quarter degree. This accuracy is needed for latitude work, but not necessary for the Sun Clock.

THE SUN'S HEIGHT ABOVE THE HORIZON

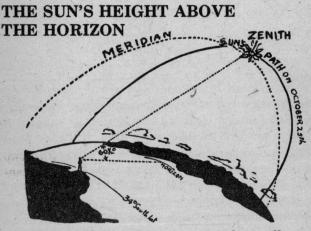

To the sun's declination you must make an allowance for your own latitude. For instance, if you are in latitude 42° North, and the date is April 21st, the sun will be 12° North, which means that at its zenith it will be 60° above the horizon. To work this out subtract your Latitude from 90°, and add the sun's declination. If the sun is on the other side of the Equator, subtract the declination.

METHODS OF OBTAINING ELEVATION OF SUN AND STARS

Latitude: A degree of longitude on the Equator equals

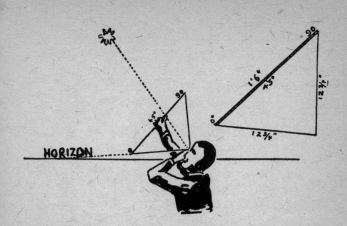

HORIZON

60 nautical miles; therefore 1 minute equals 1 nautical mile.

The elevation or height above the horizon of the sun or stars can be obtained by means of a plumb-bob quadrant—or, as Harold Gatty calls it in his 'Raft Book,' a Harp. The quadrant harp is made with two pieces of cord, and a straight piece of wood. The dimensions of both cord and wood MUST be accurate. The wood should be straight and smooth, and not less than eighteen inches long. Both ends should be flattened and a hole bored or burnt through the flattened ends. The holes should be exactly eighteen inches apart on their inside edges.

Through these two holes, two lengths of cord are passed, with a thumb knot to hold them fast. Two pieces of cord are tied together at almost exactly 12¾ inches (or if 36 board—string must be 25.45 inches) and where they are joined a third thinner length of cord for the plumb-bob is also tied so that it swings from the joining of the two cords of the harp. This plumb-bob cord should be about eighteen inches long. To the lower ends a weight such as a clasp knife or lead sinker, or a long thin stone is tied.

From the inside edge on one hole you mark off nine inches on an eighteen-inch harp or eighteen inches on a thirty-six-inch harp, and again a second mark an equal distance from the other end. The two parts should meet exactly in the centre of the stick. On one side of the stick along the nine-inch (or 18″ side) side you mark the scale given in the margin. This scale is shown in short lengths for convenience, but for the marking on the stick you should read it as one scale. From 0 to 45° reads along one side on the stick and 45° to 90° along the other side, or alternatively you can mark the stick continuously from end to end. To use the 'Harp,' sight upwards along the cord at the 90° end till the cord is aligned with the sun or star. The plumb-bob should be swinging almost free along the stick, and when the cord is aligned the plumb-bob string will just brush against the number of degrees of elevation of the sun or star observed. You can get a reading accurate to ½ degree or less with this 'Harp.'

346

For finer readings—make the base stick 36″, the cord 25.45″ and make each degree on the scale twice as long.

(Readers interested are recommended to study 'The Raft Book' by Harold Gatty.)

IMPROVISED QUADRANT

Another method of obtaining elevation of a heavenly body is by means of an improvised quadrant, over a puddle of water, the surface of which serves as an accurate 'horizon.'

A useful measurement to remember is that a degree very nearly equals one inch on the circumference of a circle of a radius of fifty-seven inches.

A straight stick is marked off into 57 divisions of equal length. The actual length of each division is not important but the divisions must be as regular as possible. Another whippy length of cane or very pliable stick is marked off into divisions of the same length. These can be marked at five or ten division intervals to save work, but a smaller stick should be marked off into separate divisions for accurate reading between the five or ten division marks.

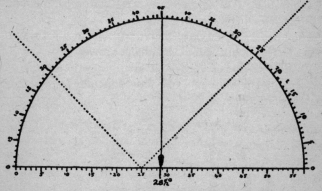

The straight stick is laid across the puddle, in line with the heavenly body to be measured, and the end of the ninety division stick is pushed into the ground so that the first mark is just level with the water surface. The stick or cane is bent right over till the other end comes to the other end of the fifty-seven division stick, and it too is pushed into the soft dirt beneath the water. The ninety division stick is then bent by hand until it assumes the shape of a semi-circle.

A degree very nearly represents one division on the circumference over a radius of fifty-seven divisions of the same length. The angle of incidence of a ray of light equals the angle of reflection, so these two facts enable you to use this bush-made 'quadrant,' and with no knowledge of spherical geometry you can measure the angle of elevation of sun or stars with reasonable accuracy.

Place your eye against one of the divisions of the semi-circle on the side farthest from the object to be viewed and looked at the surface of the water for the reflection. Move the free hand or pointer stick along the far side of the curve till it cuts off the ray of light from the heavenly body.

Count the number of divisions from the water to where the finger on stick cuts off the ray of light and also the number of divisions from the water to the one against which the eye was placed.

The total of these two will give you the angle of elevation above the horizon of the object viewed.

With care and accuracy in shaping your bow, and measuring the divisions you should be able to read to a quarter of a degree.

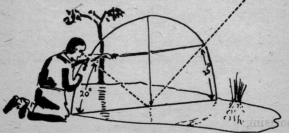

EQUATION OF TIME—AND CORRECTIONS TO STANDARD TIME

Each day every longitude of the earth passes under the sun, but because of the slight variation in the earth's path, the exact moment when the sun passes over the meridian of longitude is not precisely at twelve o'clock every day. The difference may be as much as 16 minutes of time before twelve o'clock on your clock time and fourteen minutes after twelve o'clock.

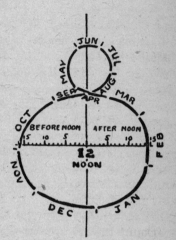

This passage of the sun over the imaginary North-south line is called 'Meridian Transit' and as you will see it differs from clock time throughout the course of the year, except for four days (April 16th, June 15th, August 30th, and December 25th).

For convenience, the time of meridian transit is averaged out over the year, and the average is called 'mean' time.

The sun's passage of the meridian is called 'solar' (sun) time. The correction of time of the two is called 'Equation of Time.'

The following simple table on Meridian Transit can be shown in the form of the figure '8' for your easy memorising.

Jan.	1 12.03	May	1 11.57	Sept.	3 11.59
	6 12.06		6 11.57		8 11.58
	11 12.08		11 11.56		13 11.56
	16 12.10		16 11.56		18 11.54
	21 12.11		21 11.56		23 11.53
	26 12.13		26 11.57		28 11.51
	31 12.14	June	5 11.58	Oct.	3 11.49
Feb.	5 12.14		10 11.59		8 11.48
	10 12.14		15 12.00		13 11.46
	15 12.14		20 12.01		18 11.45
	20 12.14		25 12.02		23 11.44
	25 12.13		30 12.03		28 11.44
Mar.	2 12.12	July	5 12.04	Nov.	2 11.44
	7 12.11		10 12.05		7 11.44
	12 12.10		15 12.06		12 11.44
	17 12.09		20 12.06		17 11.45
	22 12.07		25 12.06		22 11.46
	27 12.06		30 12.06		27 11.48
Apr.	1 12.04	Aug.	4 12.06	Dec.	2 11.49
	6 12.03		9 12.05		7 11.51
	11 12.01		14 12.05		12 11.54
	16 12.00		19 12.04		17 11.56
	21 11.59		24 12.02		22 11.58
	26 11.58		29 12.01		27 12.01
					31 12.03

A figure eight drawn to the proportions shown and with the four dates remembered when meridian transit coincides with mean time will give reasonably accurate corrections.

Note: The four dates when there is no correction are April 16th, June 15th, August 30th and December 25th, Xmas Day.

The top section of the figure 8 is about one-third the size of the lower half. The horizontal line is divided into three five-minute sections to right and left, and the right side marked PLUS to mean that the sun is ahead of mean time. The left is marked MINUS, the sun is behind mean time.

The application of this 'Equation of Time' correction will be required if you want to get accurate time from the sun, and also for correction to the sun compass-sun clock.

LONGITUDE CORRECTIONS

The other correction which you will have to make to Solar time is a correction for longitude. Time for clocks on various parts of the earth's surface is called 'Standard Time,' and is based upon the longitude convenient for a large tract of country (see page 341).

In England, time is based on Greenwich, hence the term 'Greenwich mean time.'

In other large land masses such as America, Africa, Russia and of course Australia, standard time may be defined as Eastern Standard Time, Central Standard Time, Western Standard Time, etc.

The areas of the earth and the meridian of longitude on which their standard time is based are as follows:

12h.	E	180	Siberia (E. Long. 157½ to 172½) Fiji Islands.
11h. 30m.	E	172½	New Zealand. Norfolk Island, Nauru Island.
11h.	E	165	New Caledonia, New Hebrides, Ocean Island, Solomon Islands, Siberia (E. Long. 142½ to 157½).
10h. 30m.	E	159	Lord Howe Island.
10h.	E	150	Tasmania, Victoria, N.S.W., Queensland, British New Guinea, Guam, Siberia (E. Long. 127½ to 142½).
9h. 30m.	E	142½	South Australia, Northern Territory.

9h.	E	135	Broken Hill, Area of N.S.W., Manchuria, Japan, Dutch New Guinea.
8h.	E	120	All coastal area of China, Philippine Islands, British North Borneo, Timor, Western Australia, Celebes.
7h. 30m.	E	112½	Sarawak, Java, Madura, Bali, Lombok, Dutch Borneo.
7h. 20m.	E	110	Federated Malay States, Straits Settlements.
7h.	E	105	French Indo-China, Thailand, Southern Sumatra.
5h. 30m.	E	82½	India (except Calcutta 5h. 53m. 20.8 S.), Ceylon.
4h.	E	60	Russia (Long. 40°E. to 52½°E.)
3h. 30m.	E	52½	Iran.
3h.	E	45	Iraq, Eritrea, French and Italian Somaliland, Madagascar, Russia (West of Long. 40°E.).
2h. 45m.	E	41½	Kenya, Palestine, Syria, Egypt, Union of South Africa.
1h.	E	15	Malta, Tunisia, Libya, Nigeria, Cameroons, French Equatorial Africa, Norway, Sweden, Germany, Italy.
0h.		0	Great Britain, Northern Ireland, Eire, France, Belgium, Spain.
+4h.	W	60	Eastern Part of Canada, U.S.A., South America.
+5h.	W	75	Parts of Canada and U.S.A., including Quebec and New York.
+6h.	W	90	Central States of Canada and U.S.A.
+7h.	W	105	Central America, Mountain Parts of Canada and U.S.A.
+8h.	W	120	West Coast of Canada and U.S.A.

To make the necessary longitude corrections, you must know whether you are set East or West of the meridian on which standard time for the locality is based.

If you are East your sun will be ahead and you must deduct four minutes for each degree you are East of the meridian of standard time. If you are West your sun time will be later than the Standard Meridian and you must add four minutes for each degree you are West.

IMPORTANT

The corrections for the equation of time and for longitude are necessary to correct conversion of sun time to standard time for accurate direction, and also for accurate reading of directions and time from the sun compass. With these corrections you should be able to get local standard time to within two minutes, and a bearing accurate to within an error of one half degree, using no equipment whatsoever.

DAYLIGHT SAVING TIME

Sometimes a country will move its time back an hour from the standard time to get more daylight in summertime, and this change, generally called Daylight Saving Time, must also be remembered when making corrections to Solar time.

The four 'Times' you now know are:—

Solar Time or Sun Time: Local time of sun over the North-south line.

Mean Time: Average of Solar time over twelve months.

Standard Time: Application of Mean Time to a given area of the earth's surface.

Daylight or Summer Time: A local adjustment to standard time.

There is a fifth 'Time' you will have to learn, and this is 'Sidereal' or 'Star' time.

If anyone asked you how many times the earth revolved on its axis between midday of New Year's Day of one year, and midday of New Year's Day the next year you would probably say 365¼ times . . . and you would be wrong.

The earth revolves on its axis 366¼ times.

The earth 'loses' one revolution in its path around the sun over the year and as a result the sun only crosses the meridians of the earth 365¼ times. This means that while the sun will only cross Greenwich 365¼ times a year, a star, which is far outside the solar system will pass 366¼ times every year.

For this reason Star or Sidereal Time is used by astronomers as being more accurate than Solar Time.

There is an extra day to be squeezed into a 'Star' year, a star day is shorter by 3 minutes 56.6 seconds than a sun day. You can work it out for yourself. There are 1440 minutes in a twenty-four-hour day and these have to be shared by all days in a star year and that means that there are nearly four minutes less in a star day than in a sun day.

One degree equals four minutes of time, and so the stars advance roughly one degree farther ahead each night.

Sidereal or Star Time or the star charts commence for each year at the day of the Autumnal Equinox, September 21st, and for general purposes you can say the stars gain two hours every calendar month.

ACCURATE TIME FROM THE STARS

The star maps shown on pages 00 to 00 show the position of the brightest stars in their various constellations. The numbers 0 to 24 indicate the position of the stars at midnight at Greenwich on September 21st, when the star year commences.

0 means midnight at Greenwich, and every number means one hour difference from Greenwich.

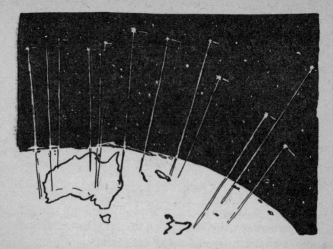

Thus ALGOL in the constellation PERSEUS is on the radial line numbered 3, which means that it is three hours ahead of Greenwich. (Chart 2.)

This position of the stars IN TIME from Greenwich is called their RIGHT ASCENSION, and their position between the poles and the Equator either North or South is called their DECLINATION.

Declination is latitude, and Right Ascension is longitude.

The declination of the stars does not vary (as does the sun) throughout the year.

The Polynesians observed this, and regarded the stars as 'fingers' pointing down to the earth and always passing over the same places and the earth revolved beneath them.

With the aid of the star map, it is easy to find and identify any star almost directly overhead. It may be slightly North or South but should not be East or West.

To find a point directly overhead, stand upright, with your head thrown well back. Rotate the body through a series of half circles and you will see the stars overhead appear to move in arcs.

The centre of the circle which the arcs form will be the point in the sky directly over your head.

Having recognised the overhead star from your Star Map, work out its right ascension, and add two hours for every odd day till the next September 21st, and add this to the time of Right Ascension.

Example. The star Antares, the very bright star in the Scorpion, you read as 16 hours 25 minutes Right Ascension. The date if it is overhead is March 25th. From March 25th to September 21st there are five months, three weeks and four days, which equal a correction of 11 hours 46 minutes. This added to the right ascension of 16 hours 25 minutes gives a total of 28 hours 11 minutes. Because the total is greater than the twenty-four hours you must deduct the twenty-four hours and the result is 4 hours 11 minutes (a.m.) Greenwich. To this you must make correction for your longitude.

This method is applicable in all latitudes and gives reasonable accuracy.

TIME FROM THE STARS— NORTHERN HEMISPHERE

In the Northern Hemisphere the stars appear to revolve anti-clockwise in the sky, and you must remember this when reading time from the stars at night. Imagine the Pole star (Polaris) is the centre of a twenty-four-hour clock dial, and the hours are numbered from Midnight 24 hours, anti-clockwise with 6 hours at the left and horizontal with the Pole star, twelve o'clock immediately below the Pole star, and eighteen hours at the right, horizontal to the Pole star. The brightest stars, Alpha and Beta, in Ursa Major (opposite the handle of the Big Dipper) or plough are the hour hands.

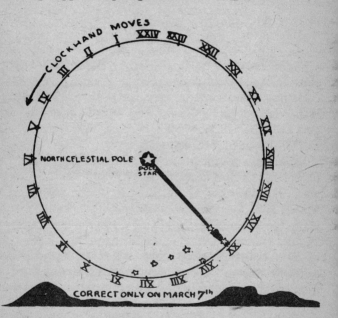

It gives correct time only on one day in the year, March 7th, thereafter it gains 4 minutes a day, or two hours a month, so that if it reads fifteen hours on June 1st, it will be seven and a half hours fast and the correct time therefore will be 7 hours 30 minutes.

357

SOUTHERN HEMISPHERE

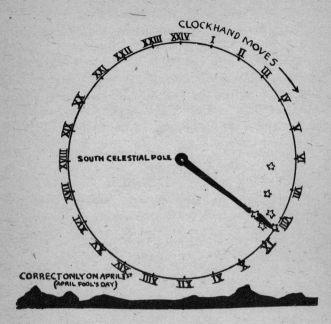

In the Southern Hemisphere the stars appear to revolve clockwise. The Southern Cross is the hour hand of a twenty-four-hour Sky Clock, and the centre of the dial is four and a half times the length of the Cross towards the foot along the longest axis of the Cross. This clock is correct on April 1st (April Fools' Day—just to fool you, but don't be fooled), and thereafter it gains at the rate of 4 minutes a day or two hours a month, so that if it reads 8.20 on September 1st it will be ten hours fast, and therefore the correct time will be 22 hours 20 minutes, or 20 minutes past ten at night.

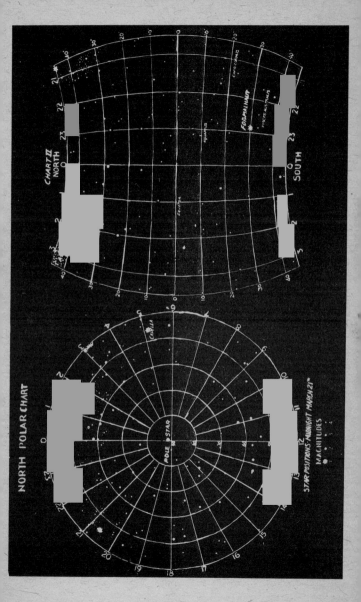

NORTH POLAR CHART

CHART II
NORTH

SOUTH

FOMALHAUT

STAR POSITIONS MIDNIGHT MARCH 21st
MAGNITUDES

POLE STAR

CAPELLA

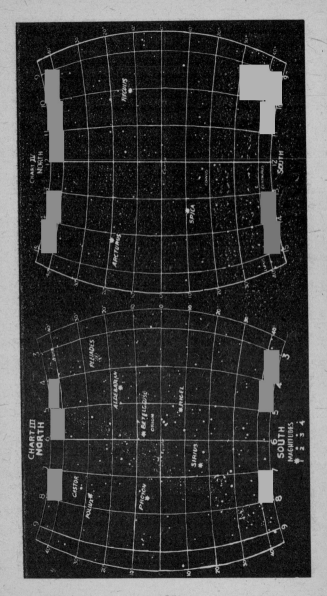

CHART IV
NORTH

REGULUS

SOUTH

ARCTURUS

SPICA

CORVUS

CENTAURUS

CHART III
NORTH

PLEIADES

ALDEBARAN

BETELGEUSE
ORION

RIGEL

SIRIUS

CASTOR

POLLUX

PROCYON

SOUTH

MAGNITUDES
1 2 3 4

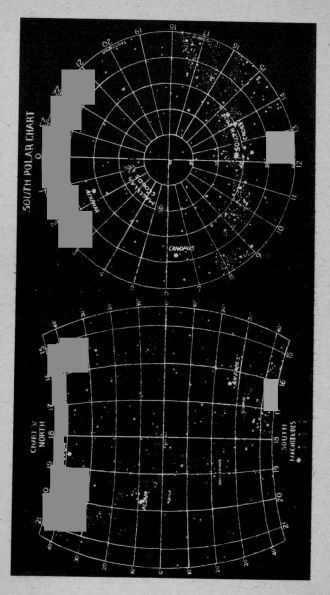

DIRECTION FROM THE STARS

In the Northern Hemisphere, direction from the stars is easy. Polaris, the Pole Star, is very nearly directly over the North Pole, and therefore wherever you see it in the sky is true North.

In the Southern Hemisphere there is no star over the South Pole and finding direction is a little more difficult.

One of the most popular methods is from the constellation CRUX, or the CROSS, better known as the Southern Cross. There are many stars which appear to make the shape of a cross in the sky, and therefore it is essential, if you live in the Southern Hemisphere, that you learn to identify the Southern Cross beyond any shadow of doubt.

Look along the Milky Way, which is unmistakable, and you will find a dark patch without a single star. This is commonly called the Coal Sack, and the Southern Cross lies right on the very edge of the Coal Sack.

To make identification more certain, the Southern Cross should show you five stars, the fifth less bright than the others, and nearly in line with the foot star, and one of the arms. Another certain identification is the two pointers, two stars of the first magnitude, lying always to the left-hand side of the Cross (when viewed as if the Cross was in a vertical position).

The longest axis of the Cross towards the foot points to the Celestial South Pole. That is, to a position over the earthly South Pole.

This, using the length of the Cross from head to foot, is almost exactly four and a half times the length of the Cross commencing from the foot.

You can measure this with fair accuracy by holding the hand at arm's length, and using the thumb and forefinger as a pair of calipers to measure the length of the Cross.

Another indicator of true South, suitable for moonless

nights is the two Magellan Clouds, which form the base
of an imaginary equal-sided triangle, the apex of which
is over the South Pole. On bright nights, when these two
clouds are not visible, the two very bright stars, Ache-
nar and Canopus, also are the base of an equal-sided
triangle with its apex over the South Pole.

THE SUN COMPASS

A Sun Compass is far quicker to read and very much
more convenient than having to refer to a magnetic
compass. The directions for working out a Sun Compass
are suitable for either working out on a card, on the
ground, or, if you prefer it, for drawing on some unim-
portant area of your map.

On a map, a Sun Compass has marked military value.

A Sun Compass worked out on the ground in a camp
becomes a Sun Clock, accurate to a minute if set down
correctly.

First draw a circle (if on the map on a place where
important information will not be obliterated) or if on
the ground the area must be clean and level and open to
sunshine throughout the day.

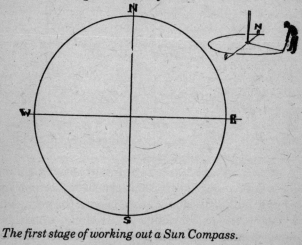

The first stage of working out a Sun Compass.

The size of the circle does not matter, six or seven inches on the map, two or three if for a card, three or four or even six feet if on the ground.

Work out carefully and accurately the true North line.

It is vitally important to have this most accurate.

If your Sun Compass or Sun Clock is wrong, it is because you have not put this North line in accurately.

If on a map this accurate North-south line will be either shown on the grid, or by the NORTH arrow head. Make sure that it is TRUE North, not magnetic.

When you have this line drawn from North to South, through the centre of the circle, draw another also through the centre from East to West, and divide the outer circumference of the circle into twenty-four equal divisions. Each of these divisions will be exactly fifteen degrees.

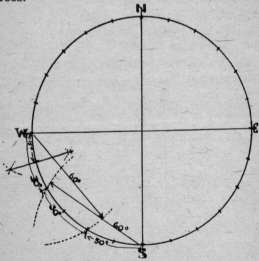

These fifteen-degree divisions can be either marked off, if on a card, with a protractor, or if on the ground by using the cord for the radius of the circle, which will divide the circle into sixty-degree divisions from the

North-south points of intersection, and into thirty degree divisions from the East-west intersections.

These thirty-degree divisions are bisected, and as a result you have the necessary twenty-four divisions of fifteen degrees each.

Lightly connect these divisions with faint lines parallel to the North-south line.

Now consult your map if you do not know your approximate latitude (within an error of five degrees) and starting on the East-west line which is zero, come up for North, down for South, along the circle till you can roughly pinpoint your present latitude North or South of the Equator.

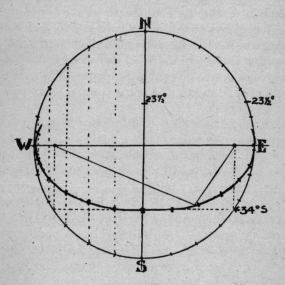

Mark off where this point comes to on the North-south line. You now have to draw an ellipse where it intersects the circle. To do this put two pins (or pegs, if you are working on the ground) on the East-west line directly in line with the two latitude points on the circle. (By directly in line is meant parallel to the North-south line.) A thread or cord is tied to each of these pins or pegs, with its length embracing the pin or peg on the latitude on the North-south line.

A pencil (or back of a knife if working on the ground) is put inside this loop, which is removed from the pin on the North-south line.

This will draw a perfect ellipse. On this ellipse mark in the hours, starting with the 12 on the North-south line, and reading to 6 p.m. of the East side, and from 6 a.m. on the West. (This is because the sun in the East throws the shadow to the West and vice versa.)

These hours are permanent and can be marked in ink, or with pegs or stakes if on the ground. (Roman figures are most suitable.)

The half and quarter hour intervals can be estimated by you with reasonable accuracy, and also marked in.

Now you must put in a declination circle to find out where the shadow stick or gnomen should be placed for any day of the year. (See page 343.)

Mark off the outer circle where the 23½ degree position is, and transfer to the North-south line. Using this as a radius, draw a circle from the centre of the big circle you drew first. Mark this off by the method given on page 343 and set your shadow stick on the North-south line opposite the appropriate date. This shadow stick should be vertical, and should be set up with a plumb-bob.

The shadow will fall across the elliptical line, and where it falls is Solar Time. This must be correct for the Equation of Time (see method on page 349), and also corrected for longitude (see page 351).

INDEX

THE BEST OF THE BESTSELLERS
FROM WARNER BOOKS!